1966

Voi

# VOICES FROM THE CLAY

*The Development of Assyro-Babylonian Literature*

# VOICES FROM THE CLAY

*The Development of Assyro-Babylonian Literature*

## BY SILVESTRO FIORE

UNIVERSITY OF OKLAHOMA PRESS : NORMAN

By Silvestro Fiore

*Über die Beziehungen zwischen der arabischen und der*
*frühitalienischen Lyrik*
(University of Cologne, 1956)
*Voices from the Clay: The Development of Assyro-Babylonian*
*Literature*
(Norman, 1965)

The paper on which this book is printed bears the University of Oklahoma
Press watermark and has an effective life of at least three hundred years.

*Library of Congress Catalog Card Number: 65-11233*

Copyright 1965 by the University of Oklahoma Press, Publishing Division of the University. Composed and printed at Norman, Oklahoma,
U.S.A., by the University of Oklahoma Press. First edition.

*Honori et meritis Patris Matrisque*
*librum dedicans*

# PREFACE

𒌓𒈾𒈨𒌉𒉆𒁄𒉡𒌇𒂼𒀀𒉌𒉡𒌅𒄉

*ud- na-me dumu nam- tag nu- tuk ama- a-ni nu- tu- ud*
"Never a child without fault any mother has born."[1]

IN PRESENTING THIS BOOK TO THE PUBLIC, the writer is well aware of the distance that lies between his work and perfection. One of the difficulties in the path of achievement is the ultimate impenetrability of an ancient world which not only time, but, most of all, the dif-

---

[1] Text and transliteration by S. N. Kramer, *Supplements to Vetus Testamentum,* III (Leiden, 1955), 170–82, pl. I ff.

ference of conceptions separate from our own epoch; the other difficulty is that of human limitations in facing a task that is all the more arduous because the scant material which generations of archaeologists have brought to light is scattered in the museums of four continents, and therefore to a large extent inaccessible.

This book is not a popular edition of Mesopotamian literature, nor is it a specialized study for the exclusive use of Assyriologists; the work is intended chiefly for students of peripheral disciplines, such as non-Akkadian Semitics, theology, and the humanities.

The writer hopes furthermore that the comprehensive presentation of Assyro-Babylonian poetry and its spiritual background will provide useful information for all those who have a serious interest in the oldest layer of human civilization and its ramifications in the culture of today.

During the preparation of this book, the writer has gratefully followed suggestions made by several European and American Assyriologists, especially the late Professor Theo Bauer, Professor Marcel Leibovici, Professor Leo Oppenheim, and Professor Samuel N. Kramer. Feeling deeply indebted to these distinguished scholars, he assumes at the same time the entire responsibility for the opinions here expressed.

While doing research on a related subject in the University of California at Los Angeles and Berkeley, the writer has had occasion to recur to the unfailing helpfulness of Professor G. E. von Grunebaum, director of the Near Eastern Center, to whom he presented the first draft of this work.

A special debt of thankfulness is furthermore due to Professor J. Brunet, former chairman of the Foreign Languages Department in the University of Florida, for his humane comprehension and for the addition of oriental research material to the University Library.

The completion of the book has been made possible through the Ford Foundation, whose generosity is most deeply appreciated.

SILVESTRO FIORE

*Gainesville, Florida*
*April 15, 1965*

# FOREWORD

THE SIGNIFICANCE OF THE ASSYRO-BABYLONIAN WORLD has for a long time been hidden by the radiance of the Hebrew and Greek civilizations, the "two pillars" of Western culture. But it now becomes more and more apparent that both Israel and Hellas had their roots in the spiritual realm of ancient Mesopotamia. The theological and ethical revolution of the Hebrew people, the message of Greek poets and philosophers, are not a *creatio ex nihilo;* they are milestones on the road of human evolution, a road which started five thousand years ago in the "Land of the Two Rivers."

Unlike Egypt, whose culture remained largely confined to the oasis of the Nile Valley, Mesopotamia was the heart of the most extensive civilization in the ancient Near East. Side by side with the military conquests of Assyro-Babylonian kings, and with the trade activity of Semitic merchants beyond the boundaries of the realm,[1] the concepts of spiritual life evolving in Mesopotamia spread over neighboring regions; cuneiform writing and Akkadian poetic traditions penetrated Asia Minor, Syria, Persia,[2] and Egypt. Thus the propagation of Assyro-Babylonian culture paved the way for the erection of new civilizations in Canaan[3] and Caphtor.[4]

The main object of the present study is the Semitic poetry of ancient Mesopotamia. It has seemed advisable to the writer that the literary part of the book be preceded by a sketch of the cultural background upon which epical and speculative poems have been projected.

The first chapter provides, in a rapid survey of prehistory and history, the framework of exterior events that determined the ethnical as well as the political development in the "Land of the Two Rivers."

The second chapter attempts to present the tissue of spiritual conceptions, including religion, kingship, and the mythopoeic precursors of science: magic and divination.

The third chapter briefly introduces the system of cuneiform script, instrument of literary expression, and surveys pictorial art, complementary discipline of writing in the domain of iconographic testimony.

[1] Concerning the merchant colony of Kanesh (Kültepe) in Asia Minor, founded in Old Assyrian times, cf. G. Contenau, F. Thureau-Dangin, and J. Lewy, *Les Tablettes Cappadociennes,* séries 1–3 (Paris, 1920–37), in *Textes cunéiformes,* Musée du Louvre, Département des Antiquités Orientales, IV, XIV, XIX–XXI.

[2] Cf. the tablets with cuneiform script found in Boghazköi, Ras Shamra, Susa, and El-Amarna.

[3] For the continuance of Mesopotamian ritual features in Hebrew literature, see pp. 234–35 below. Concerning the relationship between the Flood episode of the Akkadian Gilgamesh epic and the Biblical Deluge account, cf. A. Heidel, *The Gilgamesh Epic and Old Testament Parallels.*

[4] The connection between the Greek Dionysus festivities and the Mesopotamian Tammuz cult with its lamentations and rejoicings is discussed in the Conclusion below, p. 233.

A striking parallel exists also between Enkidu's tossing of the celestial bull's thigh in the face of Ishtar (see Part II below, tablet VI of the Gilgamesh epic) and Ctesippus' hurling of a bull's foot at Odysseus (Homer *Odyssey* 20. 299).

The second part of the book deals with the poems themselves[5]; the text of each single opus is accompanied by a detailed, step-by-step comment which takes into account the spiritual background and the mythical implications of the compositions.

The Conclusion considers the continuance of the Assyro-Babylonian heritage in the civilizations of the East Mediterranean, with particular emphasis on Hellas.

Elements in both form and contents of Greek dramatic art and mythology have been traced back to early Mesopotamia, in reconstitution of the spiritual bridge that links the oldest Semitic culture with our own age, and it will become apparent that the "Greek miracle" was not an isolated phenomenon, unrelated to all that preceded it, but that it owed much to the thriving and varied culture of the peoples of Mesopotamia in the "Land of the Two Rivers."

SILVESTRO FIORE

[5] The choice has been limited to narrative and speculative poems, as representing the two most extensive and characteristic genera of Semitic literature in Mesopotamia. For a study of the Sumero-Akkadian genre of hymns and prayers, cf. A. Falkenstein and Wolfram von Soden, *Sumerische und Akkadische Hymnen und Gebete.*

# CONTENTS

# ILLUSTRATIONS

# DRAWINGS

# MAPS

# ABBREVIATIONS

| | |
|---|---|
| *Advancement of Science* | *AS* |
| *American Journal of Archaeology* | *AJA* |
| *Analecta Orientalia* | *AO* |
| *Annales de Chimie* | *AC* |
| *Annales de l'Institut de Physique du Globe* | *AIPG* |
| *Ancient Near Eastern Texts* | *ANET* |
| *Annals of Archaeology and Anthropology* | *AAA* |
| *The Antiquaries Journal* | *AJ* |
| *Bulletin of the American Schools of Oriental Research* | *BASOR* |
| *Der alte Orient* | *DAO* |
| *Journal Asiatique* | *JA* |
| *Journal of Near Eastern Studies* | *JNES* |
| *Journal of the American Oriental Society* | *JAOS* |
| *Journal of the Royal Asiatic Society* | *JRAS* |
| *The Museum Journal* | *MJ* |
| *Revue d'Assyriologie* | *RA* |
| *Studies in Ancient Oriental Civilization* | *SAOC* |
| *Zeitschrift für Assyriologie* | *ZA* |

# PART ONE
*The Cultural Setting*

...Βαβυλῶνος δὲ ταύτης, ἥντινα
εἶδε πόλεων τῶν τότε μεγίστην
ἥλιος οὐδὲν ἔτι ἦν εἰ μὴ τεῖχος...

Pausanias Periegeticus, VIII, 33

# CHAPTER I

*Prehistoric Prelude and Historic Background*

THE FERTILE "PLAIN OF THE TWO RIVERS," though apparently separated from surrounding regions by such remarkable natural barriers as the mountain chains in the north and east, the Persian Gulf in the south, and the great Syrian desert in the west, has been since earliest times the scene of more or less peaceful encounters between native and immigrant populations, but certain abrupt changes in the different stages of its early culture illustrate that these contacts must sometimes have been violent and destructive.

Even at the summit of their splendor, Assyro-Babylonian monarchs were seldom allowed a period of complete peace, but had to subdue rebellious vassals, fight petty enemies at their borders, and wrestle with powerful rivals in Egypt, Palestine, and Anatolia.

## PREHISTORY

About the oldest struggles on Mesopotamian soil we have no written information at all. Our only knowledge of this prehistoric period derives from archaeology and is necessarily fragmentary and subject to frequent readjustments in chronology and also in the interpretation of the material found in many of the mounds extending over the plain of modern Iraq.

Since the Turinese diplomat P. E. Botta discovered the first vestiges of the legendary Assyro-Babylonian empire at the site of modern Khorsabad in 1843,[1] archaeological methods of excavation have greatly changed. In the beginning only well-preserved objects were thought to be worthy of the museums, and aesthetic rather than strictly archaeological considerations decided the selection of vessels, reliefs, statues, etc., which underwent an invisible restoration before being put on display.[2]

Later excavators, however, attached a much higher importance than their predecessors[3] to tiny potsherds, which, for all their insignificant appearance, often revealed to the archaeologist invaluable evidence about the first primitive settlements in Mesopotamia.

Mural paintings, previously neglected, were now given special attention. Many of them had to be removed to museums from sites difficult of access, but such a transfer was an exceptionally delicate procedure because the painting could not be separated from the wall. To make the transfer, the precious surface was first covered with a piece of waterproof cloth and then with a thick coat of cement or plaster. After the latter had hardened, the "double" wall with the painting inside was

---

[1] J. Mohl, *"Lettres de M. Botta sur les découvertes à Khorsabad près de Nineve,"* *JA* (1843–45); also published in book form (Paris, 1845).

[2] Early excavators often unwittingly destroyed invaluable archaeological evidence, and it happened that clay tablets were thrown away because their importance went unnoticed, since the signs were covered with dirt (e.g., during the excavations at Nimrud made by Austen H. Layard, 1845–47).

[3] Henri de Genouillac makes the following observation in his report *Fouilles de Telloh* (Paris, 1934), 35: ". . . *les échantillons de céramique semblent si pauvres dans un musée comme le Louvre!"*

4

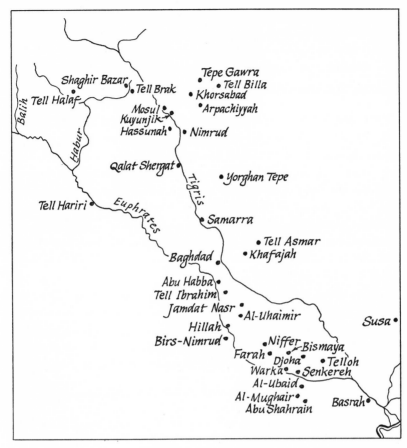

Modern Mesopotamia

sawed into segments, which were then with due care transported to their new destination and finally very skillfully restored to their primitive condition.[4]

In 1918 the German archaeologist Walter Andrae used, during his exploration of the ancient site of Ashur,[5] a new method of delimiting

[4] Such a procedure has been adopted for paintings in Dura-Europos on the Euphrates.

[5] *Die archaischen Ischtar-Tempel in Assur (Wissenschaftliche Veröffentlichungen der deutschen Orient-Gesellschaft,* No. 39, 1922); and, by the same author, *Das wiedererstandene Assur.*

the excavated layers from the surface down to virgin soil. This system of stratification has been of inestimable value for establishing chronology and is now applied in all modern archaeological operations.

Another new field technique was used by Sir Leonard Woolley during his Ur excavations in southern Mesopotamia.[6] He was able to recover the shape of numerous objects made of perishable materials which had left a more or less precise impression in the surrounding fill. By pouring liquid plaster of Paris into these cavities, he obtained exact replicas of the vanished objects.[7]

Since 1918 the discovery of many ancient sites, especially in desert regions, has been accomplished through aerial photography. A view from the perspective of high altitude not only permits obtaining a cohesive picture of scattered lines[8] but also makes it possible to discern outlines of ancient buildings and other structures that have been almost completely leveled in the course of time and covered with sand and grass.[9] Aerial photography has also revealed the plan of the ancient port of Tyre, which was completely immersed in coastal waters.[10] The existence of ancient ruins under a thick and smooth layer of cultivated soil can be determined from high altitude through the different shades of a vegetation pattern. For example, old trenches and wells, filled in later times with loose earth, will produce lines and patches of deeper color

[6] C. L. Woolley, "The Royal Cemetery," *Ur Excavations,* II (London, 1934).

[7] Through the use of this method, it has been possible, for instance, to reconstruct the "wooden harp" with its strings, contained in the "Tomb of the Queen" (Royal Cemetery of Ur) of the third millennium B.C.

[8] High altitude photography has been an important means of tracing, in a net of rice fields separated by innumerable dikes, the outlines of ancient buildings in Siam. See P. R. Williams "Irregular Earthworks in Eastern Siam—An Air Survey," *Antiquity,* Vol. XXIV (March, 1950), 30–36.

[9] Ruins of ancient cities and irrigation canals in Mesopotamia have been discovered through aerial photography by G. A. Beazeley, "Air Photography in Archaeology," *Geographical Journal,* Vol. LIII (October, 1919), 330–35; other photographers of ruins in desert regions are A. Poidebard, *La trace de Rome dans le désert de Syrie* (Paris, 1934), 213, pl. 161; T. Wiegand, *Photographs of Sites in the Sinai Peninsula and South-Palestine* (Berlin, 1920); J. Baradez, *"Fossatum Africae,"* *Arts et Métiers* (Paris, 1949), 377; and O. G. S. Crawford, "Rhodesian Cultivation Terraces," *Antiquity,* Vol. XXIV (June, 1950), 96–98.

[10] A. Poidebard, *Un grand port disparu: Tyr* (Paris, 1939), 78, pl. 29.

Harp of the Queen, Al-Mughair

G. Contenau, *La Civilisation d'Assur et de Babylone*

in a field of ripe wheat, whereas remnants of walls and fortifications will produce a lighter color.[11]

The most controversial problem in archaeological research is dating the remains of a given site. Many attempts to work out a reliable system have been made since the beginning of the last century,[12] but only in recent years has substantial progress been achieved. The best-known modern method is the carbon–14 dating technique developed by W. F. Libby,[13] of the University of Chicago, and his associates.[14] It has been established that radioactive carbon is constantly formed in the higher atmosphere by the collision of nitrogen with cosmic rays; through reaction with the oxygen of the atmosphere, carbon–14 is transformed into a gas, a measurable part of which is absorbed, together with normal carbon–12, by plants, and, through these, by animals until their death. Starting from the fact that the radioactive carbon–14 isotope disintegrates to stable carbon–12 in a period of $5,570 \pm 30$ years (the so-called "half-life" as accepted by the International Radiocarbon Dating Conference of 1962), it is possible to calculate the time elapsed since the death of a plant or an animal by measuring the radioactive carbon–14 dioxide[15] in the remains.

As this technique requires that the samples be large,[16] uncontami-

[11] O. G. S. Crawford, *Air Photography for Archaeologists* (Ordnance Survey *Professional Papers,* NS, No. 12, Southhampton, 1929).

[12] Already in 1806, two French chemists, A. F. Fourcroy and L. N. Vauquelin (*"Recherches faites sur l'ivoire frais, sur l'ivoire fossile et sur l'émail des dents pour rechercher si ces substances contiennent de l'acide fluorique,"* AC, Vol. LVII [1806], 37–44) discovered that certain substances absorb fluorine when buried in the ground; this discovery led in 1844 to Middleton's affirmation that the rate of fluorine absorbed by bones was proportional to their age. See "On Fluorine in Bones, Its Source, and Its Application to the Determination of the Geological Age of Fossil Bones," *Proceedings of the Geological Society of London,* IV (London, 1844), 431 ff.

[13] "Atmospheric Helium Three and Radiocarbon from Cosmic Radiation," *The Physical Review,* Vol. 69, No. 11–12 (December, 1946), 67; and *Radiocarbon Dating* (2d ed., Chicago, 1955).

[14] E. C. Anderson, of the Institute for Nuclear Studies, University of Chicago; S. Weinhouse, A. F. Reid, A. D. Kirshenbaum, and A. V. Grosse, of the Houdry Process Corporation at Marcus Hook, Pennsylvania.

[15] The radiocarbon content in living matter has been found to be 15.3 carbon–14 atoms disintegrating every minute in each gram of carbon.

[16] The minimum quantity of a wood or charcoal sample is 65 grams; 200 grams are

8

nated by objects of more recent epochs, and lightly carbonized,[17] it can be applied only in limited cases. It does, however, provide fairly precise dating, and the method is being improved continually.[18]

Supplementary evidence may be gathered through several other methods of dating prehistoric material. The age of unburnt osseous fossils and the inner part of teeth[19] can under certain circumstances be determined by measuring their fluorine content.[20] Bones and teeth buried in the ground absorb a small quantity of this element from the surrounding soil[21] at a steady rate. Since the amount of fluorine varies considerably from region to region, no absolute measures can be established; but it is possible to sort mixed bone fossils of various ages, found at the same site, and to ascribe them to the corresponding epochs.[22]

As prehistoric pottery, often the only testimony of an ancient phase of civilization, cannot be dated by any of the above-mentioned tests, some

required for samples of other vegetable substances. To establish the age of teeth, 2,200 grams are necessary, since only the enamel can be utilized. Animal shells must be submitted in samples of at least 700 grams, and 500 grams are required for horns and similar substances. (Amounts may vary depending upon the laboratory.) Each sample is entirely destroyed in the process of analysis.

[17] If bones have been incinerated, they cannot be utilized for experiments, since the carbon has been totally consumed; if, on the other hand, no combustion whatever has occurred, the osseous matter is usually decomposed to such an extent that a suitable sample cannot be obtained.

[18] Recently two scientists of the Boston University School of Medicine extracted the gelatin of 12,000-year-old deer antlers, which yielded a 96 per cent pure sample for carbon-dating.

[19] Tooth enamel is impenetrable to fluorine ions.

[20] See note 12 above.

[21] Chemical reaction of the bone mineral with fluorine:

$$Ca_{10}(PO_4)_6(OH)_2 + 2F = Ca_{10}(PO_4)_6F_2 + H_2O + O$$

[22] Developing earlier studies of A. Carnot (1893), K. Oakley established the fluorine method for the dating of buried bones in 1948, "Fluorine and the Relative Dating of Bones," *AS*, Vol. IV (October, 1948), 336ff. A new method for the dating of bones, based on the diffraction of X rays, has recently been devised by M. Escalon de Fonton, R. Michaud, and G. Périnet, *"Étude par diffraction des rayons X de la fossilisation d'ossements préhistoriques, Premiers résultats de la détermination de l'age d'ossements préhistoriques par les spectres de diffraction X," Comptes-rendus des séances de l'Académie des Sciences,* Vol. 233 (Paris, 1951), 706ff. In the Americas, a third method of bone dating, the Abelson test, which measures the degree of degeneration of protein molecules, was used several years ago by Juan Armenta, of the University of Puebla, to establish the age of a fossilized pelvic bone, found at Valsequillo, Mexico, and believed to be 30,000 years old.

scientists have tried to devise a technique to determine how much time has elapsed since the firing of a vessel, brick, or tablet.

At the end of the nineteenth century, the Italian scholar Folgheraiter undertook extensive research concerning the magnetization of earthenware as the basis for a new dating method. After an object has been fired, the iron particles contained in the clay become fixed according to the magnetic field of the earth at the moment of cooling. However, the impossibility of calculating the intensity, inclination, and declination of the terrestrial magnetic field during prehistoric periods, together with the difficulty in finding appropriate pottery specimens, greatly reduce the prospects for a fruitful application of this method based on thermo-remanence of fired clay objects.[23]

Starting from a similar basis, more promising results have been obtained through a technique which consists of reheating, under a sensitive photomultiplier, an object fired at an unknown date and measuring the glow it emits. The intensity of the light, divided by the radioactivity of the object, will yield information concerning the time elapsed since the clay was last fired.[24]

The work of the archaeologist alone has made possible our knowledge of the ancient civilizations of Mesopotamia. While early explorers unearthed mostly vestiges of historical times, their successors recognized the importance of those strata that bore testimony of prehistoric epochs.[25] The study of potsherds, architectural remains, and the condition of tombs can be of great value for the determination of the ethnic bases that underlie the earliest cultures.

Mesopotamian prehistory is, according to the most recent scholarship,[26] divided into the following periods:

[23] Research on this technique is presently being conducted at the Institut de Physique du Globe de l'Université de Paris under the direction of Professor E. Thellier, author of a book and several articles on the subject: *Problèmes de Géomagnétisme* (Paris, 1950), 47–64; *"L'aimantation des Terres Cuites et ses Applications Géophysiques,"* AIPG, Vol. XVI (1938), 157ff.; and *"Magnetisme Terrestre et Archéologie,"* Anthropologie, Vol. XLIX (October, 1939), 494–96.

[24] This new method was developed in 1959 by G. C. Kennedy, of the University of California at Los Angeles. Research is being conducted to determine the margin of error.

[25] E.g., the excavations made by Max Freiherr von Oppenheim at Tell-Halaf (1911–13 and 1929) and the discoveries by E. Herzfeld in Samarra (1912–14).

[26] The basis of this division is furnished by the report of Robert J. and Linda Braid-

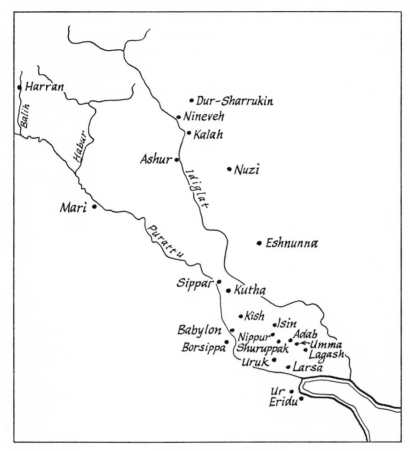

Ancient Mesopotamia

1) Prepottery period (end of sixth millennium B.C.)
2) Hassunah period (beginning of fifth millennium B.C.)
3) Halaf period (middle of the fifth millennium B.C.)
4) Ubaid period (end of fifth millennium B.C.)
5) Warka and Protoliterate periods — South (fourth millennium B.C.) Gawra and Ninevite periods—North (fourth millennium B.C.)

wood on the excavations at Qalat Jarmo in the section "Archeological News—The Near East," *AJA,* Vol. LIII (January-March, 1949), 49–51; and by A. L. Perkins' book, *The Comparative Archeology of Early Mesopotamia.*

*The Prepottery period.* In 1948, Robert J. and Linda Braidwood discovered at Qalat Jarmo, in the foothills of Kurdistan, traces of a very ancient neolithic settlement which yielded no potsherds whatsoever, only primitive artifacts such as microlithic flint tools. This is the earliest village assemblage yet found in Mesopotamia; it illustrates the neolithic change from food-gathering to food production and the transition from nomadic life to semisedentary existence. The excavators submitted several samples from the site for carbon–14 dating; the results indicate that the oldest stratum of civilization goes back to the late sixth millennium B.C.[27]

The only example in the Near East showing a similar degree of evolution is represented by the site of Jericho in Palestine, where the first traces of coarse pottery overlay a debris layer about twenty feet thick, which contains flints but no potsherds.

*The Hassunah period.* The oldest earthenware in Mesopotamia has been found in the lowest levels of Hassunah,[28] Matarra,[29] Samarra,[30] Arpachiyyah,[31] Nineveh,[32] Halaf,[33] and other northern mounds.[34] These potsherds are roughly contemporary with those found in Deir Tasa, Al-Badari, and Merimde-Banisalam in Egypt, Mersin in Turkey, Tepe Sialk in Iran, and Anau in Turkestan, as well as with the already mentioned earthenware of Jericho.

[27] The most ancient sample, consisting of snail shells from level 7 of excavation I, is supposed to be 6,707 years old (margin of error: ±320 years). The second sample, flecks of charcoal (same level), is about 100 years younger, and two other charcoal samples seem to be respectively 6,695 and 5,266 years old. See *JNES*, Vol. XI (January, 1952), 66.

[28] Seton Lloyd and Fuad Safar, "Tell Hassuna," *JNES*, Vol. IV (October, 1945), 255–89.

[29] Robert J. and Linda Braidwood, J. S. Smith, and C. Leslie, "Matarra, a Southern Variant of the Hassunan Assemblage, Excavated in 1948," *JNES*, Vol. XI (January, 1952), 2–75.

[30] E. Herzfeld, *"Die Ausgrabungen von Samarra V,"* *Forschungen zur islamischen Kunst,* Vol. II (January, 1930), 5.

[31] M. E. L. Mallowan and Cruikshank Rose, "Excavations at Tall Arpachiyah 1933," *Iraq,* Vol. II (January-April, 1935), 1–178.

[32] M. E. L. Mallowan, "The Prehistoric Sondage of Nineveh," *AAA,* Vol. XX (Liverpool, 1933), 95–104.

[33] M. E. L. Mallowan, *Survey of the Habur.*

[34] The Iraqi mounds, commonly called "tell" ("tepe" in Iran), have been formed by the debris of several successive settlements on the same site. In 1945 the Department of

The people of this period, probably still seminomadic, did not know metal tools.[35] The pottery, apparently not manufactured by trained craftsmen but by the women of each separate household, is at first very coarse and tempered with straw; later occur burnished, incised, or painted vessels, usually much better fired than the former ware. The standard ceramic material of the Hassunah period is decorated with both incisions and painted designs, in red, gray, brown, or black.

A particular style is represented by the Samarran pottery,[36] which shows a remarkable quality of design, almost entirely geometric[37] and never polychrome.

Architectural remains of four-wall buildings in Hassunah consist of construction material of pisé and mud lumps, but apparently most of the primitive dwellings were huts made of reeds and skins.

The dead are buried in sleeping position, lying on the right side, their bodies contracted. The fact that the graves contain various objects suggests a primitive conception of an existence after death.

Some very crude clay figurines representing women have been found in levels corresponding to this period; they seem to be the earliest testimony of a mother-goddess cult in this region.

*The Halaf period.* Here we enter an era during which metal begins to be known but is not yet used for the manufacture of tools and weapons.[38]

The pottery characteristic of this period shows polychrome decoration, in red, brown, black, or bister. The vessels are thin walled and very well fired, almost porcelain-like in appearance. This ware has been

Antiquities in Baghdad estimated the number of "tells" that represented sites of ancient civilizations at 2,886. So far, excavations have been made in approximately sixty-five Mesopotamian tells.

[35] An implement of iron and various pieces of copper found at Samarra are supposed to be intrusive and to belong to the Islamic epoch. Cf. E. Herzfeld, *Archäologische Mitteilungen aus Iran,* V (Berlin, 1935), 29ff.

[36] In Matarra no other pottery than the Samarra-style earthenware has been found.

[37] There are, however, a few highly stylized figures of birds, fish, serpents, deer, and women.

[38] A piece of lead and two fragmentary copper ornaments were found in Arpachiyyah; a copper bead of Shaghir Bazar belongs to the same period.

found in Halaf, [39] Arpachiyyah,[40] Tepe Gawra,[41] Hassunah (levels above the pottery of the preceding period),[42] Nineveh,[43] Tell Brak,[44] and Shaghir Bazar.[45]

The architecture of this epoch exhibits a rather peculiar feature—most of the recognizable buildings are circular, and some of them have an attached rectangular antechamber. The constructions, which bear a striking resemblance to the Mycenaean beehive tombs, did not, however, have a sepulchral function, nor do they appear to be secular dwellings.[46]

Burial customs have not changed; bodies lie in sleeping position, with pottery or other objects at their side.

At almost every site were found crude clay figurines, which apparently represent pregnant women or women in the squatting position of childbirth. They probably belong, like the Hassunah idols, to the mother-goddess cult.

*The Ubaid period.* The first culture for which evidence has been found in the South dates from this epoch. It is characterized by a prevalence of monochrome pottery, mostly greenish ware decorated with black geometric designs.[47]

This aeneolithic (or Chalcolithic) civilization extends over a far greater area than the preceding one; not only does it cover all Mesopotamia, but its vestiges are found also in Syria and northern Turkey.

[39] Max Freiherr von Oppenheim, *Tell Halaf I, Tell Halaf II,* and *Tell Halaf III* (These three books are in the series *Die prähistorischen Funde,* edited by H. Schmidt, and were published respectively in 1943, 1950, and 1955, in Berlin).

[40] Mallowan and Rose, "Excavations at Tall Arpachiyah 1933," *Iraq,* Vol. II (1935) 1–178.

[41] E. A. Speiser, *Excavations at Tepe Gawra,* Part I (Philadelphia, 1935); and A. J. Tobler, *Excavations at Tepe Gawra,* Part II (Philadelphia, 1950); hereafter cited as one work.

[42] Lloyd and Safar, "Tell Hassuna," *JNES,* Vol. IV (October, 1945), 255–89.

[43] Mallowan, "The Prehistoric Sondage of Nineveh," *AAA,* Vol. XX (Liverpool, 1933).

[44] M. E. L. Mallowan, "Excavations at Brak and Chagar Bazar," *Iraq,* Vol. IX (January to December, 1947).

[45] M. E. L. Mallowan, "The Excavations at Tall-Chagar Bazar," *Iraq,* Vols. III (January, 1936), and IV (June, 1937).

[46] Mallowan thinks they are shrines, possibly pertaining to the mother-goddess cult attested almost everywhere since the Palaeolithic age. See "Excavations in the Balih Valley," *Iraq,* Vol. VII (June, 1947), 111–59.

[47] The colors may vary according to the composition of the clay and the degree of firing.

*Hassunah*

*Halaf*

*Ubaid*

 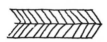 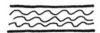

*Jamdat Nasr*

*Nineveh V*

Prehistoric Pottery Designs

The typical monochrome painted pottery has been excavated in southern sites (Ubaid,[48] Al-Mughair,[49] Abu Shahrain,[50] Warka,[51] Telloh,[52] etc.) as well as in northern mounds (Tepe Gawra,[53] Arpachiyyah, [54] Hassunah,[55] Halaf, [56] Nineveh,[57] Yorghan Tepe,[58] etc.).

However, a trend towards a differentiation between North and South is visible: in the South, glyptic art was hardly practiced, while it reached a very high degree of skill in the North.[59] On the other hand, certain objects found in considerable quantity in the South, such as clay sickles, figurines, and cones, occur only rarely in the North.

The traces of architecture in both northern and southern Mesopotamia reveal a fair level of religious life, since several temple remains have been excavated at Tepe Gawra and at Abu Shahrain.[60] The northern site, however, shows certain changes in the structure of religious buildings; after several edifices of rectangular outline, the circular tholoi are once more to be found, and it is quite possible that they represent

[48] C. L. Woolley, "Excavations at Tell Obeid," *AJ*, Vol. IV (October, 1924), 329–46.

[49] Woolley, *Ur Excavations*, II.

[50] Seton Lloyd and Fuad Safar, "Eridu," *Sumer*, Vol. III (April, 1947), 84–111; Seton Lloyd and Fuad Safar, "Uruk Pottery," *Sumer*, Vol. IV (April, 1948), 39–51; and R. Campbell Thompson, "The British Museum Excavations at Abu Shahrain in Mesopotamia in 1918," *Archaeologia*, Vol. LXX (April, 1920), 101–44.

[51] J. Jordan, *Vorläufiger Bericht über die von der Notgemeinschaft der Deutschen Wissenschaftler in Uruk unternommenen Ausgrabungen* (Berlin, 1930–41); and E. Heinrich, *Ausgrabungen der Deutschen Forschungsgemeinschaft in Uruk-Warka*, I–V (Berlin, 1936–53). (Both these books are in the series *Abhandlungen der preussischen Akademie der Wissenschaften.*) See also H. Lenzen, *"Ausgrabungen in Uruk,"* *Sumer*, Vol. X (January, 1954), 86–88 and (April, 1954), 100–101.

[52] A. Parrot, *Tello—Vingt campagnes de fouilles 1877–1933* (Paris, 1948).

[53] Speiser and Tobler, *Excavations at Tepe Gawra*.

[54] Mallowan and Rose, "Excavations at Tall Arpachiyah 1933," *Iraq*, Vol. II (1935), 1–178.

[55] Lloyd and Safar, "Tell Hassuna," *JNES*, Vol. IV (October, 1945), 255–89.

[56] Oppenheim, *Tell Halaf I*.

[57] Mallowan, "The Prehistoric Sondage of Nineveh," *AAA*, Vol. XX (Liverpool, 1933), 95–104.

[58] Richard F. S. Starr, *Nuzi; Report on the Excavation at Yorgan Tepe Near Kirkuk, Iraq*.

[59] Almost 600 seals and seal impressions, dating from the Ubaid period, have been found in Tepe Gawra.

[60] Northern temples usually show a tripartite plan, while the southern varieties consist of several rooms grouped around a court.

some other kind of temple. Still later, religious structures are completely missing, while we find a number of long rectangular bins, supposed to have been storage rooms, which do not occur elsewhere.

At a level in Gawra corresponding to the end of the Ubaid period was found a group of three temples and, later, another building (probably of religious character) called the "White Room." These last structures show traces of violent destruction, evidently wrought by invaders who afterwards created the civilization of the next levels.

All thirteen temples of Abu Shahrain belonging to the Ubaid period have rectangular outlines; the tholos is unknown in the South. The last five temples are built on a platform; three of these shrines follow a tripartite plan, with a large central "cella" and smaller rooms on either side.

The changes in northern architecture have their counterpart in the burial customs. While during the first period of the Ubaid age occur mostly simple inhumations with bodies contracted in sleeping position,[61] there are at the time of the three temples and the "White Room" in Tepe Gawra mostly urn burials.[62]

In the South we find a striking change in the burial customs of the Ubaid period: the inhumations excavated in Abu Shahrain (about two hundred) as well as the Al-Mughair graves show, without exception, the dead buried in an extended position. This new practice, which made its appearance around the end of the epoch, seems to indicate an invasion by other populations.

Quite a number of figurines, almost exclusively female, have been found in southern mounds. Most of them have heads resembling the snout of a reptile. There are also a few male specimens with similar serpentine features.

*The Warka period.* The earliest civilization following the culture of the Ubaid period in the South has been identified so far only in Warka and Al-Mughair. This age is characterized by only two new styles of pottery: one style consists of unpainted ware, always handmade, light

[61] The excavations of the Ubaid levels in Tepe Gawra yielded also three supine burials.

[62] Perkins (*Comparative Archeology*, 73) divides the northern Ubaid period into two parts: "Northern Ubaid I" (first temples, tholoi, bins; contracted burials) and "Northern Ubaid II" (three-temple group, "White Room"; urn burials).

in color, rather coarse, and less well fired than the Ubaid vessels; the second style is represented by red or gray ware, mostly wheel-made, burnished or dark slipped. This last variant of the Warka pottery was probably produced by firing the clay in smother kilns, where the smoke, created by a lack of oxygen, gave a gray or black color to the ware.

It is possible that the two techniques were used by two distinct elements of the population, the producers of the dark ware slightly preceding those of the unpainted light-colored pottery. That the Ubaid civilization had not completely disappeared is shown by the fact that monochrome-painted vessels coexist with the vases of the new period.

Architecture was not yet as highly developed as in the Protoliterate period. The "White Temple" in Warka shows a plan which resembles that of almost all the later prehistoric temples in the South. On a high platform[63] built of mud bricks, a tripartite structure was erected, with the cella in the middle and a row of small rooms on each side. The walls are made of mud bricks plastered with clay and then covered with a whitewash, whence the name of the temple.

In other sites there are no architectural remains which can be attributed to the Warka age with any degree of certainty.

About the burial customs of this period we are only poorly informed. Warka has yielded no tombs at all; the Mughair graves are simple pits in which the bodies are buried in a supine position. At the sides of the dead are red or drab unpainted ware and a few specimens of cuplike painted vases.

Glyptic seems to have been now more frequent in the South; besides several stamp seals of good workmanship, the first cylinder seals appear in Warka, and one other specimen has been found in Al-Mughair.

Stone sculpture begins in this period, as attested by the figures of a wild boar and a woman; these statuettes were excavated respectively in Al-Mughair and Warka.

*The Protoliterate period.* This civilization,[64] which preceded the

---

63 The platform is commonly designated by archaeologists as the "Anu *Ziqqurat*," although it is not certain at all that this terrace was ever dedicated to Anu, nor can the structure be called a *ziqqurat*.

64 About 3100–2900 B.C.; as indicated above, the Warka culture has been identified

Early Dynastic epoch, is particularly important since it was responsible for the oldest written documents of Mesopotamia.

The Protoliterate age is divided into four phases.[65] The first pictographic tablets of Warka belong to phase B, while the preceding phase A is considered the formative period of the new civilization. Phases C and D are periods of chiefly architectural and glyptic achievements.

The pottery of the Protoliterate epoch, found in Warka,[66] Al-Mughair,[67] Abu Shahrain,[68] Ubaid,[69] Telloh,[70] Farah,[71] Jamdat Nasr,[72] Tell Uqair,[73] Khafajah, and Tell Asmar,[74] is of various styles. There are, as in the levels of the Warka culture, plain vessels, either burnished or slipped. The occurrence of gray and red ware is another common feature of the two periods. But there is also a new kind of pottery, decorated in the Jamdat Nasr style,[75] which shows polychrome painting or a peculiar plum-red slip.

The true progress, however, is not represented by this last Proto-

only in Warka and Al-Mughair. In all other southern sites the Protoliterate period seems to come right after the Ubaid levels.

[65] P. Delougaz, *Pottery from the Diyala Region.*

[66] Jordan, *Vorläufiger Bericht über die von der Notgemeinschaft der Deutschen Wissenschaftler in Uruk unternommenen Ausgrabungen;* Heinrich, *Ausgrabungen der Deutschen Forschungsgemeinschaft in Uruk-Warka;* and Lenzen, *"Ausgrabungen in Uruk," Sumer,* Vol. X (January, 1954), 86–88 and *ibid.* (April, 1954), 100–101.

[67] Woolley, *Ur Excavations,* II.

[68] Lloyd and Safar, "Eridu," *Sumer,* Vol. III (April, 1947), 84–111; Lloyd and Safar, "Uruk Pottery," *Sumer,* Vol. IV (April, 1948), 39–51; and Campbell Thompson, "The British Museum Excavations at Abu Shahrain in Mesopotamia in 1918," *Archaeologia,* Vol. LXX (April, 1920), 101–44.

[69] Woolley, "Excavations at Tell Obeid," *AJ,* Vol. IV (1924), 329–46.

[70] Parrot, *Tello.*

[71] E. F. Schmidt, "Excavations at Fara," *MJ,* Vol. XXII (October, 1931), 192–245.

[72] E. Mackay, *Report on Excavations at Jemdet Nasr, Iraq.*

[73] Seton Lloyd and Fuad Safar, "Tell Uqair," *JNES,* Vol. II (June, 1943), 132–58.

[74] Henri Frankfort, *Tell Asmar and Khafajah* (Oriental Institute *Communications,* Chicago, 1932–36).

[75] The particular style of this pottery induced archaeologists until a few years ago to consider the Jamdat Nasr ware as characteristic of an independent prehistoric period which followed the cultures of Ubaid and Warka; according to the same opinion, the Warka period was supposed to have covered the entire area of western Asia. This outdated view is expressed, for example, by G. Contenau in *Les civilisations anciennes du Proche-Orient* (Paris, 1955), 89.

literate variety, because the ware thus decorated is quite coarse and the designs are far from artistic. But the already known light-colored unpainted vases are now much better made, mostly on the fast wheel, and there are a number of new forms, often gracefully shaped.

The red and gray wares are frequently decorated with fingernail incisions, and a new technique, known as the "reserved slip" method,[76] is introduced; it flourished chiefly in the Early Dynastic period, right after the Protoliterate phases.

The great variety of the pottery possibly reflects the presence of several elements of population; it is therefore especially difficult to find out which people was the creator of writing in Mesopotamian culture.

Other than a very old tablet found at Al-Uhaimir,[77] inscribed with almost undecipherable pictographs, the first collection of written documents was discovered at Warka.[78] Although these 570 tablets also bear pictographic script, the meaning can be more or less guessed, since they consist almost exclusively of numerical signs, with the addition of a few depicted objects.

Another collection of thirty-four tablets has been excavated in the succeeding Warka level.[79] Here we stand at the dividing point between Protoliterate and Early Dynastic periods; the signs are better developed and might be considered semipictographic.[80] Contemporaneous and on the same level of development with this last collection is a group of 194 tablets found at Jamdat Nasr.[81] There has been a controversy about the nature of the language used in these early groups of tablets, but it now seems incontestable that both the Warka III tablets and the Jamdat

[76] Part of the slip is wiped away when still fresh, so that the original color of the surface is visible, forming a pattern against the darker slip. Sometimes painted decoration is applied to the reserved areas.

[77] S. Langdon, *Excavations at Kish* (Oxford, 1924), 1–2, pl. XXI.

[78] *Level IV of the Eanna precinct* (J. Jordan, *Vorläufiger Bericht über die von der Notgemeinschaft der Deutschen Wissenschaft in Uruk unternommenen Ausgrabungen,* 24 ff.).

[79] Level III of the Eanna precinct (*ibid.,* II, 27ff.).

[80] G. R. Driver, *Semitic Writing,* 6: ". . . the texts from Jamdat Nasr have the first use of a sign with determinative value."

[81] S. Langdon, "Pictographic Inscriptions from Jemdet Nasr," *DAO,* Vol. XXVI (January, 1927), 73.

Nasr texts are written in Sumerian.[82] Thus it is highly probable that writing in Mesopotamia was actually invented by the Sumerians.

Turning to architecture, we see that it has developed to an amazing extent. In Warka several new techniques are used in both construction and decoration. While the plan of the Protoliterate temples continues to be essentially tripartite, the number of doorways increases, and in various temples there occur walls and wallbeds of limestone. A new kind of wall decoration makes use of many-colored limestone or clay cones inserted into the plaster to form mosaics of geometrical design; this decoration has been found on outer as well as on inner walls. Another temple presents the first example of free-standing columns, all of them covered with a thick layer of clay and decorated with black and white clay-cone mosaics. Some of the next temples are built on terraces, and a unique structure, the so-called "labyrinth," makes its appearance, erected on a plan totally different from that of the tripartite temples. This building consists of a number of small rooms, some of which could evidently be entered only through circuitous ways of access; there are no corridors or courts to connect the rooms. The location of the "labyrinth" in the sacred Eanna precinct seems to indicate a religious function of this complex. In a shrine at Tell Uqair we find for the first time painted frescoes which show both geometrical designs and animal or human figures.

About the burial customs during the Protoliterate period we know only little, since no graves have been found in most of the sites. The tombs from Al-Mughair and Farah may be attributed to the Early Dynastic period; the bodies lay in sleeping position and had probably been wrapped in reed matting; the pottery found in the graves likely held food offerings.

The art of stonecutting stands on as high a level as the architecture of this period. Vases as well as stamp or cylinder seals testify to a remarkable perfection in draftsmanship and artistic co-ordination.

---

[82] A. Falkenstein, *"Archaische Texte aus Uruk," Vorläufiger Bericht über die von der Notgemeinschaft der Deutschen Wissenschaft in Uruk-Warka unternommenen Ausgrabungen*, II (*Abhandlungen der preussischen Akademie der Wissenschaften*, Phil.-hist. Klasse, Berlin-Leipzig, 1936), 37–43.

## A. Tholoi from Arpachiyyah

## B. Group of Three Temples from Tepe Gawra

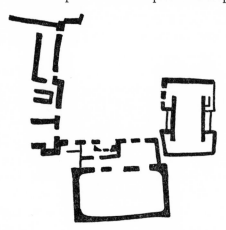

Prehistoric Architecture

One very finely carved alabaster vase excavated in Warka represents the earliest evidence of Mesopotamian cult scenes and is therefore important also for our knowledge of the religious customs pertaining to this culture.[83] On the seals we find animal or human motifs, while

[83] See Chapter III below, "Pictorial Art"; and Woolley, "Excavations at Tell Obeid," *AJ,* Vol. IV (October, 1924), 329–46.

geometrical design is predominant in the cylinders belonging to the Jamdat Nasr style.

The first specimens of monumental sculpture-in-the-round date from this period. The statue of a woman (Khafajah), several stone animals (Al-Mughair and Telloh), and a magnificent human head of marble (Warka) illustrate the high degree of artistic achievement in this early period.

Most of the metal vases and tools excavated in the area are made of copper, a few of gold and silver.

While southern Mesopotamia enjoyed a relatively high culture during this age, the northern sites show the vestiges of a contemporary civilization both different from and inferior to that of the Protoliterate period just examined.

*The Gawra and Ninevite periods.* The period which follows the Ubaid civilization of the North and precedes the beginning of history in northern Mesopotamia appears by no means as homogeneous as the southern sequence of the Warka and the Protoliterate levels. It does not seem as if the region were inhabited by only one or even two elements of population, since there is a considerable lack of coherence between one site and another, even between such settlements as Nineveh and Tepe Gawra, which are only a few miles apart. Vestiges of these cultures have been found in Nineveh,[84] Tepe Gawra,[85] Yorghan Tepe,[86] Shaghir Bazar,[87] Tell Brak,[88] Tell Billa,[89] and Grai Resh.[90]

The invaders who destroyed the "White Room" in Gawra and put an end to the Ubaid civilization were apparently of a lower cultural level than the previous occupants. This is evident from the much poorer

[84] Mallowan, "The Prehistoric Sondage of Nineveh," *AAA*, Vol. XX (Liverpool, 1933), 95–101.

[85] Speiser and Tobler, *Excavations at Tepe Gawra.*

[86] Starr, *Report on the Excavations at Yorgan Tepe.*

[87] Mallowan, "The Excavations at Tall-Chagar Bazar," *Iraq*, Vols. III (January, 1936) and IV (June, 1937).

[88] Mallowan, "Excavations at Brak and Chagar Bazar," *Iraq*, Vol. IX (January to December, 1947).

[89] E. A. Speiser, "The Pottery of Tell Billa," *MJ*, Vol. XXIII (Philadelphia, 1932).

[90] Seton Lloyd, "Iraq Government Soundings at Sinjar," *Iraq*, Vol. VII (January, 1940), 13–19.

quality of the pottery introduced by the new populations. The vessels, mostly handmade,[91] are coarse, thick walled, and made of dark clay tempered with sand or straw; there is no connection at all with southern styles of decoration. Only the early Ninevite pottery has a red slip similar to that of the Warka ware. Later on there appear in Nineveh[92] several new techniques: we find not only simply but also elaborately incised vases showing relief work and made of light-colored, very well-fired clay. Besides this class there is another group of vessels more popular than the first: the entire surface of the pots, which are of coarse light-colored clay, is covered with dark or bright red designs of awkwardly drawn birds and other animals.

The motifs of the Gawra painted vessels are mostly geometrical, in contrast to the designs of animals and humans on the Ninevite ware. Elaborately incised pots are not present at all. Among the other northern sites yielding Ninevite-style elaborately incised as well as profusely painted ceramics are Tell Brak, Tell Billa, and Shaghir Bazar.

One wonders why the two sites of Nineveh and Gawra, apparently in a very close neighborhood, have so little in common as far as their earthenware is concerned. Furthermore, the painted ware and the elaborately incised pottery, both found in Nineveh V, seem to be the products of different ethnic elements; in Tell Billa, the two styles are stratigraphically separated.

Thus the wares of the Ninevite and Gawra periods show a heterogeneous picture, reflecting probably the many different components of the population that settled in the North during the last prehistoric phases.

That the coexistence of these groups of inhabitants was not always peaceful seems to be borne out by some of the architectural remains. While we have encountered only religious buildings and some private houses in the South, there appear in the North certain structures which seem to have been used for defense. One of them is the round, thick-walled edifice called the "Round House" in Tepe Gawra. It belongs to the period which immediately followed the destruction of the settlement around the "White Room." Another building probably used for

---

[91] The introduction of the fast wheel is attributed to Gawra levels IX–VIII.
[92] Ninevite level V.

defense appears in the next period, and there are remnants of watch-towers in many other levels as well as masses of unusually thick brick walls.

Many temples also existed in this period, almost all erected on the usual tripartite plan. The most striking of them is the "Eye-Temple" in Tell Brak, so called after the design of a human eye on the copper paneling of the central room. The shrine stands on a platform consisting of the leveled ruins of three older temples (named respectively the "Red Eye-Temple," "Gray Eye-Temple," and "White Eye-Temple") and shows the remnants of a remarkably well-decorated altar.

Judging from the burials of the Gawra and Ninevite periods, one might suppose that a part of the inhabitants corresponding to the Ubaid civilization had survived the invasion of the new conquerors. The vessels of the Gawra graves are in fact mostly specimens showing the style of the last Ubaid levels. Most of the dead lay in the customary sleeping position; a small group of urn burials was found, along with an isolated grave containing a supine body.

In Tell Billa, the difference in the two pottery styles is matched by a change in the burial customs: the dead of level VI are not buried in the customary sleeping position, as were the bodies of the previous stratum.

Among the objects found in the tombs, there are in the later levels of Tepe Gawra some particularly beautiful stone vases, thin walled and very finely ornamented. Cylinder seals were found in Tell Billa in almost every grave, while in Tepe Gawra they are limited to the last level. Some seals of the same form were excavated in the "Eye-Temple" of Tell Brak. However, stamp seals are much more common than cylinder seals; the latter type had probably been introduced by southern merchants. The most significant feature of the cylinders is the adoption of the geometrical style characteristic of a group of Jamdat Nasr seals.

Monumental sculpture existed only at Tell Brak, where four stone masks of marked geometrical stylization have been found under the ruins of the "Eye-Temple." Other sites yielded the customary clay figurines representing females and sometimes males.

The only metal vessel unearthed in the north is a bronze vase from Tell Billa. Tools and weapons do not occur frequently, but perhaps

25

many were made of perishable material and are lost to the excavators.

The sporadic material evidence of Mesopotamian prehistory, as well as the still embryonic state of dating techniques, make it very difficult to establish an absolute chronology for the time that elapsed between the Neolithic age and history,[93] but it is possible to guess, on the basis of excavation reports, the relative duration of each period and to estimate the temporal extent of coexistence between the cultures of neighboring regions.[94]

## HISTORY

Ancient Mesopotamian history begins at the onset of the third millennium; passing successively through the Pre-Babylonian, Old Babylonian, Assyrian, and Neo-Babylonian periods, it comes to an end in 539 B.C., when the country was conquered by the Persians under their King Cyrus the Great.

The Pre-Babylonian (or Early Dynastic) time continues the evolution of the Protoliterate period, adhering to the same political, religious, and artistic patterns of this rich civilization. The assumption that the Sumerians were the masters of early Mesopotamian culture seems to be confirmed by the fact that the first written documents, found in the last prehistoric levels, render Sumerian dialects.[95] It is by no means certain, however, that the Sumerians preceded the Semites chronologically in the habitation of the Plain; the identification of several Semitic loan words[96] in very old Sumerian texts speaks in favor of a Semitic temporal priority. We must therefore consider the possibility that the Semites, too, played a role in the creation of the first high culture in Mesopotamia. Furthermore, the population of the Pre-Babylonian period probably contained a substratum of a third ethnic element which was responsible for the peculiarities of the Sumerian *"eme-sal"* dialect.[97]

[93] For a tentative dating of the principal periods see Robert J. and Linda Braidwood, *AJA*, Vol. LIII (January-March, 1949); and Perkins, *Comparative Archeology*.

[94] See the diagram in Perkins, *Comparative Archeology*, table 3.

[95] A. Falkenstein, *"Archaische Texte aus Uruk,"* Vorläufiger Bericht über die von der Notgemeinschaft der Deutschen Wissenschaft in Uruk-Warka unternommenen Ausgrabungen, II, 37–43.

[96] A. Poebel, *"Sumerische Untersuchungen,"* ZA, Vol. XXXIX (June, 1930), 149, n. 2.

[97] See Chapter III below, n. 13.

Many suppositions have been made concerning the racial composition of the earliest Mesopotamian inhabitants. The divergence of opinion among the Assyriologists is due in part to the scarcity of archaeological material on which to base any conclusion. On the other hand, scholars have been using a variety of names to designate ancient Near Eastern peoples, borrowing geographical terms or Biblical appellations. Names such as "Subarians,"[98] "Japhetites,"[99] or "Asianics"[100] are mostly meant to identify one and the same population group; terms such as "Amorites" (or "Amurru"),[101] "Kishiotes,"[102] "Arameans,"[103] and the like refer to subdivisions of the Semites.

On the basis of the evidence gained from the excavations, judging especially from the different pottery styles, it is perhaps justifiable to assume that the creators of the unpainted light-colored pottery which was found in Warka levels contemporary with and anterior to the first pictographic tablets were the Sumerians.

The slipped red and gray vessels, which appear at the same time in Warka and Al-Mughair but show inferior workmanship, are possibly the product of the Elamites, who were culturally eclipsed by the Sumer-

98 A. Ungnad, *"Die ältesten Völkerwanderungen Vorderasiens,"* *Kulturfragen,* I (Leipzig, 1923); and *"Subartu,"* *Beitrage zur Kulturgeschichte und Volkerkunde Vorderasiens* (Berlin, 1936); the term "Subarians" is later used in a more restricted sense by I. J. Gelb ("Hurrians and Subarians," *Studies in Ancient Oriental Civilization,* Vol. XXII [1944]), who connects the Subarians with the Guti, Elamites, and Lullu, and opposes them to the group of Hurrians and Urartaeans. S. A. Pallis (*The Antiquity of Iraq,* 452) sees in the Subarians a people who invaded the southern part of Mesopotamia during the early Dynastic period.

99 E. A. Speiser, *Mesopotamian Origins.* The "Japhetites" comprise "Hurrians" and "Elamites." The term "Japhetites" has been used by the Russian scholar N. Marr to designate Asianic peoples, Etruscans, and Basques, under the assumption that they had once formed one linguistic family. In the publications of the Institute of Japhetite Research (Leningrad, 1922ff.), the epithet "Japhetite" refers to the Indo-European languages.

100 Most recent, and now generally accepted term for a number of not otherwise classifiable languages of the ancient Near East comprising Hurrian, Urartaean, Elamite, Hatti, Sumerian, etc. See M. Cohen, *Les Langues du Monde* (Paris, 1952).

101 A. T. Clay, *Amurru, the House of the Northern Semites* (Philadelphia, 1909); and *The Empire of the Amorites* (New Haven, 1919).

102 Pallis, *Antiquity of Iraq.*

103 S. Schiffer, *Die Aramäer* (Leipzig, 1911); R. A. Bowman, "Arameans, Aramaic and the Bible," *JNES,* Vol. VII, (April, 1948), 65–90; and A. Dupont-Sommer, *"Les Araméens,"* *L,Occident ancien illustré,* Vol. II (Paris, 1949).

ians, but whose early presence in southern Mesopotamia can be deduced from ancient non-Sumerian place names.[104]

For an identification of the Semites with the makers of the coarse, polychrome painted earthenware of Jamdat Nasr style there is no sure evidence. It is very probable that the Semites were already present in the Plain during the Warka period.[105] Leading at first the primitive existence of nomads, they used, perhaps exclusively, waterskins and leather containers; later, after adopting a sedentary way of life, these tribes presumably started the making of pottery at the beginning of the Protoliterate age. Between the coarse, crudely painted, and inexpertly fired Jamdat Nasr ware and the other styles of painted pottery usually attributed to an Iranian origin[106] no connection is possible, since neither the Samarran nor the Ninevite V vessels show polychrome decoration; furthermore, the motifs and their co-ordination are quite different. Therefore, a supposition linking the Jamdat Nasr vessels with the Semites may not be entirely discarded.[107]

*The Pre-Babylonian period (ca.2900–1800 B.C.).* The names of the oldest Mesopotamian monarchs are known to us through a Sumerian text[108] which lists all the early rulers, as well as the length of their reign, until the epoch of Utu-Hegal, king of Uruk (about 2250 B.C.). The ancient scribe divides the "history" of his country into an antediluvian and a postdiluvian period. The first kings of the list, often gods or mythological heroes, are credited in the text with reigns that extend over such fantastic periods as 36,000 or 43,000 years. The numbers ap-

---

[104] E.g., Shuruppak, Larak, Zimbir, and Zarar (for the etymology of these place names, cf. Speiser, *Mesopotamian Origins*, 38ff.

[105] Cf. Poebel, *"Sumerische Untersuchungen,"* ZA, Vol. XXXIX (June, 1930), 149, n. 2.

[106] For a connection of the northern painted pottery styles (Samarra, Nineveh V, and Gawra) with Persian sites, cf. D. E. McCown, *The Comparative Stratigraphy of Early Iran* (Studies in Ancient Oriental Civilization, Vol. XXIII, Chicago, 1942).

[107] It is generally assumed that the Ubaid culture, with its overfired, monochrome-painted pottery, was that of a pre-Sumerian Asianic people, perhaps the Hurrians; cf. A. Parrot, *Archéologie mésopotamienne*, II (Paris, 1953). No counterparts outside Mesopotamia have been found for the Halaf pottery nor for the elaborately incised ware of Nineveh V.

[108] The different versions of this document have been collected by Thorkild Jacobsen, *The Sumerian King List.*

proach a degree of probability only with the third dynasty after the Flood, Ur I: Mesannipadda, its founder, is said to have reigned eighty years. This same king opens for us the chapter of documented history, since his actual existence is attested by a cylinder seal found in a tomb of the Royal Cemetery of Ur.[109]

Probably contemporary with Mesannipadda's successors was the powerful dynasty of Lagash[110] (about 2700 B.C.) founded by Ur-Nanshe. The most famous ruler of the house is Eannatum, hero of the Vulture Stela.[111] He claimed to have defeated "Ur, Uruk, and Umma, as well as Kish." This last city, ancient stronghold of the Semites, played an important role in the struggles among the city-states.[112]

Eannatum was in turn defeated by Kish and killed in battle. The King's successor, Entemena, recognized the ruler of Kish as "his overlord."[113] The last monarch of the Lagash dynasty, Urukagina, introduced severe reforms directed against the corruption of the priesthood. Protecting the rights of the poor, the King strove to establish peace and prosperity in his city.

Urukagina's efforts, however, were nullified by Lugalzaggesi, who, starting from Umma, annexed successively "Uruk, Ur, and Lagash," forming thus under his hegemony the first confederation of Sumerian cities.

After twenty-five years of reign, Lugalzaggesi's ambition was

---

[109] Woolley, "The Royal Cemetery," *Ur Excavations,* II.

[110] The dates of this chapter follow the chronology proposed by W. F. Albright ("A Third Revision of the Early Chronology of Western Asia," *BASOR* [1942], 28–33). The writer is aware of the divergence of opinion concerning the accurate dating of Mesopotamian history and has adopted Albright's theory as the most convincing chronology, in accordance with I. J. Gelb, F. Weidner, E. Cavaignac, W. von Soden, M. Rutten, and G. Contenau, etc.

[111] Louvre Museum; E. de Sarzec and L. Heuzey, *Découvertes en Chaldée* (Paris, 1884ff.), pls. 3–4.

[112] Mesannipadda, after having defeated Kish, prefers the title "King of Kish" to the appellation "King of Ur." Later on, Sargon I, sovereign of an empire, lays specific claim to the title "King of Kish." Even Neo-Assyrian kings include among their titles the appellation "King of Kish" (G. A. Barton, *The Royal Inscriptions of Sumer and Akkad* [New Haven, 1929]). For the political implications of this title see J. Lewy, *Hebrew Union College Annual* (1946), 476.

[113] Cf. F. Thureau-Dangin, *"Die sumerischen und akkadischen Königsinschriften,"* *Vorderasiatische Bibliothek,* I (1907), 63ff.

broken by Sargon I,[114] the Semitic ruler of the newly founded city of Agade and "king of Kish," who about 2450 B.C. conquered all Mesopotamia and extended his empire to the Amanus in the west, the Zagros in the east, and the Taurus in the north.

Under Sargon's successors, Manishtusu and Naram-Sin, the vast kingdom maintained itself at the peak of its power; but when Sharkalisharri ascended to the throne, the country fell prey to the Guti, a barbarous mountain people of the Zagros. The Semites and Sumerians had to submit to the ruthless dominion of the pillaging tribes, until in 2250 B.C. Utu-Hegal, king of Uruk, succeeded in freeing the land from the oppressors.

The Sumerians rose thereupon to a new height and attained a splendid level of culture. Ur-Nammu, who governed Ur as *"shagub"* (*GIR₃-NITA*) under the suzerainty of Utu-Hegal[115] assumed, after seven years of vassalage, the kingship of Ur and thus founded the famous Ur III dynasty.[116] Ur-Nammu was not only a political conqueror, who subjugated the majority of the other Sumerian and Akkadian citystates, but also a conspicuous builder. Temples, steptowers, and city walls were erected under his rule in Ur, Uruk, Nippur, Eridu, Adab, and Larsa. Ur-Nammu was also a legislator and drew up the first law code in Mesopotamia.[117]

A contemporary of Ur-Nammu, and perhaps of his son Shulgi, was Gudea, famous "ensi of Lagash." Until recently it had been believed that Gudea lived much earlier than the Ur III rulers and was a vassal of the Guti, but the preamble of Ur-Nammu's code gives us new information concerning the city of Lagash,[118] placing Gudea's reign in the epoch after the liberation from the Gutian yoke. This modified

[114] Concerning the legendary birth and youth of Sargon, see L. W. King, "The Legend of Sargon," *Chronicles Concerning Early Babylonian Kings,* II (London, 1907), 87ff.

[115] G. Castellino, "Ur-Nammu. Three Religious Texts," *ZA,* Vol. LII (January, 1957), 1 ff.

[116] No historical record of a second Ur dynasty has as yet been discovered.

[117] The fragmentary text has been published by S. N. Kramer, "Code of Urnammu," *Orientalia,* Vol. XXIV (1954).

[118] The text mentions that Namhani, ensi of Lagash, was killed by Ur-Nammu. Namhani is known to have preceded Gudea in the reign of Lagash. Gudea must therefore be considered a contemporary of Ur-Nammu or of Shulgi, perhaps of both.

Ashurbanipal Mounted—British Museum

Collection of Theo Bauer

Pictographic Tablet from Kish

S. H. Langdon, *Excavations at Kish*

Pictographic Tablet from Warka IV

A. Falkenstein, *Archaische Texte aus Uruk*

Semipictographic
Tablet
from Warka IV

A. Falkenstein,
*Archaische Texte
aus Uruk*

Semipictographic Tablet from Jamdat Nasr

A. Falkenstein, *Archaische Texte aus Uruk*

Code of Hammurabi—the Louvre
This basalt stela was excavated in Elam and contains
the *Dinat-mesharim* laws compiled by Hammurabi,
king of Babylon.

Furlani, *Leggi dell'Asia anteriore antica*

Stela of Ashurnazirpal III, from the Temple of Ninib

Kleinmann, *Assyrian Sculptures*

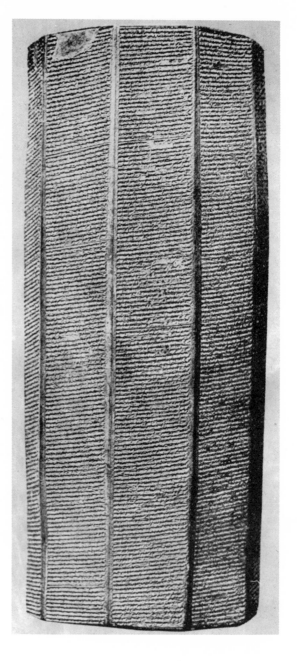

Prism of
Ashurbanipal—
British Museum

Collection of
Theo Bauer

Cylinder of Nabonidus—British Museum
This cylinder was found in the temple of Sin at Mughair. For other
cylinder seals see *Keilschriftliche Bibliothek* and Langdon,
*Neubabylonische Königsinschriften,* No. 1, 281ff.

Idol of Mother-
Goddess Cult—
the Louvre

Léon Heuzey, *Les origines
orientales de l'Art*

chronology lends quite a different background to the ensi's building activities, which had hitherto been inexplicable in view of the rapacious character of the Gutian oppressors. The main achievement of Gudea's reign was the erection of a temple in honor of the city-god Ningirsu; for this purpose the ensi imported cedar wood, marble, gold, silver, copper, and ebony from all over western Asia.

This cultural splendor of Ur and Lagash was but the twilight which preceded the setting of Sumerian political power. The last monarch of Ur III, Ibi-Sin, succumbed to the attacks of Elamites and Semites; the Sumerian heritage was divided between the Semitic monarch of Isin and the Elamite king of Larsa. The ensuing rivalry between the two non-Sumerian dynasties came to an end when, around 1750 B.C., Rim-Sin of Larsa subjugated Isin. But his triumph was of short duration: a few years later, Rim-Sin was himself vanquished by Hammurabi, king of the newly emerging dynasty of Babylon.

*The Old Babylonian period* (about 1800–1530 B.C.). While the kings of Isin and Larsa battled over the spoils of the Sumerian Ur III monarchs, a new city-state rose in the Akkadian plain. Sumu-abum, a Semite, founded the new Amorite dynasty of Babylon around 1830 B.C. Until then, the Semites had been an ethnic minority in the plain of southern Mesopotamia. Semitic cities such as Kish,[119] Mari,[120] or Eshnunna[121] exercised their influence in the course of early history, but the dominant force in the country was the Sumerians. Sargon's empire[122] was doomed

[119] Kish was, according to the Sumerian king list, the most ancient postdiluvian dynasty. For the role of Kish in early Sumerian history, see n. 112 above.

[120] The importance of Mari has become evident through the excavations of A. Parrot (*"Les fouilles de Mari,"* Syria, Vol. XIX [1938], 183ff.); of particular interest is the rich correspondence found in the three archives of the Zimrilim Palace (cf. G. Dossin, *Archives Royales de Mari* [Paris, 1941 ff.]). See also Wolfram von Soden, *"Das altbabylonische Briefarchiv von Mari,"* Die Welt des Orients (Berlin, 1946), 187ff.

[121] H. Frankfort, *Excavations in Tell Asmar* (Chicago, 1933–36); and Seton Lloyd, *The Gimilsin* [Shu-Sin] *Temple and the Palace of the Rulers at Tell Asmar,* (Oriental Institute *Publications,* Vol. XLIII, Chicago, 1940), have unearthed the vestiges of a kingdom which, shortly before Hammurabi's reign, exercised a brief sovereignty over Assyria, until it was suffocated by the impact of greater Semitic powers.

[122] Cf. E. Weidner, *"Das Reich Sargons von Akkad,"* Archiv für Orientforschung, Vol. XVI (January, 1952), 1 ff.

from the very beginning because it imposed Semitic suzerainty on a non-Semitic majority.

The new Semitic dynasty of Babylon found different conditions in the Plain: a steady stream of Amorite immigrants had, during the last centuries, greatly increased the Semitic proportion of the population. The Sumerian language, an unwieldy instrument of expression, was more and more supplanted by the much clearer, subtle idiom of the Semites. In the pantheon, Sumerian deities appeared under Semitic names (e.g., Ishtar, Sin, Shamash). The time was ripe for Semitic hegemony in Mesopotamia.

When Hammurabi ascended the Babylonian throne a century after the founding of the dynasty, he set about to create an empire which would combine military power with economic prosperity and cultural brilliancy. The idea of national unity, still nonexistent in the agglomeration of Sumerian city-states, found an emphatic expression in the formation of Babylonian religion: Marduk, an insignificant local deity, was promoted to the position of supreme god of Babylonia through the skillful redaction of a poem[123] and a new organization of the "temple ritual." It is significant that Enlil, the chief god of Sumer and patron deity of Nippur, a city which was important only as a religious center,[124] was then supplanted by Marduk, patron deity of Babylon, the city which combined the features of a sanctuary and a political metropolis.

Hammurabi extended his realm by gradually conquering all the southern city-states, including Larsa, Mari, and Eshnunna.[125] Subartu in the North, where Shamshi-Adad I dreamed of creating an Assyrian empire, did not resist Hammurabi's armies. Thus the Babylonian king ruled over all Mesopotamia, impressing on its inhabitants the indelible stamp of Semitism.

Unlike Sargon, who had dedicated all his energy to military conquests, Hammurabi conscientiously promoted the welfare of his people. He dug canals and enlarged the irrigation system of the Plain, and his law code guaranteed equitable treatment of the poor and the defense-

---

[123] "Enuma Elish" or "The Epic of Creation" (see Part II below).

[124] See Chapter II below.

[125] The Semitic kingdom of Kish had already been conquered by Sumu-abum, founder of the Babylonian dynasty.

less; his firm administration[126] established peace and prosperity in the land.

The cultural achievements of Hammurabi's age are known to us through a number of tablets which show that not only the Creation epic was composed at this time, but also the most famous secular poem of the ancient Near East, "The Epic of Gilgamesh."[127] Several other literary fragments[128] dating from this epoch illustrate the intensity of spiritual life in the Old Babylonian empire.

Though not attaining the renown of Hammurabi, the later rulers of the dynasty succeeded in upholding the empire by imitating the lines of the great king's policies. Even when in the sixteenth century B.C. the destructive waves of foreign invaders swept over Babylonia and broke the political power of the realm, the firm foundations of civilization laid by Hammurabi resisted the suzerainty of the Barbarian overlords and assured the continuity of Semitic culture until the Neo-Babylonian Renaissance.

*The Kassite Interregnum* (*ca.*1530–1170 B.C.). The middle of the second millennium B.C. is characterized by a vast migration movement over all the Near East, caused by the advance of the Indo-Europeans[129] towards Persia and India. From the main stream of these migrating people, small groups of invaders separated and turned towards Syria, Asia Minor, and Mesopotamia, carrying along the hordes of Asianic people whom they had previously overrun. Thus there sprang up in various regions of western Asia new kingdoms, with a society which consisted of an Asianic core and an Indo-European aristocracy, essentially military in character.[130]

---

[126] Cf. A. Ungnad, *Babylonische Briefe aus der Zeit der Hammurabi-Dynastie* (Leipzig, 1914).

[127] Also called *"Ša nagba imuru"* (He who saw everything); see Part II below.

[128] E.g., Old Babylonian versions of the "Atrahasis epic." See Part II below, the "Myth of Zu" and the "Etana Legend."

[129] Presumably already in the third millennium, Indo-European tribes (the so-called "Achaeans") passed through Greece and the Aegean Islands, crossed the Hellespont, and invaded Phrygia. Cf. G. Glotz and R. Cohen, *"Histoire Grecque," Histoire Ancienne,* Vol. I (Paris, 1925–47).

[130] The rapidity of the Indo-European advance was due mostly to the use of the horse and the war-chariot; in the Near East the horse had been unknown until then,

These new nations emerged like volcanoes: after having reached heights of impressive political grandeur, they were, within a few centuries, once more swallowed up by the ancient Semitic soil, leaving behind nothing but their names, and their ambitious plans came to a premature end.

The Hittites, an Asianic people governed by an Indo-European military caste,[131] created an empire in Asia Minor.[132] Under their king Mursili I, they descended into Mesopotamia and overwhelmed Babylonia. In 1531 b.c., the rich Semitic capital was ravaged and sacked, and the last king of the Hammurabi dynasty, Samsuditana, perished in the catastrophe.

Before the Semites could recover from the blow of the Hittite invasion, a new host of conquerors poured onto the Mesopotamian plain. The Kassites, like the Hittites a conglomerate of Asianics and Indo-Europeans, occupied the land and established themselves as the new rulers of Babylon.[133] Their dynasty reigned over the Semitic country for almost four hundred years, but the vanquished Babylonians subdued the Kassites culturally. The uncivilized foreign warriors dared not change the pattern of spiritual life in the "Land of the Two Rivers"; religion, language, and writing remained unaltered.

The Kassites limited their activity to the promotion of trade and the defense of their dominion against Elamites and Assyrians; their administration, more and more decentralized,[134] weakened the empire

---

except for a period in Early Dynastic Sumer, as is attested by mention of the horse in a song of Shulgi, second king of the Ur-III dynasty. (See Chapter III below, n. 41.) Cf. also A. Salonen, *"Hippologica Accadica,"* *Annales Academiae Scientiarum Fennicae* (Helsinki, 1956).

131 The Hittite language is attested by documents excavated in Boghazköi; they render two distinct, yet closely related Indo-European idioms: cuneiform Hittite (deciphered by B. Hrozný), and hieroglyphic Hittite (deciphered by H. T. Bossert, E. Forrer, Ignace J. Gelb, B. Hrozný, and P. Meriggi).

132 Cf. A. Goetze, *"Das Hethiter-Reich,"* DAO, Vol. XX (January-April, 1919).

133 The Kassites abandon the name "Babylon" for the appellation "Karanduniash"; the center of their power was, however, a newly founded city, Durkurigalzu (modern Aqarquf, near Baghdad).

134 Concerning the ever increasing privileges of the Kassite rural nobility, see F. X. Steinmetzer, *"Über den Grundbesitz in Babylonien zur Kassitenzeit,"* DAO, Vol. XIX, 1–2 (January, 1918).

Kassite Document from the Time of Merodach-Baladan, Excavated
Near Baghdad in 1873—British Museum

L. W. King, *Babylonian Boundary Stones and Memorial Tablets in
the British Museum*

35

so much that Babylonia receded from the political stage and became a secondary power in Mesopotamia; leadership was destined to be taken over by a new Semitic nation emerging in the North—the empire of Assyria.

*The Assyrian period* (*ca.*1170–612 B.C.). About the same time that the Hittites and Kassites established their kingdoms in the Near East, another people of Asianic stock began their rise to power in the Mesopotamian plain: the Hurrians.

Under the leadership of Indo-European equestrians, they created the realm of Mitanni, situated between the rivers Habur and Balih.[135] The new kingdom rapidly achieved astounding strength and dealt on a basis of equality with Egypt.[136]

But the young nation was soon subjugated and annexed by the expanding Hittite empire. The Hittite king, Hattusil III, concluded, in turn, an alliance with the Egyptian Pharaoh.[137] However, the power of the Indo-European state was of brief duration. About 1200 B.C., a new wave of invaders from the Aegean Islands and the Balkan swept over Asia Minor[138] and completely engulfed the Hittite empire. Thus, the twelfth century B.C. saw the end of the Indo-European nations that had come into power in western Asia after the Old Babylonian age.[139] Not until the second half of the last millennium B.C. did the Indo-Europeans become significant in Near Eastern history, when Medes and Persians,

[135] West of the Mitanni was situated another Asianic-Indo-European nation, the kingdom of Hurri; it stood more or less under the influence of the Mitannians and was only of secondary importance.

[136] Mitannian princesses were the wives of Thut-mose IV, Amen-hotep III, and Amen-hotep IV.

[137] A Hittite princess, daughter of Hattusil III, was the wife of Ramses II.

[138] It is possible that the siege of Troy was an episode of this Phrygian migration. (Cf. H. Glotz *Histoire Grecque*, I, 95.)

[139] Presumably at the beginning of this same period of migration occurred the exodus of Abraham and his clan from Ura towards Canaan (concerning the geographical situation of Ura, see C. B. Gordon, "Abraham and the Merchants of Ura," *JNES* [1958]): Shortly afterwards, Egypt was invaded by the Hyksos, a partly Semitic people; the Pharaoh protector of Joseph (Gen. 41:40) probably belonged to their race. When native Egyptian kings once more ruled the land, the Semites were treated with hostility (Ex. 1:8).

in a reversal of the earlier migration movement, invaded the Plain from the east.[140]

During the turbulent period which witnessed the rise and fall of the Hittites, Mitannians, and Kassites, the Indo-European and Asianic tribes were incessantly at war with the northern Semites. Through the second millennium, the Assyrians had seen their aspiration to self-determination thwarted again and again. The attempt of Shamshi-Adad I to create an Assyrian empire had been defeated by Hammurabi; after an obscure existence during the Old Babylonian age, the northern Semites were subjugated by the kingdom of Mitanni. Only when the powerful, yet ephemeral, Hurri-Indo-European nation became annexed by the Hittites did the Assyrians shake off their yoke.[141]

The unrest that characterized the prehistoric culture of northern Mesopotamia perpetuated itself in the vicissitudes of the Middle Assyrian age; periods of great power alternated with intervals of weakness.

Tukulti-Ninurta I (1235–1198 B.C.), the "Ninos" of Greek mythology, was in many respects a prototype of Sennacherib; like the Neo-Assyrian ruler, Tukulti-Ninurta led a destructive campaign against Babylon and tore down the city walls; Marduk, Babylon's patron deity, was deported by the enraged king to Ashur. When Tukulti-Ninurta met violent death at the hands of his own son, the murder was believed to have been Marduk's revenge for the King's crime against the "holy city."

The empire disintegrated rapidly under the patricide Ashur-nadi-napli and his successors; Assyria fell once more under the dominion of its southern rival. In the twelfth century B.C. Ashur-Dan joined the

---

140 S. N. Kramer supposes that Indo-Europeans were in southern Mesopotamia as early as the Ubaid period (Warka XVIII–XVII), coming from southwestern Iran ("Heroes of Sumer," *Proceedings* of the American Philosophical Society, Vol. XC, No. 2 [Philadelphia, 1947], 120–30; and by the same author, "New Light on the Early History of the Ancient Near East," *AJA*, Vol. 52 [June, 1948], 156–64). The pre-Sumerian people, whose vestiges are visible in ancient place names (see Chapter I above, n. 104) and in the dialectal peculiarities of the *"eme-sal"* idiom, are, according to Kramer's theory, Indo-European vikings.

141 While under Hittite suzerainty, the Mitannians had to pay tribute to Adad-Nirari I, king of Assyria. Under Shalmaneser I, Adad-Nirari's son, the land of Mitanni, now called Hanigalbat, became a province of the Assyrian kingdom.

Elamite King Shutruk-Nahunte to drive the last Kassite monarch from the Babylonian throne; but a new ruler, Nebuchadnezzar I of the Semitic Isin II dynasty, brought the Assyrians again under Babylonian hegemony.

The foundations of Assyrian imperialism were laid by Tiglat-Pileser I (1116–1090 B.C.), who threatened Syria, Asia Minor, and Armenia with his armies and aspired to make the Assyrian god the overlord of the entire world.[142]

Ashurnazirpal II (883–859 B.C.) and Shalmaneser III 858–824 B.C.) extended the dominion of Assyria in all directions, conquering Syria, Palestine, Armenia, Elam, and Babylonia.

Through the deportation and forced resettlement of huge population groups,[143] the Middle-Assyrian kings succeeded in preventing nationalist upheavals in the annexed provinces of their empire; making Assyria the melting pot of numerous heterogeneous elements, they laid the ethnic foundation for a stable realm under the triumphant rule of the Sargonides. Tiglat-Pileser III (745–727 B.C.) added to this a reform of the administrative system: the power of local officials was drastically reduced and all the provinces were brought under the control of the central government.[144]

Sargon II (721–705 B.C.) initiated the last and most powerful Assyrian dynasty. Like his predecessors and his ancient namesake "Sargon of Agade," the monarch directed his chief attention to exterior conquests. He subdued the unruly Urartaeans in Armenia, vanquished an Egyptian

---

[142] Tiglat-Pileser I is the first Assyrian king to have written the annals of his military conquests, following a custom of the Hittite rulers. The clay prisms that contain the accounts of the King's activity during the first five years of his reign were incorporated in the corners of the Anu-Adad temple in Ashur. Cf. W. Andrae, *Der Anu-Adad-Tempel in Assur (Wissenschaftliche Veröffentlichung der Deutschen Orient-Gesellschaft,* Vol. X, Leipzig, 1909).

[143] E.g., Shalmaneser I deported 14,000 inhabitants of the Hanigalbat province; Tukulti-Ninurta I resettled 28,800 subjects of the western frontier. Ashurnazirpal II uses mass deportation not only to destroy national unity of conquered lands but also to bring together communities of artisans; such a colony was organized, e.g., in Kalah, where Ashurnazirpal had a new palace erected. Cf. A. H. Layard, *Nineveh and its Remains* (2 vols., London, 1848–49).

[144] Cf. E. Forrer, *Die Provinzeinteilung des assyrischen Reiches,* (Leipzig, 1920); also L. Waterman, *Royal Correspondence of the Assyrian Empire* (Ann Arbor, 1930–36).

army in Palestine, and defeated the kingdom of Samaria: thirty thousand Israelites were deported, in accordance with the traditional practices of Assyrian statesmanship.

Sennacherib (704–681 B.C.), Sargon's son,[145] was less fortunate in his military enterprises than his father. The siege of Jerusalem in 701 B.C. had to be called off because pestilence broke out in the royal army. Furthermore the astutely planned attack from the sea against Elam dissolved into a fiasco. The frustrated immoderately ambitious king set his mind on two extravagant projects: he created a new capital of fantastic splendor in Nineveh, seat of a famous Ishtar sanctuary; and turning from construction to destruction, Sennacherib brought about the complete annihilation of Babylon,[146] the city which had incessantly fomented rebellion against its Assyrian overlords.[147] Marduk's statue was brought to Nineveh, and the god's temple underwent total devastation. To justify the sacrilegious action before the people, a tendentious new myth was composed, in which Marduk is depicted as being submitted to a humiliating trial before all the gods.[148]

Sennacherib's death at the hands of his own son[149] alarmed the King's family, who saw in the murder a token of Marduk's wrath against the destruction of Babylon. The new monarch, Esarhaddon (680–

---

[145] The hostility between Sargon II and Sennacherib is apparent from the fact that the latter, contrary to Assyrian habit, never calls himself "son of Sargon" and shuns the mention of his filiation.

[146] The raging king achieves the destruction of Babylon in 689 B.C. by making the Euphrates flood the entire city.

[147] Sennacherib's father, Sargon II, was defeated at the beginning of his reign by Merodach Baladan, king of Babylon; after the campaigns in Palestine and Armenia, Sargon succeeded in putting to flight the Babylonian rebel ruler. The Assyrian victor, however, was careful not to touch upon the Marduk cult; the Esagil temple was spared, and Sargon named as his personal gods the triad of "Ashur, Marduk, and Nabu."

[148] Concerning this text, which had been interpreted until recently in a very different sense, see Chapter III below, n. 73.

[149] Cf. II Kings 19:36ff.; it has been suspected that Esarhaddon, whom Sennacherib had chosen for his successor, secretly instigated the murder of his father. See H. Hirschberg, *Studien zur Geschichte Esarhaddons, Königs von Assyrien* (Ohlau, 1932); also B. Meissner, *Neue Nachrichten über die Ermordung Sanheribs* (*Sitzungsberichte der Preussischen Akademie der Wissenschaften*, Phil.-hist. Klasse, Berlin, 1932), 250 ff.; and *"Wo befand sich Asarhaddon zur Zeit der Ermordung Sanheribs?" AO*, Vol. XII (October, 1936), 232ff.

669 B.C.), and his mother, Naqia,[150] therefore set about at once to rebuild the city and to reconstruct the Marduk temple. After overcoming a revolt of his older brothers, Esarhaddon dedicated himself to military conquest. He not only occupied Armenia and Persia but also subdued the Phoenician cities of Sidon and Tyre. Marching into Egypt, the King subjugated Taharka, the Memphite Pharaoh. But when he returned to Egypt for a second campaign, he fell a victim to pestilence.

Esarhaddon's empire was divided between his third son Ashurbanipal (668–626 B.C.), who received the throne of Assyria, and his second son Shamash-shum-ukin,[151] who became governor of Babylonia. While Ashurbanipal prepared for his conquest of Thebes, his brother stirred up a revolt in Babylon against the Assyrian suzerainty. The King, hastily returning from Egypt, succeeded in bringing the rebellious country under his control; Shamash-shum-ukin—Byron's Sardanapalus—perished in the flames of his besieged palace.

Elam, the ally of the seditious Babylonia, was punished by Ashurbanipal with unusual severity: the King utterly destroyed the land, profaned the royal tombs, and carried away all works of art. Thus the age-old foe of the "inhabitants of the Fertile Plain" was wiped out and never reappeared in Near Eastern history.

Ashurbanipal was the last great king of Assyria. His importance lies not only in the impressive number of his conquests but also in the particular attention he devoted to the literature of his land. The collection of over thirty thousand clay tablets, which the excavators found in the rich library of Ashurbanipal's palace in Nineveh,[152] is our chief source for the knowledge of Mesopotamian myths and legends.

Under the reign of Ashurbanipal's successors, the empire disintegrated rapidly. The declining realm was unable to withstand the attack of Nabopolassar, chief of the Babylonians and ally of the Medes, like-

[150] Concerning the role in Babylonian politics of this highly influential queen of Palestinian origin, see H. Lewy, "Nitokris-Naqî'a," *JNES*, Vol. XI (October, 1952), 264ff.

[151] Since Esarhaddon's first son, Sin-iddina-apla, had died before his father, the succession to the throne was open to any of the other sons. (See Chapter IV below, "The Creation Epic.")

[152] Cf. C. Bezold, *Catalogue of the Cuneiform Tablets in the Kouyunjik Collection of the British Museum* (5 vols., London, 1889–99), Supplement by L. W. King, 1914.

wise insurgent vassals of Assyria. Nineveh, the hated symbol of Sennacherib's hybris, was destroyed in 612 B.C., and the North Semitic kingdom lost forever its independence to become a province of the renascent empire of Babylon.

*The Neo-Babylonian period (ca.612–539 B.C.).* This last epoch of Semitic greatness in the ancient Near East saw the struggle of two hostile parties. One was the voice of Babylonian nationalism, newly erupting after the humiliating period of subjection under Assyrian hegemony. The other comprised the disciples of Assyrian influence, which was still strong in Babylonia owing to the skillful diplomacy that had been exerted by Naqia, Esarhaddon's mother, whose gesture of reconstructing the "holy city" after Sennacherib's assassination as well as her non-Assyrian descent[153] facilitated a reconciliation between herself and the rancorous Babylonians.[154]

After the destruction of Nineveh, accomplished by Nabopolassar with the help of the Medes, the nationalists prevailed in Babylonia. To their party belonged Nabopolassar's son, Nebuchadnezzar II (605–562 B.C.), who proved to be a worthy successor of the Sargonide conquerors. He defended the Assyro-Babylonian empire against aggressors from Egypt, Syria, and Palestine, subjugated Tyre, and in 587 B.C.[155] destroyed Jerusalem, deporting the Hebrew kings Jehoiachin and Zedekiah to Babylon, together with a great number of their subjects.

Nebuchadnezzar also devoted considerable time to the restoration

[153] Naqia was, according to ancient documents, an Aramean princess from Palestine. See H. Lewy, "Nitokris-Naqi'a," *JNES,* Vol. XI (October, 1952), 264 ff.

[154] Naqia's supporters had also helped Ashurbanipal, her favorite grandson, overcome Shamash-shum-ukin, the rebel who was foolhardy enough to defy his powerful grandmother.

[155] A new way is being devised for ascertaining the exact date of events that occurred during the Neo-Babylonian period (e.g., the deportation of the Israelites); the scribes, when recording such events on their tablets, usually added indications concerning the constellation of the day. From calculations made recently by B. Tuckerman with the help of an electronic computer, we can now determine the positions of the sun, the moon, and five planets in Babylon corresponding to each day of the last six centuries B.C. Through the comparison of these figures with the astronomical indications of the Neo-Babylonian scribes, it will be possible to ascertain the date of each recorded event with fair accuracy.

of Babylon[156] and favored the increase of trade relations between his city and all parts of the ancient world.[157]

After the reign of three other kings of minor importance,[158] the dynasty of Nabopolassar came to an end; Nabonidus (555–539 B.C.), remote offspring of Naqia and the candidate of the philo-Assyrian party, usurped the throne of Babylon.[159]

The ambition of this singular monarch was not so much the political expansion of the Babylonian empire as the establishment of a new religious cult. He restored a great number of minor temples all over Mesopotamia and paid particular attention to the worship of astral deities. His erection of a Sin temple in Harran[160] was violently resented by the Babylonian clergy[161] because the new shrine openly proclaimed the supremacy of the moon-god, who had been the tutelary deity of the Assyrian royal family, over Marduk, king of the pantheon and symbol of the Babylonian nation. The substitution of Sin for Marduk during the reign of Nabonidus is apparent also in a memorial[162] to the monarch's mother,[163] in which Sin appears as the "King of Gods," while Marduk is not even mentioned.

On account of this religious contrast, which reflects the political

---

[156] In all probability, Nebuchadnezzar had wrongly been credited by miso-Assyrian scribes with the erection of buildings which were in reality the work of Naqia.

[157] The Biblical account of Nebuchadnezzar's madness (Dan. 4:33) probably refers to Nabonidus, who is reported to have resided for several years in Tema, a city in the Arabian desert, while the crown prince Belshazzar administered Babylonia.

[158] Erba-Marduk, Neriglissar, and Labashi-Marduk.

[159] Herodotus mentions Nabonidus as the only Neo-Babylonian king; the omission of the names of Nabopolassar and Nebuchadnezzar is probably due to the fact that the informants of the Greek author belonged to the philo-Assyrian party who recognized only Nabonidus and his ancestress Naqia (Nitokris).

[160] Harran, a city in northern Mesopotamia, had been the last stronghold of the Assyrian army, which, after the destruction of Nineveh, resisted Babylonian attacks until 608 B.C.

[161] The hostility of the priests is evident in the "Verse Account of Nabonidus." Cf. S. Smith *Babylonian Historical Texts Relating to the Downfall of Babylon* (London, 1924), pls. V–X.

[162] H. Pognon, *Inscriptions Sémitiques de la Syrie, de la Mésopotamie et de la région de Mossoul* (Paris, 1907), pls. XII–XIII.

[163] It is also possible that the appellation, "offspring of my womb," recurring in the text with reference to Nabonidus, stands for "grandson" instead of "son," according to similar usage in other Semitic languages.

conflict between the Babylonian nationalists and the friends of Assyria, the priests of the Marduk temple welcomed Cyrus as a liberator when the city was conquered by Persian troops in 539 B.C.

After its military breakdown, Babylon still retained some of its importance as an administrative center of the Near East. Cyrus made it a capital second only to Susa, and Alexander of Macedonia planned to establish his permanent residence in the ancient "city of Hammurabi." But the center of gravity had now shifted from the Orient to the Occident; after a glorious existence extending over one and one-half millennia, Babylon gradually sank into total oblivion. Only in A.D. 1899 did an expedition of German archaeologists headed by R. Koldewey bring part of the sunken metropolis to the light of the modern world.[164]

[164] R. Koldewey, *Das wiedererstehende Babylon.*

# CHAPTER II

*Spiritual Life in Mesopotamia*

THE STUDENT WHO TRIES TO PENETRATE the essence of Assyro-Babylonian literature will have to put aside all conventional methods of examination. The remote period which he approaches is entirely unlike our modern times; yet it is amazing to see that, in spite of the different conditions that presided over the formation of poetry then and now, the ancient Mesopotamian often wrestled with much the same problems that still torment the modern spirit. The inexorable necessity of death,[1] the doubt about the usefulness of terrestrial exist-

[1] In the "Epic of Gilgamesh." See Chapter IV below.

ence,[2] and the despair of the virtuous who suffers injustice[3] are stings which are acutely felt by the man of today, and it is through the universal value of its ideas that the poetry of more than four thousand years ago still appeals to us and stirs, besides admiration, a deep human interest in our minds.

Yet we must not look at the spiritual realm of ancient man with modern eyes or apply modern patterns of thinking to a world which was governed by entirely different rules. The Mesopotamian had never learned that art could exist for the sake of beauty alone; for him, art was the servant of cult. He never dreamed of considering the laws of nature from the point of view of science; the behavior of the elements was, for him, ordered by the gods. He could not conceive that the teachings of the clergy might be questioned; religion was the absolute master of his daily life and permeated all his activities.

Ancient man had not undergone any of the great spiritual revolutions that have fixed the modern trend of speculative thought. But he was not a savage without any imagination beyond the necessities of material existence; the abundance of myths emerging from the dawn of prehistory testifies to the creativeness of his mind.

For the Mesopotamian, the entire world which surrounded him was filled with life. Every contact between man and nature was an encounter between two living entities facing each other and pitting their will power against each other. In the words of H. and H. A. Frankfort,[4] it was a relationship between "I" and "Thou."

When confronted with a natural phenomenon, man could not intellectually detach himself from it, because he was too deeply involved in the rhythm of the cosmic forces which determined every instance of his existence. Each natural event, even when repeated with seasonal regularity, was the result of an individual, unique, and "willed" act; it therefore could not be connected with other similar events, provoked by the same causes and subject to a general law. This would be reason-

---

[2] In the pessimistic "Dialogue between Master and Servant." See Chapter V below.

[3] In the "Dialogue about Human Misery" and the poem "I Will Praise the Lord of Wisdom." See Chapter V below.

[4] "Myth and Reality," *The Intellectual Adventure of Ancient Man,* 5ff.

ing in a modern way, and ancient man did not reason as we do; he clothed his thoughts in the imagery of myth.

Turning once more to the words of H. and H. A. Frankfort, we can define myth as "a form of poetry which transcends poetry in that it proclaims a truth; a form of reasoning which transcends reasoning in that it wants to bring about the truth it proclaims; a form of action, of ritual behavior, which does not find its fulfilment in the act but must proclaim and elaborate a poetic form of truth."[5]

The attitude of man, when confronted with the "Thou," is neither passive nor active; it is in between. Here we come to one of the most problematic aspects of mythopoeic thought: How did ancient man react to the cognition that he was a small particle in the great realm of nature? Had he a concept of hierarchy in the order of the living world? Did he feel superior or inferior to his fellow creatures, which included natural phenomena as well as minerals, plants, animals, and human beings? Was there any way for him to control nature and subdue it under his own will?

In order to find the solution to these problems, we now must limit the idea of "ancient man" to the more specific one of "Mesopotamian man." For the inhabitants of the *Zweistromland* chose a different road from that, for example, of the Egyptians, whose conditions of life were similar.

Never afterwards were spiritual evolutions so strongly influenced by natural environment as in the dim past of prehistory. The mind of man experienced his world profoundly, but only his particular world, the one he knew. If the Mesopotamian plain was yearly inundated by the Euphrates and the Tigris, it was the world which was flooded, not just a region of it. If nature behaved in an unpredictable manner in Mesopotamia, its inhabitants conceived all of nature as acting under the impact of violence, threatening destruction, against which all human labor was powerless. The attitude of the Mesopotamian, therefore, had to be different from that of the Egyptian,[6] whose existence was regulated

5 *Ibid.,* 8.

6 In the Egyptian mind the cosmic order was static; resting upon the unchanging rhythm of the seasons, it had first been established at the moment of creation and could never really be disturbed. The belief that the earthly ruler of the country was a god incarnate intensified the Egyptian's confidence in the nature that surrounded him.

by the Nile's periodic inundations, which brought only blessings to the country, never destruction; the unfailing seasonal recurrence of the life-giving flood increased not only man's prosperity but also his confidence in himself and in his ability to pit his will against the will of nature and eventually be its master.

Ancient man had a subjective view of nature, limited to that aspect of it which he himself experienced and judged through the necessities of his own existence. The Mesopotamian's relation to the sun, for instance, was a double one: in the morning and in the evening the sun's effect was beneficent; it gave light to the world as antithesis to darkness; the regularity of its rising and setting inspired the idea of divine order and immutable justice. But at noon the sun's effect was very different: the heat it exhaled scorched the land and struck the imprudent wanderer with tormenting headache. The midday sun bred the germ of pestilence, and death was hidden in its devastating scald.

The Mesopotamian therefore conceived two different deities incarnating these two aspects of one and the same star: one was Shamash, the god of justice and of divination; the other was Nergal, the king of the Nether World and god of pestilence and death.

When the first myths crystallized in Mesopotamia, the gods were the incarnations of natural phenomena: Enlil, god of the winds; Enki or Ea, god of the earth and of the water; Nanna (Sin), the moon-god, and his son Utu (Shamash), the sun-god; and over them all Anu, the god of the sky, which was imagined as a solid vault.

All these gods reflected the conditions of nature in the land of Sumer. A peculiar feature, proper to Mesopotamian soil, characterized Ea-Enki: he was the god of the sweet waters[7] but also of the earth. These elements, usually quite distinct, were vaguely identical in the marshlands which extended from one Sumerian city to another. Enlil, the god of the winds, who personified the sweeping tempest, was considered the national god[8] before Marduk usurped his role in a later period.

7 The very nature of water, which chooses to overcome an obstacle by circumfusion rather than direct conquest, suggests the association of this element with Ea as the personification of shrewdness and magical knowledge.

8 Enlil's holy shrine, the "Ekur," had been erected in Nippur; this fact gave to the city a special prestige throughout the Early Dynastic period, although it was politically quite unimportant. The presence of the Enlil temple made Nippur the religious capital of all

But was this pantheon of the divinized forces of nature, featuring the particular climatic conditions of Mesopotamia, the oldest layer of Sumerian religion? If we want to discover the primitive form of worship, we have to go back, not to the myths, but to the rites. It is the rite which survives the longest, even after the creed which inspired it has fallen into oblivion. And the ancient Mesopotamian rites all point in one direction, to the cult of the mother-goddess and the young fertility god. This cult underlies the practices of the *hieros gamos* and of the vase of overflowing waters.

Such a figuration of the divine powers in nature is a very general one; it did not surge from the specific physical conditions of Mesopotamia, but is the common heritage of a very large group of people. Perhaps it was proper to the widely scattered family of the Asianics,[9] but it might have extended even further.[10] In the preceding chapter we saw that idols pertaining to the mother-goddess cult had already appeared in the early fifth millennium during the Halaf civilization[11] and were quite numerous in the following millennium, during the Ubaid period. The young fertility god was sometimes imagined as husband of the mother-goddess, sometimes as her brother or son.[12]

Traces of this ancient cult are to be found in many of the old Sumerian myths. The mother-goddess has many names (Ninhursag, Mami, Aruru, Nintu, and others), and the young fertility god may be called Enki or Dumuzi (Tammuz), etc. The god's two functions of generation and irrigation merged into one,[13] until in the later myths

Sumer; it was the place where all the gods were believed to assemble in order to "fix" the destinies, or to make decisions in moments of crisis.

[9] Cf. also the Hittite "Telepinus Myth," which probably goes back to proto-Hittite (Asianic) traditions. A Göetze and H. Otten, *Keilschrifturkunden aus Boghazköi,* (*Wissenschaftliche Veroffentlichungen der deutschen Orient-Gesellschaft*, Vols. XVII and XXXIII, Berlin-Leipzig, 1938–43).

[10] The worship of the female principle of fecundity has been attested in the palaeolithic caves of southern France, Cantabrica, and Asturias. For details see E. O. James, *Myth and Ritual* (London, 1958), 22ff.

[11] See Chapter I above.

[12] W. W. Baudissin sees the different degrees of vitality visible in the mother-goddess and the young fertility god reflected in a distinction between two classes of Semitic verb roots. *Adonis und Esmun* (Leipzig, 1911), 56 and 480 ff.

[13] In Egypt, the god Osiris was at the same time the personification of the sprouting

the latter prevails, and the male deity becomes the incarnation of water.

The foundation of well-organized city-states then brought about the assignment of local gods. Without losing their specific character as personifications of natural phenomena, they became patrons of particular cities: Ea ruled in Eridu, Enlil in Nippur, Anu in Uruk, Nanna in Ur, and Utu in Sippar.

A further step was taken with the elevation of Marduk, the local god of Babylon and originally a chthonian deity, who for reasons of political prestige usurped the role of Enlil in the Creation epic and gradually absorbed the attributes of all the members of the pantheon, almost showing the road towards monotheism.[14]

Divinity thus progressed from the universal idea of procreation towards the incarnation of natural phenomena proper to Mesopotamia and culminated in the social hegemony of the Babylonian city-god.

We turn now once more to the question of man's attitude towards the cosmos. The oldest traces of human life, even beyond the Neolithic age, indicate that man did not accept passively the conditions of his precarious existence. On the other hand, he was far from approaching the active attitude of the scientist of today; as was stated above, man was in a position between active and passive.

From earliest times, he had tried to influence nature, to obtain from the mysterious powers around him the favors of increasing the number of animals that provided him with food and of helping him to catch as many beasts as were needed to supply the community.

Such early traces of magical practices have been discovered in palaeolithic caverns of southern France. In the Tuc d'Audoubert near Saint-Girons in Ariège, clay figurines representing a female and a male

grain and the Nile flood. See Herman Kees, *Der Götterglaube im alten Ägypten* (*Mitteilungen der Vorderasiatisch-ägyptischen Gesellschaft,* Vol. XLV, Leipzig, 1941). Similarly, the Babylonian Tammuz is associated with both vegetation and water. A Moortgat, *Tammuz, Der Unsterblichkeitsglaube in der altorientalischen Bildkunst.* "When young, he lay in a sinking ship / When adult, he lay immersed in the grain" (H. Zimmern, *Sumerisch-babylonische Tammuzlieder,* 208).

[14] A significant approach to monotheism is made in the following passage: "Ninurta is Marduk as the god of plantation; Ilbaba is Marduk as the god of dominion and council; Nabu is Marduk as the god of destinies; Sin is Marduk as the god who illuminates darkness; Shamash is Marduk as the god of justice; Adad is Marduk as the god of rain." *Cuneiform Texts,* XXIV, pl. 50.

bison as well as phallus-shaped clay objects[15] denote an ancient fertility cult. In another cave near Montespan in Haute Garonne are depicted horses, bears, and lions with wounds on various parts of their bodies; a wild horse is represented as falling into a trap.[16] The ritual was meant to ensure a successful chase.

Magic was thus the first ally of man in his struggle for existence, and we shall find two basic features in all later practices extending over the ages: one was meant to augment procreation and is therefore positive; the other was intended to bring about destruction and is therefore negative. The complicated rites of later generations, which utilized circle and wand, knots and stones, and other expedients, all go back to the fundamental idea that by means of magic man can influence positively or negatively the surrounding nature.

But what is the essence of magic? How did ancient man arrive at the belief that humans could command cosmic powers? From the oldest evidences, it seems clear that magic could not be exercised by everybody but was a special gift conferred upon a single person, distinguishing him from his fellow beings.

We may safely assume that starting from, or coinciding with, the submissive and rogatory attitude of religion, magic gradually adopted an empirism stemming from superstition and took, in its essence, the direction towards an attitude of command and injunction. In the hands of the man capable of exercising such a power, magic therefore assumed the shape of authority. Yet the sphere of his influence extended only over such fields where domination of nature was required: fertility of the soil, abundance of crops, multiplication of flocks, and increase of the human family.

When the community, be it a tribe or village, had to make political decisions, authority was exercised by an assembly which comprised all free men. Such a form of democratic government in early Mesopotamia is mentioned by several literary texts, including the Sumerian fragment "Gilgamesh and Agga"[17] and the Babylonian "Epic of Creation."[18]

15 See *Comptes-rendus de l'Académie des Inscriptions et Belles Lettres* (Paris, 1912), 532ff.

16 See H. Breuil, *Quatre cents siècles d'art pariétal* (Montignac, 1954), 236ff.

17 Text translated by S. N. Kramer, *ANET*, 44–47.

18 See Chapter IV below.

The group of free men elected, in the case of an emergency (as when threatened by an enemy attack), a military leader on whom they conferred special power for the duration of the crisis. Once the danger was over, the leader relinquished his position of temporary authority and became once more a member of the communal assembly of free men.

Thorkild Jacobsen[19] supposes that the council of the community could elect for temporary rule not only a military leader, the *"lugal,"*[20] to cope with external danger, but also a magic chief, the *"en,"*[21] in case of an internal threat, for example, drought, pestilence, flood, famine, etc.

It seems to the writer, however, that the nature of magic is incompatible with the ideas of a merely temporary rule and the appointee's voluntary resignation of his powers. It appears much more likely that the authority of the *"en"* was a permanent institution in ancient Mesopotamia, even while democratic government was in vigor. Moreover, since primitive society saw that its precarious existence depended upon the favorable or pernicious behavior of nature long before the threat of an external enemy became important, it may be assumed that the title *"en"* was anterior to *"lugal."*[22]

With the development of the Sumerian city-states, war between rival communities became more and more a permanent way of life, and the importance of the military leader increased steadily, so that his prestige now equaled that of the *"en,"* or even surpassed it. The two aspects of this authority merged into the hands of a single chief, and we see in several Sumerian texts that many Early Dynastic rulers called themselves *"en"* as well as *"lugal."*[23]

The pattern of early Mesopotamian society is reflected very distinctly in the great politico-religious "Epic of Creation."[24] The multitude of the gods form an assembly of democratic character. When

[19] "Early Political Development in Mesopotamia," *ZA,* Vol. LII (1957), 91–140.

[20] Translated "king," literally "great man."

[21] Translated "lord," it often appears as a component of the title "ensi" (governor), literally "free lord."

[22] The chronological priority of the title *"en"* over that of *"lugal"* is supposed, though on a different basis, also by W. W. Hallo (*Early Mesopotamian Royal Titles,* 122), who believes that *"en"* is a specific title of Uruk and becomes replaced by *"lugal,"* title of Ur, after the political decadence of Uruk.

[23] E.g., Eannatum, Entemena, Urukagina, etc.

[24] Other poems that contain allusions to assemblies are the already mentioned Sumerian

enmity arises between Tiamat and her host on one hand, and the great gods on the other, both sides set up different assemblies, each group being headed by a military "leader." Marduk is the champion of the great gods, Kingu the chieftain of Tiamat's army. Having been elected in the face of an enemy attack, they hold the role of a *"lugal"* in their group and wield a special executive power (tablets I and IV). Their characteristics are strength, combativeness, prowess in battle, and heroic valor. Marduk's weapons, even though they include natural elements (as winds, fire, and floodstorm), are used like the arms of a soldier when the god meets Tiamat, whom he subdues in an open battle (tablet IV).

But both parties have also a magic chief, the *"en."* In Kingu's camp this position is held by Tiamat, who takes upon herself the task of generation and whose exclusive weapons are magic spells, venom, and charms. The *"en"* of the great gods is Ea, the all wise, who averts the danger of destruction at the hands of Apsu by reciting a spell and pouring a magic sleeping potion on his adversary.

Neither Ea nor Tiamat have been appointed by the assembly; they act of their own accord, not needing a special power to install them in their function. When the *"lugal"* enters the scene, they do not relinquish their position but maintain their rank.

After the battle against Tiamat, Marduk assumes the duties of an *"en"*: he assures the prosperity of the gods (tablet VI), commands the stars (tablet V), and shapes the earth (tablet IV) and mankind (tablet VI). The fusion of the two functions of *"lugal"* and *"en"* in the person of Marduk is consecrated by Ea at the end of the poem (tablet VII), when the water-god confers upon the young victor his own name, Ea, as a mark of supreme honor: "All my combined rites he shall administer."[25]

Throughout Mesopotamian history, the kings never renounced their *"en"* function, even when military conquest was their main ambition. In their hymns, stelae, foundation stones, codices, etc.,[26] they stressed

---

fragment "Gilgamesh and Agga," the Akkadian Gilgamesh epic (including the episode of the Deluge), the myth of Zu, the Atrahasis legend, and the tale of Nergal and Ereshkigal.

25 *ANET*, 72.

26 E.g., Hymns of Ur-Nammu (G. Castellino, *ZA*, Vol. LII [1957], 1–57), a song

their physical qualities and their soldierly achievements but called a marked attention also to their wisdom and justice; they prided themselves upon being good shepherds of their people, providers of abundance, and promoters of peace and prosperity. A particular feature pertaining to the *"en"* recurs with insistence in all royal inscriptions: each king, from the Early Dynastic rulers to the Neo-Assyrian monarchs,[27] maintains that deities are his parents, that a goddess nursed him, that he was elected to his throne by a god even before he was born. This concept of a divine predestination indicates the position of the Mesopotamian king as standing between his people and the gods, holding the role of mediator, whose duty was to preserve harmony between nature and mankind.

The practice of magic by the king[28] was, in historical times, nothing but a ritual action. The creed that once inspired these gestures goes back to a very ancient period, when the religion of the Sumerians had not yet undergone the influence of Mesopotamian environment but was dominated by the more universal cult of the mother-goddess. The people who later on worshiped the divinized elements of Mesopotamian nature had probably at that time not yet invaded the "Plain of the Two Rivers" but belonged to the great family of tribes who were, at the beginning of the Neolithic period, scattered all over western Asia, where their seminomadic existence acquainted them with a wider range of climatic conditions.

The belief in the effectiveness of magic reposes on the assumption that nature is yielding and liable to being influenced. When, however, the Sumerians settled in the Plain and experienced the violent storms,

of Shulgi (A. Falkenstein, *ZA*, Vol. L [1952], 64 ff.), the Stela of the Vultures (F. Thureau-Dangin, *Die sumerischen und akkadischen Königsinschriften,* 20), foundation stones of Entemena (E. Sollberger, *ZA*, Vol. L [1952], 14 ff.), the prologue of Hammurabi's law code (A. Deimel, *Codex Hammurabi*).

27 Lugalzaggesi calls himself "son born of Nisaba, fed by the holy milk of Ninhursag" (R. Labat, *Le caractère religieux de la royauté assyro-babylonienne*, 63–69); Ashurbanipal proclaims that he is the "offspring of Ashur and Belit . . . whom they formed in his mother's womb for the rulership of Assyria" (D. D. Luckenbill, *Ancient Records of Assyria,* (Chicago, 1927) II, §§ 765).

28 E.g., the pouring of water to bring about rain, the *hieros gamos* to ensure multiplication of the herds and abundant crops.

destructive inundations, and torrid droughts of the country, they could not but feel impotent before nature.

About the same time that the new form of worship of natural phenomena took shape, magic gradually lost its hold on the Mesopotamians as a living practice. Nature no longer appeared to be yielding to human will. It was not that nature seemed hostile, because the fertility of the alluvial soil was famous in the ancient world. But nature in Mesopotamia was unpredictable; it could bring destruction and prosperity alike to the people who depended on it for their sustenance, and there was no means of avoiding the disaster of too violent inundations or averting the vehemence of the scorching winds that dried up the land.

On such a background, magic could not thrive as before; it survived only as a ritual, a ceremony repeated with the recurrence of cult celebrations.

To the change in the attitude towards magic contributed also the political development of the country. The constant quarrels among the Sumerian city-states put an ever increasing emphasis on force. The king's authority was maintained by means of his palace troops, and the people often saw in their ruler no longer a shepherd who protected them from harm or heaped abundance on them but, rather, an enemy who exacted hard work at the city fortifications as well as excessive military service, and who added the burden of continual privations.[29]

The Creation epic illustrates the gradual ascendancy of force over magical knowledge: in tablet I, Ea overcomes his adversary with charms and spells, but in tablet IV, Tiamat sees her magic ineffective against Marduk, who overcomes the monster through force.

In Mesopotamia, the only field in which magic continued as a living practice was the exorcism of demons, who were generally considered

---

[29] See the complaint of the people of Uruk over the arrogance of Gilgamesh ("The Epic of Gilgamesh," tablet I), or the bitter report of the Babylonians on their King Nabonidus ("Verse Account of Nabonidus," ANET 312ff.): *"Law and order are not promulgated by him / He made perish the common people through want / The nobles he killed in war / The brick form and the brick basket he imposed upon them / His weary army grumbled";* At the invasion of Cyrus *"To the inhabitants of Babylon a joyful heart is given now / Liberty is restored to those who were surrounded by oppression."*

to be at the root of diseases. In order to cure a sick person, magical craft aiming at the destruction or the banishment of the demon was exercised.

The principal elements of an exorcism were: a threefold offering by the petitioner to the god Ea, to the temple administration, and to the *āšipu* priest; ritual ablutions performed by the *ramku* priest; and the reciting of an incantation. Numerous texts describe these practices, especially the twelve tablets of the series *asakkē marṣūti*.[30]

The insecurity of life in the Plain and the dependence of the inhabitants on the natural phenomena worshiped as deities favored the development of an elaborate system of divination. The adorant, afraid to offend a god by acting unknowingly against his will, tried to understand the deity's enigmatic message, which was conferred to him through an oracle, a dream, or an omen, so that he would not attract the divine wrath.

Gudea, ensi of Lagash, interpreted the fact that the Tigris had failed to rise one year as a sign of the gods. Through dreams he learned that by divine will he was to rebuild the temple of the god Ningirsu, and other dreams instructed him on every step that had to be taken in order to fulfill the wish of the gods and ward off divine displeasure.[31]

In the course of time, divination shifted to fortunetelling, in that the wish to execute the god's will was gradually replaced by the desire to gain premature knowledge of the future.

Allusions to dreams that foreshadow coming events are to be found in several Mesopotamian epics. Gilgamesh learns of his future friendship with Enkidu through two dreams (tablet I). The probable outcome of his fight against Huwawa is likewise revealed to him in dreams (tablet V). Etana, prior to his ascension towards the sky of Ishtar, foresees in a dream his arrival before the throne of the goddess (Neo-Assyrian fragment C-5).

After this comprehensive view of the elements which composed the spiritual life of Mesopotamia, we will now consider the basic structures of religious worship, political organization, magical medicine, and divinatory practices.

---

30 *Cuneiform Texts*, XVII.

31 "Gudea Cylinder A." For the text, see F. Thureau-Dangin, *Les Inscriptions de Sumer et d'Akkad* (Paris, 1905), 134.

## RELIGION

There is no poem in all of Assyro-Babylonian literature that does not deal with religion. Even hero tales such as the epic of Gilgamesh and the legend of Sargon involve gods and goddesses, much in the way of Greek mythology, in which the activities of gods and humans are continually intertwined.

This relationship reflects the Mesopotamian's close dependence on religion, which gave him the only perspective he had of the surrounding world. While modern man can explain many natural events through science and assigns religion to the realm of the supernatural, for the Mesopotamian such a distinction did not exist. A thunderstorm or the sprouting grain was as marvelous for him as the apparition of a god.

Ancient man did not distinguish between reality and appearance; what he beheld in a dream was just as true as what he saw during the day. The former might, in his eyes, even be more real, because the dream was a means of coming in closer contact with the gods. Similarly, we find no difference in the Mesopotamian's mind between identity and resemblance. The teratologic treatise "Shumma Izbu" deals with new-born humans and speculates upon whether they are lions, dogs, asses, fish, reptiles, etc.[32] This fantastic speculation, which might at the most refer to very far-fetched resemblances, established in the eyes of the Meso-potamian a relationship of identity. The importance of this view with regard to the statues of the gods in the temples will shortly become apparent.

The pantheon which underlies Assyro-Babylonian poetry is of Sumerian origin. Most of the gods have preserved their Sumerian name without adopting a Semitic counterpart. In fact, only the astral deities are known under their Semitic names: Sin (Sumerian: Nanna) is the moon-god; Shamash (Sumerian: Utu), the sun-god, and Ishtar (Su-merian: Inanna), the planet Venus. All the other major deities pre-serve their Sumerian names through the whole Assyro-Babylonian time. Marduk, the national god of the Babylonian empire, is often called by the Semitic name "Bel" (Lord), but it is more a title than a name, and it originally belonged to Enlil, who was later called "the old Bel."

---

[32] Cf. Cicero *De Divinatione* I, LIII. 121: *"Et si mulier leonem peperisse visa esset, fore ut ab exteris gentibus vinceretur ea res publica in qua id contigisset."*

As stressed previously, the members of the pantheon are incarnations of natural phenomena: Enlil, the storm-god, whose realm is the space extending between the surface of the earth and the vault of heaven, was the national god of Mesopotamia before the advent of Marduk; he was worshiped in the Ekur temple in Nippur. Ea or Enki, the water-god, who is also lord of the earth, reigns over the rivers, wells, and coastal waters of the Persian Gulf; he is said to have infinite wisdom, and is the patron of magic. He was worshiped in Eridu. Anu is the god of heaven and exercises a kind of sovereignty over the other gods, as their father. The city dedicated to his worship was Uruk. When the Semites tried to organize the intricate Sumerian pantheon, these three deities were considered the first divine triad.

Another triad was formed by the astral deities; Sin, the moon-god, passed for very wise, because he regulated time. He was worshiped in Ur and later in the Assyrian city Harran. The fact that he became the patron deity of the Assyrian royal family opposed him, during the Neo-Babylonian period, to Marduk, who, since the accession of Hammurabi, had replaced Enlil in his role of national god. Shamash, the sun-god, was the protector of justice and the patron deity of divination. He was worshiped in Sippar and Larsa. Ishtar, the goddess of the planet Venus, was a very complex personage. She was at the same time the goddess of love and the patroness of battle.[33] But it was the first of these aspects that made her cult so preponderant in Mesopotamia. As the deity promoting reproduction, she absorbed all the attributes of the mother-goddess to an extent which left the other female deities of the pantheon without significance. Although in the older texts she was considered a young maiden without maternal functions,[34] she gradually assumed the position of the mother-goddess[35] as incarnation of fruitfulness in the vegetable, animal, and human realms. There were Ishtar temples in most

[33] A similar duality appears in Song of Sol. 6:4: "Thou art fair, O my friend, as Tirzah, comely as Jerusalem, terrible as bannered hosts."

[34] Cf. the myths "Dumuzi and Enkimdu." See J. J. A. Van Dijk, *La Sagesse Sumero-Accadienne* (Leiden, 1953), 65–85; and Thorkild Jacobsen and S. N. Kramer, "The Myth of Inanna and Bilulu," *JNES*, Vol. XII (July, 1953), 160–87.

[35] Cf. the Flood episode in the Gilgamesh epic (tablet XI), in which Ishtar is said to have given birth to mankind, a function which in the epic of the Creation of Man (*ANET*, 99ff.) is attributed to Ninhursag or Mama.

of the Sumerian cities, especially in Uruk, Bad-Tibira, Nippur, and Kish. Assyrian Ishtar temples existed in Arbela, Nineveh, Kalah,[36] and other northern cities. Ishtar's association with Tammuz will be discussed later.

The Nether World was ruled by two deities: Ereshkigal, the queen of the "Arallu"[37] and hostile sister of Ishtar, and Nergal,[38] Ereshkigal's husband, who was also god of the midday sun and of pestilence. He was worshiped in Kutha.

A northern deity, Adad, was introduced into the pantheon rather early and acquired importance as the god of lightning and thunder-storm, who sent the violent rains that provoked the floods; he is said to have brought about the Deluge.[39] Together with Shamash, Adad was the patron of divination.

Among the gods who owed their importance to political circum-stances was Ashur, the national god of Assyria. In order to provide the formerly obscure patron deity of the village of Ashur with a more impressive mythological background after the village had become the capital of the Assyrian empire, Assyrian priests equated Ashur with Anshar, one of the primeval gods[40] and father of Anu. Ashur retained his supremacy after the capital changed to Kalah and finally to Nineveh.[41]

Marduk, originally a local god of agriculture,[42] attained his apex of glory under the Old Babylonian empire. An epic[43] was especially composed by the Babylonian clergy to justify his ascendancy over the other members of the pantheon; he assumed or, rather, usurped the function of Enlil as the national god.

---

[36] The temple "Kidmuri" in Kalah was very famous in the ancient world.

[37] The Mesopotamian Hades.

[38] According to the Sumerian myth "Enlil and Ninlil" (S. N. Kramer, *Sumerian Mythology*, 47ff.), Nergal was a son of Enlil, begotten after the latter had been banished to the Nether World; the Semitic legend "Nergal and Ereshkigal" (see Part II below) states that he was primarily a celestial deity but afterwards descended to the Nether World, where he accepted Ereshkigal's offer to divide the sovereignty of the *Arallu* with her.

[39] See Part II below, "The Mesopotamian Deluge" and tablet XI of the "Gilgamesh Epic."

[40] See Chapter IV below, tablet I of the Creation epic.

[41] Until the fall of Nineveh in 612 B.C., the Assyrian kings were crowned in the Ekur temple in Ashur.

[42] This origin is still visible in his emblem, the spade.

[43] *"Enuma elish"* (When on high) or the Creation epic.

Nabu, son of Marduk, achieved fame during the Neo-Babylonian period, and his cult almost supplanted that of his father. He was the patron deity of the scribes and the guardian of the Tablets of Destinies, evidently a function of Enlil.[44] He was worshiped in the temple Ezida in Borsippa.

In the Creation epic we are confronted with still another group of gods: the primeval deities that first emerged from the Chaos represented by Apsu and Tiamat (respectively the sweet and the salty waters). They are brought forth two by two:[45] first Lahmu and Lahamu, then Anshar and Kishar; it seems as if the next pair would be An and Ki (Heaven and Earth), but only An (Anu) is mentioned, as the sky-god, and he already belongs to the first triad of the great gods.

In Mesopotamian literature we often encounter collective terms like the "Anunnaki" and "Igigi"; in still other passages allusion is made to the "Seven Great Gods." The precise position of these anonymous groups is not very clear and varies according to the texts; in many poems the first two terms are used indifferently for the same group. The most common opinion held the Igigi to be the totality of the celestial gods, while the Anunnaki were considered the deities of the lower regions, especially of the "Arallu." The names of the "Seven Great Gods" are never indicated; sometimes they are equated with the Igigi;[46] sometimes they belong to the Nether World.[47]

The Assyro-Babylonians conceived their pantheon under the image of a state, and we find that the gods formed an assembly each time they were to make an important decision, just as Gilgamesh conferred with an assembly of the elders of Uruk before he set out to fight Agga[48] or Huwawa.[49]

Behind this official pantheon we perceive, however, now and then, a much older religious stratum, where anthropomorphism had scarcely

[44] See Chapter IV below, the "Myth of Zu."

[45] We have a parallel with this concept in the Egyptian precreation gods Nun and Naunet, Huh and Hauhet, Kuk and Kauket, and Amun and Amaunet.

[46] In the Etana epic.

[47] In the Sumerian myth "Inanna's Descent to the Nether World."

[48] Cf. the episode "Gilgamesh and Agga" of the Sumerian version of the Gilgamesh epic (*ANET*, 45).

[49] See Chapter IV below, tablet III of the Akkadian version of the Gilgamesh epic.

begun to transform the original conception of deified plants, animals, and even stones.

In the vegetable realm, it is especially trees which are considered divine; Ningishzida is a tree-god, as is Tammuz in one of his many aspects.[50] Gilgamesh and Enkidu are accused by Enlil not so much for having slain Huwawa, guardian of the Holy Cedar, as for having felled the sacred tree.[51]

A deity with animal form is Zu, the storm-god recorded in the "Myth of Zu," in which he is described as a bird.[52] But he was not the only ornithomorphic god; underworld deities, especially, were often said to be bird shaped,[53] and the dead themselves were clad in bird feathers.[54] It is possible that birds have been deified since earliest times. Prehistoric pottery includes several bird-shaped vases,[55] and birds are depicted on vessels of the Protoliterate and the Ninevite V periods.

Another animal often associated with gods and even identified with them is the serpent, always characteristic of chthonian deities. There are early representations of serpents on cylinder seals; the reptiles issue from the shoulders of a god,[56] or from the lower half of his body.[57] A vase of Gudea (in the Louvre Museum) is decorated with the motif of two intertwined serpents, flanked by two dragons who are the emblem of the god Ningishzida; and a Sumerian mace-head shows a serpent with seven heads.[58] This last example may allude to the realm of demons; a cylinder (Oriental Institute of Chicago) illustrates the slaying of a similar seven-headed monster. In almost all other cases, however, the

---

[50] In Greek mythology we find the same association of a god and a tree in Adonis, the Phoenician Tammuz, son of the arboreal Myrrha.

[51] The Old Babylonian term 𒀭 𒄄 𒅆 *"neir"* means "slay" rather than "fell," yet it is used to express not only the killing of Huwawa but also the extermination of the Cedar.

[52] See Chapter IV below.

[53] See Chapter IV below, "A Vision of the Nether World."

[54] See Chapter IV below, "Descent of Ishtar to the Nether World."

[55] In Arpachiyyah (Halaf level) and Khafajah (Sin temple III and Small temple VI).

[56] E.g., a cylinder seal of Gudea, showing the god Ningishzida. See G. Contenau, *Manuel d'archéologie orientale* (Paris, 1931), Vol. II, illustration 535.

[57] Cylinder seal of the Louvre (Delaporte, *Catalogue des Cylindres Orientaux du Musée du Louvre*, pl. 29).

[58] *AO*, No. 12 (1935), 108.

serpent has a positive significance, also when depicted without a divine attribute.[59]

A very ancient cult centered around a god who had the body of a fish, with an additional human head and human feet. The adoration of this god is known to us through the Babylonian historiographer Berossus,[60] who reports a Sumerian legend concerning the origin of civilization: a pisciform deity named Ὠαννῆς appeared to the inhabitants of the Persian Gulf Coast and taught them agriculture, art, science, law, architecture, and writing. The event is said to have taken place during the reign of Alulu, the first antediluvian king. In the Sumerian king list,[61] Alulu is assigned the throne of Eridu. This city was where the god Ea had his temple, and fish were an essential part of the daily sacrifice offered to the deity.[62] It is probable that Berossus refers to a very ancient Mesopotamian tradition, according to which Ea, the Sumerian water-god and personification of wisdom and magic, was originally adored under the form of a fish; in this direction points also a bronze plate[63] representing an exorcism, where the two priests who administer the magical rites are clothed in fish costumes.

The fish offerings in the temple of Eridu may be a remnant of this ancient form of the Ea cult, which is attested in prehistoric times by ichthyomorphic motifs painted on vessels of the Jamdat Nasr period and by fish-shaped amulets found in Protoliterate levels of Warka, Telloh, and Khafajah.

The cult of stones was not expanded in Mesopotamia, probably because the alluvial soil was very poor in stones. However, the tenth tablet of the Gilgamesh epic contains a passage which speaks of mysterious "Stone Things,"[64] apparently stones endowed with supernatural properties, which might be reminiscent of a worship of stones. In the Su-

[59] See Chapter IV below, "The Myth of Etana."

[60] A priest of the Esagil temple who, about 250 B.C. composed a history of Babylonia in Greek; the book has entirely perished, but parts of it are known to us through citations by Alexander Polyhistor and Apollodorus.

[61] *ANET*, 265.

[62] See Chapter IV below, "The Myth of Adapa."

[63] Frank, *Babylonische Beschwörungsreliefs* (Leipzig, 1908).

[64] See Chapter IV below, "The Epic of Gilgamesh" (tablet X).

merian myth *"Lugal-e ud me-lam-bi nir-gal₂,"*[65] Ninurta, a war-god, fights and vanquishes a number of stones who have invaded his city Nippur.

Deity Half-Serpent, Half-Human—British Museum
The deity represented on this cylinder seal is not identified.

M. Jastrow, *Bildermappe zur Religion Babyloniens und Assyriens*

In other regions of the Near East, the conception of the divinity of stones was more apparent, as in the Hittite myth of Ullikummis, in which the principal personage is a god made of diorite.[66]

In the New Year's festival, the most important religious ceremony of Mesopotamia, several cults were blended together. In its Assyrian version, the principal personage was Ashur; in Babylon, Marduk took that position. The recital of the Creation epic was an important part of the ritual and was meant to confirm Marduk's sovereignty as king of the gods.[67]

The procession carrying the god's statue to the Akitu temple outside Babylon symbolizes Marduk's marching towards the abode of Tiamat

[65] Cf. S. Geller, *Altorientalische Texte und Untersuchungen* (Berlin-Leipzig, 1917), I, 4.

[66] Cf. Job 5:23 and Isa. 57:6, in which we find faint reminiscences of a stone cult. For the Ullikummis myth, see *ANET*, 122ff.

[67] The rites of the Babylonian festival are described in detail by S. A. Pallis, *The Babylonian Akitu Festival.*

with the intention of killing her. The god's return to the Esagil temple in Babylon is greeted with joy as the victory of Marduk over the forces of Chaos.

The two divine assemblies mentioned in the Creation epic were likewise represented during the New Year's festival: the first meeting precedes the procession; it comprises all the secondary gods of Mesopotamia whose statues had been brought to Babylon for the occasion. These deities are to fix Marduk's destiny. The second assembly meets after the procession and symbolizes the divine assembly headed by the victorious Marduk, who then fixes the destinies of the other gods.

We find, however, elements of older traditions in the New Year's festival. One is the celebration of the sacred marriage of Marduk and Sarpanit, his consort, enacted by a priest and a priestess, perhaps by the king himself in his quality of high priest, and the queen, as high priestess. This practice goes back to a very ancient fertility cult and is the ritual survival of an act of sympathetic magic designed to promote the increase of cattle, crops, and human posterity.

Another ancient cult element in the New Year's festival was the fictitious disappearance of the god during the sixth and seventh days of the celebrations. The consequence is a general disorder accompanied by lamentations which last until the god makes his reappearance in the temple two days later. The Creation epic does not account for such an event; its origin lies instead in the old Tammuz festivities.

The young fertility god was believed to have died as the sown grain, and lamentations were held all over the country[68] until Tammuz rose as the new vegetation at the beginning of spring. The two times of the seasonal cycle were then celebrated together, once a year.[69] But in Uruk and Ur the older version of the New Year's festival was held twice, once at the end of the harvest and once in spring.

[68] Cf. the verse of Ps. 126: "They that sow in tears shall reap in joy."

[69] Concerning the continuance of the Tammuz cult, S. Langdon reports (*Semitic Mythology*, 336): "At Harran in Syrian territory the Arabic sect known as the Sabaeans maintained the worship of this god as late as the tenth century A.D. where the name was pronounced Tamūz and Ta-ūz. The festival of Ta-ūz was also known there as the festival of the weeping women and occurred on the first of the month Tammuz. The women of this Harranian cult wept for Tammuz whom a king had slain, ground his bones, and scattered them to the winds. . . . Hence during this festival the women ate nothing which had been ground in a mill."

Tammuz is the principal deity, besides the mother-goddess, of the oldest religious tradition. His character is rather complex, and he has been associated with trees, serpents, grain, vegetation in general, and also with the "powers in milk."[70] All these attributes point towards the character of fertility god, milk being considered in the ancient world not so much a simple nourishment as a life-giving substance producing fruitfulness. It is to be noted that no emphasis was laid upon fecundity originating in a sexual union.

This, on the contrary, was the domain of Ishtar, the goddess of love. In the myth of Ishtar's descent to the Nether World, the consequences of her disappearance from the Upper World are described as follows: "The bull springs not upon the cow, the ass impregnates not the jenny, in the street the man impregnates not the maiden."[71]

We come here to a very significant seasonal background for the Ishtar-Tammuz myth which has hitherto been overlooked. The divine influences are exercised at two opposite phases of the year: the new vegetation grows in spring, while the mating of the animals indicated above takes place in fall. The fact that Ishtar is directly connected only with the process of mating, not with the bringing forth of offspring, deserves to be stressed. Ishtar starts her activity about the same time that the harvest is gathered and the new grain is sown—when Tammuz is dead.

The myth of Ishtar's descent to the Nether World explains this double-faced effect of fertility by assigning Ishtar to the Arallu during the period between spring and fall. When she is at last released, she has to pay a ransom to Ereshkigal. As is apparent from a Sumerian tablet of the Yale Collection[72] pertaining to the same myth, it turns out that Tammuz is the ransom, and the ghosts who had accompanied Ishtar on her leaving the Arallu take the young god to the Nether World.[73] This happens in fall, when the vegetation is dead and the sown

[70] Jacobsen and Kramer, "The Myth of Inanna and Bilulu," *JNES*, Vol. XII (July, 1953), 165.

[71] Speiser, *ANET*, 108.

[72] Kramer, *ANET*, 52, n. 6.

[73] This explains also the seemingly unmotivated mentioning of Tammuz' name at the end of the Akkadian version.

grain is beneath the surface of the earth. But in compensation the mating begins in the animal realm and is effective until spring.

The Sumerian myth "Inanna and Bilulu"[74] presents another interpretation of the seasonal alternation: Tammuz is with his sheep in the fields, while Ishtar is separated from him, staying at her mother's house and longing to be at her husband's side.[75] When at last she sets out to meet him, she finds Tammuz dead, slain by robbers. The detail that matters in this connection is the fact that through a tragic coincidence (motivated by the alternation of their respective fertility functions) the union of Ishtar and Tammuz does not take place. While Tammuz is occupied with his flocks, Ishtar cannot stay with him but has to remain with her mother as Ishtar stayed in the Nether World. When at last she is about to rejoin him, it is too late; Tammuz has been killed. Thereupon Ishtar sets forth on a journey to the house of the robbers in order to avenge the slain god. (In the other myth Tammuz had been carried to the Nether World by the ghosts.)

In none of the myths, either Sumerian or Akkadian, is there any warrant for the current assumption that Ishtar descended to the Arallu for the purpose of rescuing Tammuz. No reason for Ishtar's journey is indicated in the texts, and it was probably of slight moment for the mythopoeic mind of the Mesopotamian. What mattered was to furnish a mythological account of the alternating lack of one of the fertilizing influences in nature.

Apart from the great New Year's festival, there were ceremonies in the Mesopotamian temples every day, centering around abundant food-offerings and libations for the god or the goddess. The concept of divinity was based very largely on human conditions: the gods were clothed and adorned like mortal beings,[76] and they needed food for

[74] Jacobsen and Kramer, "The Myth of Inanna and Bilulu," *JNES*, Vol. XII (July, 1953).

[75] See Jacobsen's commentary *ibid.*, 163, n. 9: "It is possible that we should imagine the relation between Dumuzi and Inanna as that of a marriage which, while concluded, has not yet been consummated, and which is to be consummated only when Dumuzi can lead Inanna from her father's house to his own."

[76] Ishtar prepares herself for her journey to the Nether World by putting on "her queenly robes" and adorning herself with "her jewels." For the Sumerian version, see *Orientalia*, Vol. XIV, NS (1945) 24ff.

their daily sustenance.[77] We see that during the New Year's festival the god and the goddess were even provided with a bridal chamber for the consummation of the sacred marriage.

The Sumerians had, from prehistoric times, statues in their temples which represented the respective deities. The statue was not a symbol of the god, but the god himself. This conception, that a man-made idol had divine character and was completely identical with the god it represented, is rather startling to modern minds. But it never disturbed the ancient Mesopotamian that the statue was necessarily imperfect and depended on a priest for voice or action. The fact that it "resembled" the respective god assured its identity with the divine personage.[78] According to the conception of the Mesopotamian, two things were identical when they shared essentials. In the ancient world, such an essential feature could be the name of the object in question; the simplest means of investing a statue with the resemblance that entitled it to be fully identical with the real personage was to confer the latter's name upon the effigy.

The name of a person or inanimate object had a singular significance for the ancient Mesopotamian. We have already seen how, in the Creation epic, Ea confers his function upon Marduk by giving his own name to his victorious son (tablet VII). Gilgamesh sees in the glorification of his name a reflection of immortality (tablet III).[79] Mesopotamian rulers, both mythological and historical, stress the importance of their names' being pronounced by a deity. In the Zu myth, the champion of the gods[80] against the thief of the tablets is promised by the divine assembly that his "names shall be the greatest." In the Creation

[77] See *Publications of the Babylonian Section of the University Museum,* Vol. V, No. 1 (University of Pennsylvania, Philadelphia, 1914), verse 211.

[78] Mesopotamian monarchs transported, during military campaigns, the statues from the temples in the hostile cities to their own country in order to assure for themselves the protection of the respective gods; thus Sennacherib transferred after the destruction of Babylon the statue of Marduk to his own capital, and Ashurbanipal, after his victory over the rebellious Elamites, took the god Shushinak "by his hand" and conducted him to the temple of Uruk (it is not explicitly stated that this was the god's statue). On the same occasion the goddess Nana (i.e., her statue), who had been brought to Elam 1,635 years before, was reinstalled in her original abode, the Eanna temple in Uruk.

[79] See also Chapter IV below, the final comment of the Gilgamesh epic.

[80] Ninurta in the Ashur text, Ningirsu in the Susa version.

epic (tablets VI–VII), the gods call Marduk by fifty names.[81] Sumerian and Akkadian monarchs proclaim in their inscriptions that their royal names have been pronounced by deities.[82] In a Sumerian text describing a coronation ritual in Uruk,[83] the king is elevated to his rank by a goddess who pronounces his "name of rulership" instead of his "name of smallness."

Inanimate things also were given names which conferred divinity even upon them. Crown and scepter, for example, have the rank of goddesses in the coronation text just mentioned and are called *"Nin-men-na"* (Lady of the Crown) and *"Nin-PA"* (Lady of the Scepter). The divine Ninshubur, vizier of Anu, was actually the door of the sky-god's shrine, and Ninshubur's son, Hedu, personified the arch in which the door swung.[84] In the Creation epic (tablet VI), Enlil fashions a bow and, calling it his daughter, confers upon it three names; he assigns to the bow a place among the gods, its brothers.[85] The giving of a name may even approach the act of creating, as is apparent from the initial lines of "Enuma elish": "When on high the heaven had not been named,/ Firm ground below had not been called by name . . ./ When no gods whatever had been brought into being,/ Uncalled by name, their destinies undetermined . . ./ Lahmu and Lahamu were brought forth, by name they were called."[86]

In the poem it is not stated that the names of heaven and earth as well as those of the primeval gods Lahmu and Lahamu had been pronounced by a divine being: the vaguely announced concept of verbal creation remains impersonal. It was the Hebrews who first formu-

---

[81] The fifty names of Marduk have been discussed in a study by F. M. T. Böhl, *Archiv für Orientforschung* (Berlin, 1936), 191–218.

[82] E.g., Shu-Sin, monarch of the third Ur Dynasty, had been named by Anu. See Frankfort, Lloyd, and Jacobsen, *The Gimilsin Temple and the Palace of the Rulers at Tell Asmar* (Oriental Institute *Publications*, Vol. XLIII, Chicago, 1938), 134 ff. Lipit-Ishtar, ruler of the Isin dynasty, calls himself "named by Nunamnir" (Enlil) ("Lipit-Ishtar Law Code," published by F. A. Steele in *AJA*, Vol. LII [July, 1948], 425ff.); Hammurabi states in the prologue of his law code that Anu and Enlil named him "to promote the welfare of the people" and expresses in the epilogue the wish that "in Esagila, which I love, may my name be spoken in reverence forever!" See Deimel, *Codex Hammurabi.*

[83] A. Poebel, *Historical and Grammatical Texts,* 76.

[84] Neo-Assyrian An-Anum list.

[85] Sultantepe fragment.         [86] Translated by Speiser, *ANET,* 60 ff.

lated the idea of a "creatio ex nihilo" performed through the word of God.

## THE EVOLUTION OF KINGSHIP

In the Sumerian king list,[87] the god Dumuzi (Tammuz) appears twice as an earthly ruler, once in Eridu, before the Deluge, and once in Uruk, after the Flood. He is said to have been a shepherd.

We find here united in one person three different aspects of the chieftain's role: Tammuz is a god, a king, and a shepherd. Nor is he the only mythological personage with these three attributes: Gilgamesh, whose name comes after the second mention of Dumuzi in the king list, is partially a god (his name is preceded in the texts by the determinative ⟜⊣ *"dingir,"* which means "divinity"[88]), a king, and a shepherd. Likewise, Etana, a legendary ruler of the first postdiluvian dynasty of Kish, is divine and exercises the functions of king and shepherd.[89]

These examples illustrate a very old conception of kingship in Mesopotamia, which goes back to the period when the ancestors of the first inhabitants had not yet fixed their abodes in the alluvial plain of Sumer but led a nomadic existence.

In the course of time, the king's role as a god and as a shepherd underwent profound changes. The idea that an earthly ruler was of divine nature became almost completely abandoned at the beginning of history.[90] Unlike the Egyptian Pharaoh, incarnation of a god, the Mesopotamian monarch was the humble servant of the gods, their steward and their soldier. The shepherd-king, who once had to lead his people to fresh pastures for their flocks, now assured the prosperity of his sedentary subjects by "digging canals" and promoting irrigation of the fields.

The king's principal task consisted of being the mediator between his people and the city-god. In this role the historical kings were much further removed from the deity than had been the legendary rulers of

[87] A Leo Oppenheim, "Historiographic Documents," *ANET*, 265ff.; S. Langdon, *Oxford Edition of Cuneiform Texts,* II, No. 1923, 444, p. 13ff.

[88] Other meanings of this sign are: star, heaven, Anu, and high.

[89] Oppenheim, "Historiographic Documents," *ANET*, 265.

[90] The pretense to divine parentage, as it appears in the royal inscriptions, was only nominal, since the kings also mentioned officially their real forefathers.

the myths. Gilgamesh, Etana, Atrahasis, and Utnapishtim had all been favored with direct "communication" imparted by a god or a goddess[91] on a conversational level[92] and had no difficulty interpreting their personal deity's wishes. The monarchs of historical times, on the other hand, had to supplicate the gods through sacrifices, prayers, and vigils for a token that would reveal the divine will. They were perpetually anxious about receiving the approval of their smallest actions from the gods and eagerly consulted a staff of priests who would assist them with the interpretation of dreams,[93] eclipses,[94] and other omens.[95]

The humility of the sovereign's position in relation to his god found expression also in the conception that all the land of the community belonged to the deity, to whom the king, as administrator of the divine property, owed an accounting.[96] A small part of the god's domain, called *"Kur"* land, consisted of allotments of various sizes which served for the sustenance of the individual members of the community, while the greater and better part of the estate, the *"Nigenna"* land, was reserved exclusively for the god. The labor was provided through *Frondienst* of each inhabitant, and the produce was assigned to the temple. A third part of the god's property, the *"Urula"* land, was leased to community members who wanted to cultivate a plot for their own use, after paying a fee to the deity.

Urukagina, ruler of Lagash prior to the invasion of the Guti, proved to be an exemplary steward of the divine estate by putting an end to abuses which tended to convert the *"Nigenna"* land to secular profit.[97]

---

[91] Gilgamesh converses with Shamash (tablet X) and Ishtar (tablet VI); Etana receives instructions from Shamash (fragment C–3); Atrahasis hears the advice of Ea (fragments B, X, and C), and so does Utnapishtim (tablet XI of the Gilgamesh epic).

[92] In the Old Testament, a divine communication takes more the shape of a revelation granted under exceptional circumstances.

[93] Gudea Cylinder A.

[94] A. T. Clay, *Miscellaneous Inscriptions in the Yale Babylonian Collection,* (New Haven, 1915), 66–75.

[95] R. Pfeiffer, *State Letters of Assyria* (New Haven, 1935), 231.

[96] A. Schneider, *Die sumerische Tempelstadt (Plenge Staatswissenschaftliche Beiträge,* Vol. IV, Essen, 1920). Cf. also A. Deimel, *"Die sumerische Tempelwirtschaft zur Zeit Urukaginas und seiner Vorgänger,"* AO, Vol. II (1931), 71–113.

[97] "The oxen of the gods tilled the onion fields of the ensi, since the onion and

The king's military campaigns were always presented as executions of a divine command.[98] The victor imposed upon the defeated people the yoke of his god[99] and severely punished the slanderers of the deity's name.[100] It was the awe inspired by the gods' fame that made rulers of distant countries pay homage to the sovereign of Assyria.[101] The regions which the Assyrian armies occupied aggrandized the territory belonging to the god Ashur.[102] The king conducted his campaigns aided by the gods who marched beside the army and overpowered the enemy by their terror-inspiring glamour,[103] blinding their opponents[104] and driving them insane.[105]

In the account of Esarhaddon's fight for the throne, Ishtar is said to have broken the bows of the hostile soldiers.[106] Ashurbanipal claims that he has been assisted in the campaign against the Arabs by Ninlil, the "lordly Wild-Cow," who "butts [his] enemies with her mighty

---

cucumber fields of the ensi were in the good land of the god" (translated from F. Thureau-Dangin, *Les inscriptions de Sumer et d'Akkad*, 74–75).

[98] Tiglat-Pileser I, of Assyria, proclaims: "At the order of Anu and Adad, the great gods, my Lords, I went to the Lebanon mountains" (Prism of Tiglat-Pileser, published by O. Schröder, *Keilschrifttexte aus Assur historischen Inhalts* (Berlin-Leipzig, 1922), II, No. 63). The same king asserts: "At the order of my Lord Ashur I was a conqueror" (Foundation Document of the Anu-Adad Temple in Ashur; Schröder, *ibid.*, II, No. 68). Shalmaneser III states: "At the order of Ashur, the great Lord, my Lord, I fought against them, inflicted a defeat upon them" (From the Black Obelisk; A. H. Layard, *Inscriptions in the Cuneiform Character from Assyrian Monuments* (London, 1851), pl. 87ff.)

[99] Sargon II declares: "In the City of Carchemish, I forced upon their neck the yoke of Ashur, my Lord" (A. G. Lie, *The Inscriptions of Sargon II, King of Assyria* [Paris, 1929], Part I, 46ff.).

[100] Ashurbanipal boasts: "I tore out the tongues of those who had cursed my god Ashur" (Rassam cylinder, H. C. Rawlinson, *The Cuneiform Inscriptions of Western Asia* [London, 1861–84], V, pl. 1 ff.).

[101] Sargon II, Display Inscription. See H. Winckler, *Die Keilschrifttexte Sargons* (Leipzig, 1889), I, 115ff.

[102] Sargon II, Annals of the Room XIV. *Ibid.*, II, pl. 26ff.

[103] Adad-Nirari III, inscription on a stone slab. Rawlinson, *Cuneiform Inscriptions*, I, pl. 35, No. 1; and Shalmaneser III, Rawlinson, "Monolith Inscriptions," *Cuneiform Inscriptions*, III, pl. 7.

[104] Sargon II, Display Inscription. See Winckler, *Die Keilschrifttexte Sargons*.

[105] Esarhaddon, Prism B. (R. Campbell Thompson, *The Prisms of Esarhaddon and of Ashurbanipal* (London, 1931).

[106] *Ibid.*

horns."[107] Esarhaddon stresses the supernatural power with which his battles are conducted by pointing out that his foes "put their trust upon their own force," while he himself "trusted Ashur [his] Lord."[108]

We see therefore that the historical king in Mesopotamia was no more than an exalted mortal, only as near to the gods as his human nature allowed. Even his position as supreme priest was challenged in the humiliating scene of reinvestment with the royal insignia, an act that took place each year during the New Year's festival[109] on the fifth day of the month Nisan: the king knelt before the high priest after having deposited scepter, ring, scimitar, and crown in front of the god's statue; he then declared that he had committed no sins, and was struck twice in the face by the priest, who then returned the royal insignia to the sovereign.

Such a scene would have been a blasphemy in Egypt, where the Pharaoh was considered a deity, ranking on an equal level with the gods of the pantheon.[110]

The Egyptian king's claim to divine parentage was not, as in Mesopotamia, a remnant of mythological custom meant only to express the degree of predilection shown by the god in behalf of a mortal, but a solemnly voiced dogma.

In his "Hymn of Victory,"[111] Thut-mose III boasts of having been established by the god Amon-Re, his father, upon the throne of Horus for millions of years; and Amen-hotep III declared, according to a building inscription,[112] that his father Amon-Re made him "to be the Re of the Two Banks."

107 Ashurbanipal, Cylinder B. See M. Streck, *Assurbanipal und die letzten assyrischen Könige bis zum Untergang,* in *Vorderasiatische Bibliothek* (Leipzig, 1916), II, 135ff.

108 Esarhaddon, Prism A. See Rawlinson, *Cuneiform Inscriptions,* I, pl. 45ff.

109 H. Zimmern, *DAO,* Vol. XXV (Leipzig, 1926), 12.

110 In Egyptian pictorial representations Pharaoh is the same size as the gods and shares their pastime (e.g., a relief of the Karnak temple, where Ramses II nets birds in company of the gods Horus and Khnum); the Egyptian king may even show the same theriomorphic features that characterize the gods: on a war chariot, Thut-mose IV is represented as a winged lion with human head (H. Carter, *The Tomb of Thoutmosis,* IV, pl. XII). Amen-em-het III appears in a sculpture under the form of a sphinx (Ludwig Borchardt, *Kunstwerke aus dem ägyptischen Museum zu Cairo,* pl. VII).

111 P. Lacau, *"Stèles du nouvel empire,"* *Catalogue général des antiquités égyptiennes du Musée du Caire* (Cairo, 1904), pl. VII, 17ff.

112 *Ibid.,* I, pl. XVff., 47ff.

Although subject to death as every other mortal, the Pharaoh possessed, in the belief of the Egyptians, everlasting life.[113] He was the incarnation of Horus, who perpetually renewed himself through rebirth as son of Osiris[114] (identified with the king's dead predecessor) and Isis (identified with the queen mother).

In Mesopotamia the primitive association of kingship and divinity appears during the historical period only in rare echoes; a Sumerian ruler might be treated as a god outside his own city,[115] but when a vanquished vassal built a temple for his victorious sovereign, the building was quickly converted to secular use as soon as the political power of the deified king had ceased.[116] The concept of the divine character inherent in kingship found expression only in the idea that the monarch was personally chosen by the gods and that the royal insignia were of heavenly origin.[117]

In royal inscriptions, the Mesopotamian ruler frequently claims that he has been selected, through decree of the gods, to be the "shepherd of the black-headed people."[118] Such a title, deriving from a time when pastoral existence was preponderant in Mesopotamia, continued in use throughout the historical period. Although, with the organization of a sedentary civilization in the "valley of the two rivers," the king no

[113] In the inscription of the Barkal Stela, Thut-mose III calls himself "Men-kheper-Re who lives forever"; G. A. Reisner and M. B. Reisner in *Zeitschrift für ägyptische Sprache und Altertumskunde*, Vol. LXIX (January, 1933), 24ff.

[114] In Egyptian mythology, Pharaoh was viewed as son of Re, sun-god and first king of Egypt, and also as son of Osiris, king of the dead.

[115] This is attested for rulers of the third Ur dynasty who took the place of their defeated enemies' city-gods. (Frankfort, Lloyd, and Jacobsen, *The Gimilsin* [Shu-Sin] *Temple and the Palace of the Rulers at Tell Asmar* (Oriental Institute *Publications*, Vol. XLIII, Chicago, 1938), 134ff.

[116] Ituria, ruler of Eshnunna, built a temple for the "divine Shu-Sin," his political overlord. After the fall of the third Ur dynasty, the temple was secularized and became part of the royal palace in Eshnunna; the god Tishpak now reigned again as "overlord" of the Eshnunna kings.

Other cities where a vassal erected a temple for an earthly sovereign were Lagash, Umma, and Drehem, as is apparent from inscriptions. See T. Fisch, "The Cult of King Dungi [Shulgi] during the Third Dynasty of Ur," *Bulletin of the John Rylands Library* (Manchester, 1927), 322ff.

[117] Cf. the initial lines of the Etana myth (Old Babylonian version, fragment A–1).

[118] E.g., in a Song of Shulgi (A. Falkenstein, *ZA*, Vol. L [1952], 64ff.); and in the epilogue of Hammurabi's law code (Deimel, *Codex Hammurabi*).

longer exercised materially the profession of shepherd, the essential features of the function were maintained.

The ancient "shepherd" had the task of assuring the prosperity of his flock by seeking out suitable pastures and watering places; he defended his sheep against attacks from the wild beasts of the steppe and safeguarded peace and order among the members of his herd.

In the historical epoch, the "shepherd" of the sedentary community provided for the sustenance of his people through the upkeep of an extended irrigation system, key to the fertility of the land. He protected his subjects from the incursions of human enemies by erecting fortifications around the city and training the inhabitants for military defense. To assure peace and order, the shepherd-king became a legislator and established long lists of written laws that were to be respected by every member of the community.

From Early Dynastic times until the Neo-Assyrian period, Mesopotamian rulers emphasized their pastoral attributes. Gudea of Lagash is the "Shepherd looked upon by Ningirsu."[119] During the third Ur Dynasty, Ur-Nammu and Shulgi repeatedly proclaimed that they were the shepherds of their people, and Shu-Sin is said to have been granted the "shepherdship of the country."[120] Lipit-Ishtar stressed his pastoral function twice in the prologue to his Law Code;[121] in a song dedicated to the king, Anu compared the people over whom Lipit-Ishtar reigned to a herd of sheep.[122] Hammurabi called himself "the shepherd named by Enlil."[123] Ashurnazirpal II, of Assyria, stated that Ishtar established him as "shepherd of men."[124] In a dialogue dating from Neo-Babylonian times,[125] the king's title is replaced by the appellation "the shepherd, sun of the people."

[119] F. Thureau-Dangin, *Les Inscriptions de Sumer et d'Akkad*, 107 (Statue B, II, 8ff.).

[120] G. Castellino, "Ur-Nammu-Three Religious Texts," Vol. LIII, *ZA* (1957), 1–5; A. Falkenstein, "Ein Shulgi-Lied," *ZA*, Vol. L (1952), 64ff.; and Frankfort, Lloyd, and Jacobsen, *The Gimilsin* [Shu-Sin] *Temple* (Oriental Institute *Publications*, Vol. XLIII, Chicago, 1938), 138.

[121] F. R. Steele, *AJA* (1948), 425ff.

[122] H. Zimmern, *König Lipit-Ishtars Vergöttlichung* (*Berichte über die Verhandlungen der Kgl. Sächsischen Gesellschaft der Wissenschaften*, Phil.-hist. Klasse, Vol. 68).

[123] Deimel, *Codex Hammurabi*, Prologue.

[124] I. Y. Le Gac, *Les inscriptions de Aššur-nasir-aplu* II (Paris, 1907).

[125] J. A. Craig, *Babylonian and Assyrian Religious Texts*, in *Assyriologische Bibliothek* (Leipzig, 1895), I, pl. 52.

Hammurabi was especially eloquent regarding his pastoral achievements.[126] The primitive task is recalled in his assertions: "I am . . . the one . . . who assigns the pastures and watering places for Lagash and Girsu. . . . I am . . . the founder of dwelling places for them . . . the shelter of the land, who gathered the scattered people of Isin . . . I . . . did not neglect the black-headed people whose shepherdship Marduk had entrusted to me, I sought peaceful regions for them."

But the king is also the "shepherd" of his sedentary people. Both Hammurabi[127] and his son Samsu-iluna[128] devoted themselves to the digging of new canals or the clearing of old ones so that the cities of the Plain were provided with abundant water supply.[129] Hammurabi "aggrandized the cultivated land of Dilbat";[130] the high walls he erected at the embankments of the Tigris and of the Euphrates[131] were probably meant to serve the irrigation system of the land.

Lipit-Ishtar had given himself the title of "farmer" besides the one of "shepherd."[132] Hammurabi stated that he stored up grain "for the great Urash," and asserted again and again that he promoted the welfare of the people.[133] Samsu-iluna went so far as to grant his subjects "freedom from taxation."[134]

As is apparent from the texts, at least in the Early Dynastic and the

---

[126] Deimel, *Codex Hammurabi*, Prologue and Epilogue.

[127] Hammurabi dug the canal "Hammurabi-is-abundance" in his ninth year and cleared it once more twenty-four years afterwards; he also redug the "Flowing Vase" canal and the Euphrates bed. Cf. A. Ungnad, *Reallexikon der Assyriologie*, II, 164–82.

[128] Samsu-iluna dug two canals in his third and in his fourth year of rulership "Samsu-iluna-is-fountain-of-prosperity" and "Samsu-iluna-is-abundance." After thirty-two years of reign, he redug the canals Durul and Taban.

[129] "Thirty-third year of Hammurabi" (Ungnad, *Reallexikon der Assyriologie*, II, 180) and prologue to the law code (Deimel, *Codex Hammurabi*).

[130] Deimel, *Codex Hammurabi*, Prologue.

[131] "Forty-second year of Hammurabi" (Ungnad, *Reallexikon der Assyriologie*, II, 182).

[132] F. R. Steele, Vol. LII (July, 1948), 425ff.

[133] Deimel, *Codex Hammurabi*, Prologue and Epilogue.

[134] Cf. E. F. Weidner, *"Ilušumas Zug nach Babylonien,"* ZA, Vol. XLIII, NF IX (1936), p. 122.

Old Babylonian periods, the king fulfilled his pastoral duty of providing abundance for his people.[135]

The old Mesopotamian myths depict the "shepherd" as the protector of his flock from the attacks of raiders and wild beasts. The Sumerian poem "Inanna and Bilulu"[136] shows the goddess praising the good shepherd Dumuzi, who lost his life while defending his sheep against the robbers Bilulu and Girgire. In the Gilgamesh epic, Enkidu joins a group of herdsmen while on his way to Uruk; during the night, he kills the lions and wolves which threaten the fold.[137]

The ancient shepherd had to possess great physical strength in order to cope, singlehanded, with predatory men and animals. In the description of Gilgamesh, particular emphasis is laid upon the hero's capability of measuring himself against the violence of wild animals,[138] even though no sheepfolds are mentioned.[139]

An echo of the ancient shepherd's defensive activity is to be found in the pictorial representations of Assyrian kings chasing and killing lions.[140] What seems to be nothing more than a royal pastime is in reality the continuance of a pastoral tradition; the king does not hunt to provide venison but, as an act of defense, chases dangerous animals.

With the switch from pastoral to urban life in the historical period, it became the king's duty to defend the people effectively against incursions and acts of violence menacing the city. The wise ruler protected his community by building thick walls and inpenetrable fortifications and by manning these armaments with soldiers.

Gilgamesh takes a special pride in the solidity of the ramparts around Uruk,[141] which were constructed under his command[142] by the

---

135 The historical texts of later epochs emphasize more the military activities of the kings.

136 Jacobsen and Kramer, *JNES*, Vol. XII (July, 1953), 160–88.

137 Gilgamesh epic, tablet II.

138 *Ibid.*, tablets VI and X.

139 As a reminiscence of pastoral life might be considered the setting out by Gilgamesh of bowls filled with honey and curds (tablet VIII), typical shepherd's fare.

140 Bas-reliefs of the royal palaces in Nimrud and Kuyunjik (British Museum).

141 Tablets I and XI (Gilgamesh epic).

142 The Sumerian king list (S. Langdon, *Oxford Edition of Cuneiform Texts* [Oxford,

people of the city.[143] Hammurabi built the walls of the town Bazu and dedicated twenty years of his reign to the erection of the walls of Sippar.[144] Samsu-iluna rebuilt the ramparts of Uruk, "the city which his father had conquered,"[145] and those of Kish.[146] The impressive size of the walls around Nineveh, built by Sennacherib, becomes apparent through the description of their ruins by Xenophon, who stated, almost two hundred years after the destruction of the city, that the rampart was fifty feet broad and one hundred feet high, with a circumference of six parasangs (about 20.5 miles), and that it stood on a foundation measuring fifty feet in width and fifty feet in height.[147]

The outer city wall of Nebuchadnezzar's Babylon was considered by Strabo as one of the "Seven Wonders of the World."[148] Built of burnt-clay bricks, the circumvallation was eleven miles long and twenty-seven feet wide, interspaced with 240 to 360 towers of an estimated height of forty to sixty feet.[149] The fortifications comprised also an inner wall twenty-three feet in width.[150]

The conducting of campaigns into foreign countries had been the task of the king acting as "the soldier of the gods." The military defense of the land against an enemy attack was the duty of the sovereign acting as "the shepherd of the people."

In the thirtieth year of his reign, Hammurabi fought against the

---

1924], II, 13ff.) names En-me-kar as the builder of Uruk; prior to the reign of this king the place consisted only of the Eanna precinct.

[143] It is possible that Gilgamesh also exacted military service from his subjects, as might be inferred from the complaint of the people (tablet I): "Gilgamesh leaves not the son to the father."

[144] Ungnad, *Reallexikon der Assyriologie,* II, 179ff.

[145] *Cuneiform Texts,* VI, pl. 9ff.

[146] Hammurabi states in the prologue to his law code that he refounded the settlement of Kish; the city had been restored earlier by Sargon of Akkad. (Poebel, *Historical and Grammatical Texts,* V, pl. 10, No. 34).

[147] *Anabasis* III, 4.

[148] Διόπερ τῶν ἐπτὰ Θεαμάτων λέγεται καὶ τοῦτο.

[149] Lucian of Samosata makes allusion to the enormous wall of Babylon in his dialogue *Charon:* Ἡ βαβυλὼν δέ σοι ἐκείνη ἐστὶν ἡ εὔπυργος ἡ τὸν μέγαν περίβολον.

[150] The numbers and measures indicated above are given by F. Wetzel, *Die Stadtmauern von Babylon (Wissenschaftliche Veröffentlichungen der deutschen Orient-Gesellschaft,* Vol. 48, Berlin-Leipzig, 1930).

army of Elam that had threatened to destroy his realm.[151] Samsu-iluna turned back incursions of the Kassites[152] and drove out the "evil usurper."[153] Lipit-Ishtar stated in his Law Code that he repressed hostility and enmity in his country.[154] Hammurabi proclaimed again: ". . . I eradicated the enemy. . . . I put an end to war. . . . I did not let the people be terrorized . . . [but] sheltered them in peace."[155]

The shepherd-king had also the duty of establishing justice among his people.[156] Like so many other conceptions of the ancient world, "justice" had a transcendent meaning in Mesopotamia. The texts refer to the *"kittum,"* the sum of immutable cosmic truths of divine origin, and to the *"mēšarum,"* the human law subject to readjustments and amendments.

Hammurabi described himself in the epilogue of his code as the "king of justice to whom Shamash entrusted the law";[157] "justice" is rendered by the word *"mēšarum,"* and "law" by the term *"kittum."*[158] The king's role was to exercise human justice by respecting the divine law. Only if he excelled in this task could he claim to be a *"šarru-ken,"* a legitimate king.[159]

Several centuries before the reign of Hammurabi, Mesopotamian rulers had already established lists of written laws for the benefit of their people. The oldest law code so far known was composed by Ur-Nammu, founder of the third Ur Dynasty. The poorly preserved text consists of a fragmentary prologue and twenty-two laws.[160] During the Isin-Larsa period, which followed the reign of Ibi-Sin, last king of

[151] Ungnad, *Reallexikon der Assyriologie,* II, 180.

[152] *Cuneiform Texts,* VI, pl. 9 (ninth year of reign).

[153] *Ibid.* (fourteenth year of reign).

[154] F. R. Steele, *AJA,* Vol. LII (July, 1948), 450.

[155] Deimel, *Codex Hammurabi,* Epilogue.

[156] Sin-idinnam, ruler of Larsa, is called "the shepherd of justice" (*sib₂ nig₂-gi-na-ge*) F. Thureau-Dangin, *Die sumerischen und akkadischen Königsinschriften,* in *Vorderasiatische Bibliothek,* 208, A–11, 13.

[157] Deimel, *Codex Hammurabi.*

[158] For the fundamental difference between these two termini, cf. E. A. Speiser, "Authority and Law in Mesopotamia," Supplement to *JAOS* (January, 1954), 12ff.

[159] Cf. Benno Landsberger, *Die babylonischen Termini für Gesetz und Recht* (*Studia et documenta ad iura orientis antiqui pertinentia,* Leiden, 1949) II, 219ff.

[160] E. Szlechter, "Code de Ur-Nammu," *RA* (1949), 169; and S. N. Kramer "Ur-Nammu Law Code," *Orientalia,* Vol. XXIV (1954), 40–51.

Ur III, another law code was written, the author of which is Lipit-Ishtar, fifth king of Isin. The text consists of a prologue, some thirty-eight laws, and an epilogue,[161] in the pattern of the Hammurabi Codex.

From Eshnunna, a Semitic kingdom which flourished prior to the ascension of Hammurabi, comes a third code,[162] representing a collection of about sixty laws. The tablets relating this code were excavated in Tell Abu Harmal near Baghdad.

The basic concepts underlying these three texts do not differ in substance from those apparent in the Codex of Hammurabi.[163] The 282 laws of the Old Babylonian king were inscribed, together with a prologue and an epilogue, on a diorite stela, which was found in Susa by Jean de Morgan at the beginning of this century. The body of the code seems to represent the sum of judgments passed over a period of several years; there are, indeed, some laws which are contradictory.[164]

The benign spirit in which the king set up the laws of his land is best expressed at the end of the code, where Hammurabi states that the purpose of his legislation is to hinder the strong from oppressing the weak, to protect widows and orphans from injustice, and to affirm every man's right to equitable treatment.[165]

Assyrian legislation is known through a number of clay tablets, which contain collectively about 115 laws.[166]

Their date of composition falls between the fifteenth and the twelfth centuries B.C., a period of political instability characterized by the passage of hostile people through Assyrian territory.[167] This may in part explain

---

161 F. R. Steele, *AJA*, Vol. LII (July, 1948), 425–46.

162 Taha Baqir and A. Goetze, *Sumer*, Vol. IV, 52–173.

163 Deimel, *Codex Hammurabi*.

164 E.g., "theft is punishable by death" according to paragraphs 6, 7, 9, 10, 22, and 25 of the code; but restitution or fines are imposed upon the thief according to paragraphs 8, 259, 260, and 265.

165 Cf. also the codex of Lipit-Ishtar, in which the king proclaims that he freed the people of his land from slavery, strengthened the family ties, and caused justice to reign in Sumer and Akkad.

166 Texts published by O. Schroeder, *Keilschrifttexte aus Assur verschiedenen Inhalts*, (*Wissenschaftliche Veröffentlichung der deutschen Orient-Gesellschaft*, Vol. XXV, Berlin, 1920); and E. F. Weidner, *Archiv für Orientforschung*, Vol. XII (1937) 50 ff.

167 Especially the Hittites, Kassites, and Mitannians.

Guardian of Sacred Tree, Excavated in
Susa—the Louvre

G. Contenau, *Le Déluge babylonien*

Priest in Fish Costume, a Wall
Decoration Excavated in
Nimrud—British Museum

A. H. Layard, *Monuments of Nineveh*

The Demoness Lamashtu

F. Delitzsch, *Beiblatt zum Jahrbuch der Königlichen Preussischen Kunstsammlung*

Expulsion of Demons (both faces)—De Clercq Collection (similar
example at the Museum of Istanbul)

Frank, *Babylonische Beschwörungs reliefs*

Document of Hepatoscopy—British Museum
This document was found in the temple of Sippar
and pertains to the period of Hammurabi, 2000 B.C.

Boissier, *Note sur un monument babylonien se rapportant
a l'Extispicine*

Statue of Gudea with Vertical
Inscription—the Louvre
This statue was excavated in Telloh;
De Sarzec found the head in 1881,
and Cros discovered the
body during the expedition of 1903.

Gaston Cros, *Nouvelles Fouilles de Telloh*

Ashurnazirpal Hunting Lions, an Assyrian Relief Excavated in
Calah—British Museum

Gilgamesh Slaying a Lion, a Relief Excavated in Nippur—
Museum of Istanbul

H. V. Hilprecht, *Explorations in Bible Lands during the XIX. Century*

Archer Hunting Birds, an Assyrian Relief—the Louvre

Bompiani, *Dizionario delle Opere*

Assyrian Horse Breaker, an Assyrian Bas-Relief—the Louvre

Bompiani, *Dizionario delle Opere*

the difference of attitude discernible in the Middle Assyrian laws; they exhibit a much greater severity than their Old Babylonian counterpart and are often tinged with outspoken cruelty.[168] It is probable that the king's role as "pastoral administrator" of justice gradually became that of a sovereign who kept his unruly subjects in curb.

Of the Neo-Babylonian laws only an exiguous portion has been preserved. The sixteen paragraphs of the extant tablet[169] do not contain harsh judgments but appear to follow the benign trend of the Hammurabi legislation, safeguarding the right of widows and protecting the weak from oppression, in a spirit befitting the king to whom "the gods entrusted the shepherdship over the black-headed people."

Turning now to consideration of the titles assumed by Mesopotamian rulers, we encounter an evolution that parallels the gradual extension of the royal domain.

When the first inscriptions of Sumerian monarchs open the path of history, the ancient distinction between the two titles *"en"* and *"lugal"*[170] conferred upon the sovereign of a city-state have almost become obliterated.

The rulers of the Lagash dynasty founded by Ur-Nanshe use the titles *"lugal"* (great man) and "ensi" (free lord) side by side. It is possible that the appellation "ensi" still retained to a certain extent the religious connotation visible in the ancient ideogram ‡ ◇ ⏀ *PA-TE-SI* transliterated *"en₅-si"*;[171] the first two elements, *PA (gidri)* and

---

[168] The *"lex talionis"* was current (tablet A, paragraphs 50 and 52): a man who causes a free woman or a prostitute to have a miscarriage must compensate with a life, either with his own, or with that of his unborn child. Tablet C, paragraph 3: if a nobleman who has been sold into a foreign country as a pledge dies abroad, his seller must compensate with a life. Tablet A, paragraph 55; a virgin's ravisher must give his wife to be ravished. Physical mutilations were frequently imposed (e.g., tablet A, paragraphs 4, 5, 8, 9, 15, 18, 19, 24, 40, and 44): cutting of nose, ears, fingers, and lips; tearing out of eyes, piercing of ears, pulling out of hair, mutilation of the whole face, and castration.

[169] F. E. Peiser, *Sitzungsberichte der preussischen Akademie der Wissenschaften* (Berlin, 1889), 823–28, and pl. VII.

[170] See notes 20 and 21 above.

[171] Cf. E. Sollberger, *ZA*, Vol. L (1952), 13–14. The transliteration *"ensi₂"* was proposed by A. Falkenstein, *ibid.*, 1934, pp. 152–54. G. Dossin thinks that it is also plausible to read the ideogram phonetically *"pa-te-si"*; the reading *"en"* for the first two components might have been the later work of Babylonian philologists (*ibid.*, p. 13, n. 3).

79

*TE* (*temen*), represent the "scepter" and the "temple terrace," symbols of a combined secular and religious power.[172]

It might be assumed that at the onset of history the sovereign emphasized his *"lugal"* title when he was engaged in an enterprise of conquest.

Ur-Nanshe, a *"lugal,"*[173] in all probability gained the throne of Lagash after a military action. Akurgal, his successor, bore the title "ensi"[174] as well as that of *"lugal"*;[175] possibly he still had to consolidate his power in the land. His son Eannatum governed Lagash as "ensi" and later became *"lugal"* of Kish[176] through conquest. Entemena was, like his father, an "ensi,"[177] but he claimed to have been granted, by the god Nanshe, the "Lugalship" (*nam-lugal*)[178] of the realm. The last ruler of the Lagash dynasty, Urukagina, called himself "ensi" as well as *"lugal"*;[179] the god Ningirsu bestowed upon him the "Lugalship" (*nam-lugal*) of Lagash,[180] and the goddess Bau foreordained him for the "shepherdship" (*nam-sipa*) of the land.[181]

The first Sumerian king who augmented his royal title was Lugal-zaggesi. Initially the ruler of Umma, he extended his domain over all Sumer by conquering successively Uruk, Ur, and Lagash. Thus he assumed the title "King of the Lands" (*lugal ḳur-ḳur-ra*).[182] When this first attempt at Mesopotamian unity came to an end, to be replaced by the erection of an Akkadian empire under Sargon I and Naram-Sin, the royal title made new progress: the Semitic sovereign was now the "King of the Four Quarters" (*šar ḳi-ib₂-ra-tim ar-ba-im*).[183]

---

[172] Sollberger (*ZA*, Vol. I [1952], 13–14) translates *"ensi"* with the word "pontiff."

[173] Votive tablet of Ur-Nanshe and his family (the Louvre). See E. de Sarzec and L. Heuzey, *Découvertes en Chaldée*, pl. 2.

[174] Inscription on Head of Lion (the Louvre), *ibid.*, pl. 54.

[175] Stela of the Vultures (the Louvre), *ibid.*, pls. 3–4.

[176] Thureau-Dangin, *Die sumerischen und akkadischen Königsinschriften*, A, V–VI.

[177] Foundation Stone of Entemena, British Museum, No. 115858.

[178] *Ibid.*

[179] Thureau-Dangin, *Die sumerischen und akkadischen Königsinschriften*, Cone A, I.

[180] *Ibid.*, Cones B, VII–VIII.

[181] W. Förtsch, *ZA*, Vol. XXXI (1917), 138.

[182] Thureau-Dangin, *Die sumerischen und akkadischen Königsinschriften*, p. 219, I, 36.

[183] Stela of Naram-Sin (Louvre), Jean de Morgan, *Mémoires de la Délégation en Perse* (Paris, 1900), I, pl. X.

After the interregnum of the Guti, the Akkadian title was taken up again by Utuhegal of Uruk and Shulgi of Ur III, who called themselves "King of the Four Quarters of the World" (*Lugal an-ub-da-limmu-ba*).[184] In Assyria, the royal title "King of the Universe" (*šar kišati*) was adopted by Shamsi-Adad I;[185] after the secession of the country from Babylon in the fourteenth century B.C., this designation recurs in all the inscriptions of Assyrian rulers up to the time of Sennacherib. Besides this title, we encounter such appellations as "Lord of Lords," "King of Kings," "Prince of Princes," but also *"išakku* (ensi) of Ashur" and "Appointee of Enlil."[186]

The conservation of these titles testifies that Assyrian kings, even when they had attained the apex of glory, never relinquished the religious connotation of their princely rank but continued the Sumerian tradition, according to which kingship was of heavenly origin, bestowed by the god upon his chosen servant.

Some Sumerian and Akkadian legends[187] allude to a body of citizens invested with a certain degree of political authority. A similar institution is mentioned in myths that deal with gods who convene in a general assembly.[188] These passages of Mesopotamian poetry are probably reminiscences of a primitive form of collective government, either tribal or local. The absence of documentary evidence in historical records[189] concerning the functioning of democracy in ancient Mesopotamia corroborates the assumption that in the second half of the third millennium B.C. such a phase had already been superseded by a politico-religious form of single government which might be defined as a theocratic monarchy. The historical rulers of Mesopotamia do not appear to have

---

184 F. Thureau-Dangin, *RA* (1913), 99ff.; and A. Falkenstein, *ZA*, (1952), 64 ff.

185 W. von Soden, *Der alte Orient* (Leipzig, 1937), 20.

186 K. L. Tallquist, *Der assyrische Gott* (edited by Societas Orientalis Fennica, *Studia Orientalia*, Vol. IV, Sec. 2, Helsinki, 1932).

187 Cf. "Gilgamesh and Agga" (Sumerian text: S. N. Kramer, *AJA*, Vol. LIII (January, 1949), 1 ff.) "Epic of Gilgamesh" (see Part II below, tablets III, VIII, XI).

188 See Part II below: "The Epic of Creation," "The Myth of Zu," "The Atrahasis Epic," "The Legend of Nergal and Ereshkigal," and Tablet XI of the Gilgamesh epic (account of the Deluge).

189 Traces of an indication concerning a group government might be found on some very old semipictographic tablets which contain the signs for "elder" and "assembly." Cf. H. Frankfort, *Kingship and the Gods*, 216, n. 4.

been influenced in any way by an assembly of elders. Already the legend-ary Gilgamesh preferred to follow his own inclination instead of heeding complaints or counsel of the citizenry.[190]

Once the office of monarch had become permanent and even hered-itary, the power of the assembly experienced a severe retrogression and finally disappeared altogether. Yet the king did not rely exclusively on his own judgment when an important decision had to be made but turned for advice to a person whose position stood halfway between the function of a vizier and that of a friend.

The Semitic languages express the notion of "friend" by a word which designates a social function rather than an emotional attitude. The Hebrew term רעה is used to characterize, for example, the posi-tion of David's "friend" Hushai,[191] who was above all a trusted official of the king. Quite a different word—translated as "brother" in the King James Version of the Bible—expresses the relationship between David and Jonathan, whom the grieving sovereign calls his אח.[192]

In the Akkadian Gilgamesh epic, Enkidu is defined as the king's "friend" (*"ra'u"* or, more rarely, *"ru'u"*) when he acts as Gilgamesh's counselor, but the emotional bond between the two heroes is expressed by the word *"ibru,"* which applies to Enkidu as well as to Gilgamesh.[193]

Enkidu, though inferior to his king, is not exactly a servant[194]; with him Gilgamesh discusses every project, trying to win his approval but never demanding his obedience.

Gilgamesh often shows himself dependent on his friend's advice, as in their joint combat against Huwawa; the king, though inclined to spare the guardian's life, heeds Enkidu's contrary counsel and kills Huwawa.[195]

A similar position as a king's "friend" or "vizier" existed also in

---

[190] Akkadian version of the Gilgamesh epic, tablets I and III. (See Part II below.)

[191] II Sam. 15:37 and 16:16.

[192] II Sam. 1–26.

[193] *"en-ki-du$_{10}$ i-bi-ir-su"* = "Enkidu, his friend"; and *"eb-ri"* = "my friend (Gilgamesh)."

[194] In the Sumerian version, Enkidu is sometimes called the servant of Gilgamesh; but in II Sam. 15:34, and 16:19, Hushai, too, is qualified as David's servant, while in other verses (cf. verses mentioned in note 191 above), he appears as David's friend.

[195] Tablet V (Gilgamesh epic), see Chapter IV below.

divine society: Mummu, the vizier of Apsu; Gaga, the vizier of Anshar; Ninshubur,[196] the vizier of Ishtar; and Namtar, the vizier of Ereshkigal. They often have considerable influence on their masters; thus Mummu is responsible for Apsu's decision to kill the younger gods,[197] and Namtar is said to be the creator of the decrees in the Arallu.[198]

That the relationship between the gods and their viziers was not as formal as that between a king and any of his servants but approached the attitude of "friendship" can be seen in the words with which Anshar greets his vizier: "O Gaga, my vizier, who cheerest my soul,"[199] and still more in Apsu's reaction to his vizier's counsel: "As for Mummu, by the neck he embraced him, as that one sat down on his knees to kiss him."[200] Nergal says to Namtar, the vizier of the Nether World, "May thy heart take delight in me."[201] Ishtar describes her vizier in the following words: "My messenger of favorable words, filled the heaven with complaints for me, cried out for me in the assembly hall, rushed about for me in the house of gods, dressed for me in a single garment like a beggar . . . he brought me to life."[202] This may not equal the still closer relation between Enkidu and Gilgamesh, visible in the king's lament at Enkidu's death: "On a couch of honor I made thee lie, I placed thee on the seat of ease, the seat at the left, that the princes of the earth might kiss thy feet! Over thee I will make Uruk's people wail and lament . . . and when thou art gone, I shall cover my body with uncut hair, and, clothed in a lion skin, I shall wander over the plain."[203]

In that it approached friendship, the bond between a vizier and his master in Mesopotamia—whether in a king's court or in a god's abode—was different from the relationship existing between an Egyptian vizier and the godlike Pharaoh. From a text containing the autobiography of a vizier of Thut-mose III, we gather that the vizier's principal duty was

196 In the Akkadian version: Papsukkal.

197 Tablet I (Creation epic), see Chapter IV below.

198 "Kumma's Vision of the Nether World," see Chapter IV below.

199 Tablet I (Creation epic), see Chapter IV below.

200 *Ibid.*

201 "Nergal and Ereshkigal," see Chapter IV below.

202 Text by S. N. Kramer in *Proceedings* of the American Philosophical Society (Philadelphia, 1942), 293–323, pls. I–X.

203 Tablet VIII (Gilgamesh epic), see Chapter IV below.

to maintain justice in the country, but not to counsel Pharaoh. There is no evidence that the relationship between the Egyptian king and his vizier ever exceeded the formal sphere, except during the period when the Hyksos, a partly Semitic people, reigned over Egypt.[204] In Egypt several high officials of the same Pharaoh bore the appellation of "Royal Friend," but this was merely an honorific title that was never limited to only one person, while in Mesopotamia and in Israel there existed only one "Friend of the King" at a time.

In Khorsabad, American excavators found, besides the famous palace of King Sargon II, another palace used by the king's vizier.[205] The importance of the vizier in Mesopotamia may be inferred also from the "Synchronistic Chronicle,"[206] in which several viziers are mentioned among the Assyro-Babylonian kings.

It seems from all this evidence that in Mesopotamia the sovereign was more liable to be influenced by a vizier who approached the position of a friend than by an assembly.

When we consider the concept of kingship as it evolved in the great civilizations of the ancient Near East, we find that the Mesopotamian ruler stood halfway between two extremes, Egypt and Israel. Pharaoh was a god incarnate, exalted far above the sphere of common mortals. Counting as a member of the pantheon, his person was the symbol of the divine power that governed Egypt's destiny. The Hebrew king, on the contrary, was no more than a military leader and an arbiter of justice.[207] The only link between himself and God[208] was the priest's act of anointing the sovereign's head in token of divine approval. The king stood before his Creator on exactly the same level as his people and was subject to severe criticism by priests and prophets, who did not hesitate to rebuke him in the name of God.[209]

204 Cf. the episode of Joseph in the last chapters of Genesis.

205 For these excavations, see Oriental Institute *Communications*, No. 16, 17, 19, and 20, and Oriental Institute *Publications*, Vols. XXXVII and XL.

206 *ANET*, 272.

207 I Sam. 8:5, "make us a King to judge us like all the nations"; and I Sam. 8:19–20 "We will have a King over us / That we also may be like all the nations, and that our King may judge us and go out before us and fight our battles."

208 The covenant between Yahweh and David was personal, not general, and did not apply to other Hebrew kings.

209 I Sam. 15:25 (Saul) and II Sam. 12:11 (David), etc.

The Mesopotamian king's position was less exalted than that of Pharaoh but far superior to the place of the Hebrew monarch. The Sumerian "ensi" as well as the Assyrian "Lord of the Universe" maintained a humble attitude toward their gods, but their authority over the people was unchallenged because it had been sanctioned by divine command.

Although the institutions of kingdom in Egypt and in Mesopotamia were separated by fundamental differences of concept, they shared one essential feature: both Pharaoh and the Assyro-Babylonian monarch were charged with the task of upholding the harmonious integration of their people with nature. The basic belief in the immanence of the divine sharply differentiated the creeds of Egypt and Mesopotamia from the revolutionary religion of Israel, whose proclamation of God's transcendence destroyed the ancient bond between man and nature.

The institution of royalty had been a necessity in Egypt and in Mesopotamia because of the king's being instrumental in maintaining harmony between his subjects and the surrounding cosmos; in Israel, royalty remained forever a secondary institution, created by the people in an artificial imitation of neighboring civilizations.[210] The Hebrews achieved peace not by living in harmony with nature but by obeying their God; the divine will was revealed to them through priests and prophets, and there was no place in their religious system for a king who had no part in the relationship between the human and the divine.

### THE ROLE OF MAGIC

The evolution of religious conceptions in the "Land of the Two Rivers" was determined to a large extent by the Mesopotamian landscape. The unpredictable behavior of nature and the violent and often destructive influence of the elements discouraged any attempt at the arrogation of magical powers over cosmic forces.

Only a god could exercise control over nature; therefore the Mesopotamian limited himself to prayer, fully aware of his impotence in the face of the elements. Even the king could only implore the gods to grant favors and avert disasters; an attitude of deliberate injunction and command towards a deity was unthinkable in Mesopotamia.

[210] I Sam. 8:5 and II Sam. 16:6–10; I Sam. 8:19–20.

After the Sumerians had settled in the Plain, "magic" could survive only under the form of ritual, a once active creed continued as a mere aggregate of gestures and formulas, and its sense had gradually fallen into oblivion.

Thus the king and his people practiced those "rites" which in the dim past had been considered propitious for a favorable destiny. The past achievements of mythological deities which had ensured abundance of food and security of life were kept alive in regular celebrations: the union of the mother-goddess and the fertility god, which in time of yore had caused the earth to bring forth new life in the form of crops and increase of cattle, was re-enacted each year[211] during the New Year's festival. Likewise, the victorious battle of the storm-god against the watery Chaos[212] was repeated in its ritual form during the same festival, and the recital of the epic describing the beneficent action of the god strengthened the effectiveness of the primeval victory for the coming year.

In the realm of myth, Adapa, the wise priest of Ea in Eridu, could break the wings of the South Wind through the uttering of a curse, recurring thus to a magical action.[213] But no document shows any of the historical kings, either Sumerian or Assyro-Babylonian, boasting of having overcome an enemy by magical means. When they attribute their victories to the supernatural guidance of their gods, they are aware that divine help cannot be extorted by means of magic, but is granted to them as a favor, as a reward for their piety.

The gods themselves repeatedly use magic in either a positive or a negative way. Ea renders Apsu, the primeval father of all the gods, defenseless by a magical spell and kills him without effort.[214] Marduk, in order to test the efficacy of his new authority, makes a garment appear and then disappear by the power of his words.[215] Of magical potency also are the Tablets of Destiny, which the bird Zu has stolen from Enlil, the king of the gods; the possession of the tablets renders

211 In some Sumerian cities, such as Ur and Uruk, there were two New Year's festivals, one in spring and one in the fall.

212 Enlil, in the pre-Babylonian period, who was afterwards replaced by Marduk in Babylon and by Ashur in Assyria.

213 See Chapter IV below, "The Myth of Adapa" (XI).

214 Tablet I, "Creation Epic"; cf. Chapter IV below (I).     215 *Ibid.*, Tablet IV.

the thief invulnerable to the attacks of the gods, who try in vain to regain the precious talisman that lends the words of Zu the effectiveness of magic.[216]

The only field in which the Mesopotamian might hope to gain control over natural forces was the fighting of demons, because here he acted as an ally of the great gods whose help he could invoke. Evil spirits were believed to be at the origin of diseases, and the practices aimed at their expulsion might to a certain extent be considered the antecedent of medicine in the ancient world.

Besides these evil spirits that could be brought under control by an appropriate exorcism, there existed for the Mesopotamian another group of demons of much greater mythological importance, and often recurrent in the poems.

Their hostility, either towards the gods or towards mankind, was not always as well defined as that which characterized the originators of plagues and diseases, and the mythical demons were frequently considered deities.

The first demon of the universe was Tiamat, who had brought forth the great gods, her "first-born"; but after the outbreak of hostilities between her and her divine offspring, she created and bore monsters and demons to help her in the combat against the gods.[217] Her evil host, however, also qualified as "divine," and their leader was Kingu, equally a god.

After Tiamat had been vanquished and her army defeated, Marduk admitted the followers of Tiamat to the divine assembly; here, instead of dividing the gods into the black and the white sheep, he counted the formerly rebellious gods and his own followers as equals.[218]

There is no evidence that, when Marduk did divide the gods into groups, they corresponded to the vanquished and the victorious parties. Marduk stated expressly that the two groups were to be "alike revered," and the gods who had been assigned to the lower regions were by no means in hostile opposition to the celestial gods. Punishment was reserved only for Kingu, the leader of the evil gods, who was to be killed before the assembly.

216 Cf. "The Myth of Zu"; see Chapter IV below (IX).
217 Tablet I, "Creation Epic"; see Chapter IV below (I).
218 Tablet VI, "Creation Epic," *ibid.*

This concept is fundamentally different from the description which is offered in the Book of Enoch dealing with the rebellion of Lucifer and his host against Yahweh and his angels. The revolt of the evil spirits makes them forever different from the faithful angels, and their banishment to hell has been inflicted upon them as a punishment. Lucifer himself, as chief of the evil spirits, is in eternal opposition to Yahweh and his angels, whose abode is in heaven.

In Mesopotamian mythology, the queen of the Nether World, Ereshkigal, is described in terms which befit a demon rather than a goddess; however, she is the sister of the great gods, whose attitude towards her is respectful and even affectionate. They even invite her to partake of the divine banquet and are quite ready to deliver Nergal into her hands.[219] The deadly enmity existing between Ereshkigal and her younger sister, Ishtar, is an isolated feature and quite secondary; it is only the logical antipathy existing between the goddess of death and the goddess of life.

Ereshkigal's husband, the god Nergal, has likewise the features of an evil demon. Besides being the king of the Arallu, he is also the god of the devastating midday sun, of pestilence and epidemics. If, in spite of these exclusively negative attributes, he was nevertheless worshiped in Sumer, especially in the city of Kutha, the reason is certainly to be found in the fear which his awesome power inspired. This can be gathered from the final passage of the Assyrian myth "A Vision of the Nether World," in which Kumma, after awakening from his dream, praises Nergal and Ereshkigal so that they may not carry out their threats against him.

Returning now to the minor demons who are at the origin of plagues and diseases, we find that they were never equated with gods, though they might claim a divine descendance, like the female demon Lamashtu, who was said to be a daughter of Anu.

In the Mesopotamian mind, the evil nature of these demons was clearly defined, and the priest called upon the gods to help him in his combat against the malefic spirits.

As long as a man possessed divine protection, the demon could not

[219] "Nergal and Ereshkigal"; see Chapter IV below (VI), Fragment A (obverse) and Fragment B.

harm him. But if a man had the misfortune to incite the deity's wrath either because of little zeal in worship or because of an unknowingly committed offense, the god withdrew his protection, and the mortal being was exposed to the tortures of the demons.

The most formidable among the evil spirits was the already mentioned demoness Lamashtu. She was responsible for a large number of plagues and diseases and for stillborn children and the death of women during childbirth.

Among the other demons there are two main groups: The first group comprises the seven *"Utukku,"*[220] who provoked headaches or intestinal fever, attacked a man's shoulder, hand, throat, or breast, or slew him in the Plain. The other is formed by the *"Edimmu,"* originally restless spirits of deceased mortals who haunted the living either because they had not received proper burial and funeral food-offerings or because their lives had not been fulfilled at the time of their death. The *"Edimmu"*[221] and the *"Utukku"* had their abode in the region of the west, the mountains which every day "swallowed the sun." The priest who expelled a demon from the body of a possessed person sent the "evil spirit" back to the mountains, offering him symbolically the means of accomplishing this journey: an ass to traverse the desert and a boat to cross the Ḫubur, the mythical "River of Death."

Since the reason for having been "invaded" by a demon was to be sought in the wrath of the god who had withdrawn his protection from the man, the first step to be taken on the road towards recovery was to propitiate the god.[222] The possessed man therefore confessed his sins[223] to the *"ašipu"* priest, who purified the patient through specific expiation rites *"kuppuru takpirta."* The list of possible sins is quite heterogeneous.

---

[220] E.g., mentioned in the twelve tablets of the series *"asakke marsūti"* (*Cuneiform Texts,* XVII).

[221] "Edimmu" became all those who had been murdered, women who had passed away before their marriage or before their delivery, and men who had been victims of some accident. Besides these evil spirits, there were also good ones, the "Lamassu" and the *"šēdu";* they were principally protectors of the abodes of men *"ilū bīti,"* or had the role of tutelary genii.

[222] The ceremony of exorcism was preceded by sacrifices and by ritual ablutions which the *"ramki"* priest performed in the *"bīt rimki,"* a particular shrine of the temple.

[223] In the Neo-Assyrian period, the confession of sins appears on a higher moral level, since an attitude of contrition is required.

Some concern worship, but there were also a large number of sins in a social sense, which were liable to prosecution by human law. These included theft, rebellion, adultery, fraud, burglary, trespass, and other offenses. Another large group consisted of sins against ritual purity, which were committed by touching an unclean person, looking at water intended for handwashing, treading in a libation spilled on the ground, standing near an enchanted person, or sleeping in the bed or eating from the place of an enchanted person, and similar actions.

Since in the frame of Mesopotamian religion there were so many occasions for committing a sin, and especially for committing it unknowingly, the patient adopted the safe method of enumerating as many sins as possible in order to be sure that the offense which had caused the god's wrath, was included.

After the priest had absolved the possessed man from his sins, making him once more worthy of his god's protection, the exorciser proceeded to expel the demon from the patient's body. First, he pronounced the name of the demon who had taken possession of the man, and, as in the case of the confession, he enumerated the names of all known demons, in order to be sure that the right one would be mentioned.

To know and pronounce the demon's name was the means of bringing the evil spirit under the priest's power. The exorciser, after threatening the discovered demon with magical destruction, also cajoled him, through the promise of jewelry, clothes, food, and means of transportation, into giving up his present abode. The priest might even go so far as to offer the demon another victim, such as a suckling pig.

The ceremony was then concluded with the pronunciation of the magical formula or incantation, the *"siptu,"* which invoked the assistance of Ea, Marduk, Tammuz, Ishtar, or other gods in expelling the demon from the patient's body.[224]

This part of the exorcism could be accompanied by symbolical actions: the priest burned a piece of wool or a vegetable substance which took the place of the demon,[225] or he unraveled knots in which

[224] Each month there were particular days, *"Umu limnu,"* considered unfavorable for the celebration of an exorcism. Cf. B. Landsberger, *Der kultische Kalender der Babylonier und Assyrer, Leipziger Semitistische Studien* (Leipzig, 1915), VI, 120.

[225] This part of the ceremony has given the name to the two series of exorcism texts

the patient was supposed to have been imprisoned by the evil spirit. He also used a magical wand made of cedar or palm wood, endowed with the power of Ea or Tammuz, and traced around himself a protective circle that kept out evil influences.

If the demon were particularly powerful, the priest fashioned a likeness of the malefic spirit and destroyed it by burning or breaking the figurine. In the case of Lamashtu, the priest placed a clay image representing the demoness on the person's head. After three days, the figurine was pierced with a dagger and buried outside the house.

It is to be supposed that such a ceremony was not only complicated but also expensive and that not everybody could afford a complete exorcism ceremony. The ceremony was therefore often replaced by an iconographic substitute, which, in the opinion of the Mesopotamian, was just as effective as the real ceremony.

Such a substitute we have in a bronze plate belonging to the De Clercq Collection.[226] The five registers into which the obverse of the plate is divided contain all the elements of an exorcism in pictorial form. The uppermost shows the emblems of the gods whose assistance lends validity to the exorcism. The next register represents a series of seven theriocephalous demons, probably the *"utukku."* The scene in the middle of the plate depicts the sick man lying in bed and two priests robed in fish costumes, who presumably are reciting an incantation. At one side of this scene is a lamp which serves to burn the animal or vegetable substances assimilated to the evil spirit. On the other side stands a *"lamassu,"* a good spirit, fighting against two demons (probably belonging to the group of the register above). The lower part of the plate shows—except for the last register which consists of fish designs, emblems of the god Ea—two major demons. One is Lamashtu, holding a serpent in each hand and kneeling on an ass, with two smaller animals, pigs or dogs, attached to her breasts. The ass stands upon a boat, both ass and boat being gifts offered to Lamashtu in order to induce her to return over desert and death river to the mountains of the West. Other gifts, mostly provisions, are depicted on her side. The other

*"šurpū* (H. Zimmern, *Assyriologische Bibliothek* [Leipzig, 1896], XII) and *"maklū"* (K. L. Tallqvist, ed., *Die assyrische Beschwörungsserie Maklū* [Helsinki, 1894]).

[226] *Revue Archéologique,* NS, Vol. XXXVIII, pl. XXV.

demon is Pazuzu, the wind of the Southwest, originator of colds and fevers, standing behind Lamashtu. The same demon, Pazuzu, seen from behind is represented, in relief, on the whole other side of the plate. His grinning head, surpassing the talisman, overlooks the five registers described above.

The priest's exorcism might be directed not only against demons but also against humans who practiced illegitimate, or black magic, *"lisānu limnu"* and *"pū limnu,"* and thereby acted in much the same way as the demons. Gudea, ensi of Lagash in the Pre-Babylonian period, purified the site of the temple he was to build by expelling from the surroundings all sorcerers and witches.

How ill the practice of black magic was judged, even until the first millennium B.C., can be inferred from a Middle Assyrian law[227]: "If either a man or a woman made up magical preparations and these are found in their possession, when they have prosecuted them and convicted them, they shall put the maker of the magical preparations to death."

From prehistoric times, the Mesopotamian tried to protect himself against the influences of malevolent spirits and sorcerers by wearing amulets[228] or keeping talismans[229] in his home. These magical objects were directed against the influence of the Evil Eye (*pānu limnu*), which provoked frigidity. This demon, often conjured by sorcerers, was driven away by phallus-shaped talismans and by clay figurines representing nude females.[230]

The practice of legitimate magic in Mesopotamia was purely defensive, directed either against demons or against sorcerers. What in later times might be considered the object of magic—contriving to obtain riches, youth, high position, love, or military and spiritual victories—was not the function of the Assyro-Babylonian priest. It is possible that certain wizards pretended to have the power of realizing

[227] Otto Shroeder, *Keilschrifttexte aus Assur verschiedenen Inhalts* (*Wissenschaftliche Veröffentlichungen der deutschen Orient-Gesellschaft,* Vol. XXV, Leipzig, 1920).

[228] They had only a protective effect and mostly represented the demons themselves or the beneficent images of a god or a genius.

[229] These exercised an active influence as a countercharm (e.g., the bronze plate of the De Clercq Collection, R. arch. XXXVIII, pl. XXV).

[230] E.g., clay figurines of the Halaf and Ubaid periods.

such desires, but their practices and pseudo-achievements are not recorded in any document preserved from this epoch.

In the course of the second and the first millennia b.c., the ceremony of exorcism began to be accompanied by rude therapeutic practices. An incantation against toothache, dating from the Neo-Babylonian period but going back to a much older document, contains a sentence which indicates that a surgical practice accompanied the magical treatment:[231] "Fix the pin and seize its foot."[232]

Already in Sumerian times, sick persons had recourse to a physician, who was called *"a-zu"* (water expert) or *"ia₃-zu"* (oil expert).[233] In the Neo-Assyrian period therapeutic treatment had developed to such a degree that the incantation was reduced to a formal accessory. Ashurbanipal divided the medical texts of his library into three groups: (1) *"bultitu"* (therapy), (2) *"šipir bēl imti"* (surgery), and (3) *"urti mašmaššē"* (magical medicine). About the practice of surgery there is surprisingly little evidence in Assyro-Babylonian documents. But we have at least four texts containing allusions to operations with a lancet.[234] One of them is to be found in the Code of Hammurabi,[235] in which it is stated that the surgeon exposed himself to the risk of losing his hand if, by opening a patient's temple,[236] he destroyed his eye, or if, by some other operation with a lancet, he caused the patient's death.

The Assyro-Babylonian texts dealing with medicine are exclusively collections of observations and treatments destined to provide the physician with practical material; they never attempt to establish any theory, as in Greece or in India.[237]

---

[231] In the Neo-Assyrian period existed a clear distinction between a priest practicing exorcism and a physician. In the case of sickness the services of both were requested.

[232] R. Campbell Thompson, *Cuneiform Texts*, XVII, pl. 50; and Speiser, *ANET*, 101.

[233] Pallis, *Antiquity of Iraq*, 734.

[234] R. Labat, *"A propos de la chirurgie babylonienne,"* JA (1951), 207.

[235] *Codex Hammurabi*, paragraphs 218–20.

[236] Interpretation of R. Labat; W. von Soden translates "eye-brow," and T. Meek renders "eye socket," as do V. Scheil and G. Contenau.

[237] Cf. J. Filliozat, *"Pronostics médicaux Akkadiens, Grecs, et Indiens,"* JA, Vol. CCXL (July, 1952), 299ff.; and W. Kirfel, *Die fünf Elemente (Beiträge zur Sprach- und Kulturgeschichte des Orients,* Walldorf, 1951). Kirfel supposes that there existed in ancient times in the whole area between the Mediterranean Sea and India the idea that the human body was ruled by pituite and gall, to which blood was added in a later conception; this

One of the most complete documents of the ancient Near East concerning medicine is a treatise in Akkadian.[238] The first [239] and the last[240] of the five parts into which the text is divided deal mostly with divination[241] and have no real medical value. The second part consists of a list of all the organs of the human body and the diseases to which they may be subject. The symptoms indicated here are supposed to point out the supernatural originator of the disease; this shows that demonology was still an important part of Mesopotamian diagnosis. The third part, however, which deals with prognosis, does reveal a certain amount of critical spirit. The physician judges the affection according to the symptoms shown by the patient during the first day of sickness, taking into consideration also the psychic condition of the victim. The treatise contains some aetiological indications, e.g., "fever caused by the drought." This feature indicates considerable progress, since the disease is here viewed independent of demoniacal influence. The fourth part is a mixture of medical and magical considerations; it deals with the malign influences of a demon during the course of the affection—with magical therapy—and with prognoses based on hallucinations experienced by the patient.

Since the first essays of therapy in Mesopotamia proceeded from the assumption that the patient's body was inhabited by an evil spirit, the sick man was forced to swallow bitter, rotten, or other nauseating substances so as to render the demon's abode distasteful.

The next step in pharmaceutical evolution was the relating of a remedy to the affection to be cured because of an exterior resemblance between the remedy and some symptom of the disease. For instance, physicians recommended carrots or other yellow-colored substances against jaundice and similar liver troubles; certain stones were supposed

---

would correspond to the existence in metaphysics of a primitive couple, Water and Fire, to which was added later the Wind as third element. The idea of the opposition of water and fire is also to be found in the Chinese conception of *"yin"* and *"yang."*

238 R. Labat, *"Traité akkadien de diagnostics et pronostics médicaux,"* *Académie internationale des Sciences* (Paris, 1951).

239 Prognosis based on presages previous to the physician's arrival at the patient's house.

240 Prognosis concerning the sex of a child before its birth and its future attitude towards its mother.

241 See last part of this chapter.

to have a beneficent influence on sick organs, the shape of which was similar to that of the stone.

Empirical therapy discovered the healing or analgesic properties of many plants that are still used today for the compounding of medicaments, such as henbane and hemp, the opium poppy, the belladonna nightshade, the mandrake root, and other herbs.[242]

The potions which the Assyro-Babylonian "physicians" prescribed often contained high percentages of poisonous substances, and the patient's risk in swallowing such a drug is evident from the following letter of an Assyrian royal physician: "As for the remedy about which the king wrote to me, it is perfectly good. As the king has commanded, we will make slaves drink [the remedy]. Afterwards, the crown prince may partake of it.[243]

During the Neo-Assyrian period, the scientific character of medicine—always empirical—increased, turning more and more from the demonological viewpoint. Prognosis and diagnosis were then almost completely independent of presages and exorcistic methods, and the road for the Greek Hippocratic school was thus paved.

While the practices of magic, as apparent in exorcism, were unchanged since historical times began, medicine developed from its position as *ancilla magiae* to an independent discipline. The medical documents that have been discovered in Assyria and in Babylonia prove conclusively the groundlessness of Herodotus' statement that Babylonia knew neither medicine nor physicians.[244] On the contrary, Mesopotamian medicine, after its liberation from the concepts of demonology, was a worthy predecessor of the Hippocratic school.

## ASPECTS OF DIVINATION

The metaphysical basis upon which divinatory practices rested in Mesopotamia was the belief in the immanence of the gods in nature. Atmospherical phenomena such as wind, lightning, or thunderstorm were considered manifestations of the divine; also the behavior of plants and animals, or the great and small events of human life, counted as

---

[242] The word *"šammu"* means "herb" as well as "drug."
[243] Cf. R. Pfeiffer, *State Letters of Assyria.*
[244] *History* I. 197.

the result of a deity's premeditated action, the hidden expression of a god's design.

Since the revelation of the divine will was neither direct nor plain, the devoted Mesopotamian who aspired to a peaceful relationship between himself and his god had to use the services of the *"bārū"* priest, whose experience made possible the interpretation of omens.

That compliance with the god's intentions was judged to be vitally necessary is apparent from the extraordinary extent of divinatory practices in Mesopotamia. In a land where life was so insecure and so dependent on many unpredictable circumstances, man deferred only too readily to the authority of the priests. If a farmer saw his crops menaced by a drought, he tried to find out what had caused the deity to punish him; by making due amends, he might hope to avert the disaster.

When Sennacherib was murdered by one of his own children, the cause of this violent act was ascribed to the wrath of Marduk "against the destructor of Babylon,"[245] and the king's widow set about at once to reconstruct the city in order to reconcile the god and to avoid the destruction of the whole dynasty. In the poem *"Ludlul bēl nēmeqi,"*[246] the sufferer asks the priest in vain for an explanation of the divine wrath; since he is aware of no fault committed against the rules of worship, he arrives at the desperate conclusion that his pious behavior is disagreeable to his god, who persecutes him with "sickness and misery."

The methods of divination were not, in the belief of the Assyro-Babylonian, arbitrary human practices but revelations made by the "Gods of Divination," Shamash and Adad, to the legendary king Enmendur-Anna, of Sippar, seventh monarch before the Deluge.[247] The chief source for divination, however, was the large collections of oracles, dreams, and presages that the priests had accumulated since the beginning of history.

One group is represented by oracles which were granted to kings by gods and goddesses. The divine message could have been transmitted directly, as the one given by the goddess Ninlil to Ashurban-

---

[245] Cf. B. Meissner, *"Neue Nachrichten über die Ermordung Sanheribs," Sitzungs-Berichte der preussischen Akademie der Wissenschaften,* Phil.-hist. Klasse (1932), 250 ff.

[246] See Chapter IV below, Poem I, Tablet II.

[247] In Greek mythology this monarch appears as "Evedorachos," king of Pantibibla.

ipal;[248] or it could have been communicated through the vision of a "medium," as when Ishtar of Arbela spoke to the same king by means of a "seer."[249] A third possibility might be the conferment of the oracle by the mouth of a woman, presumably a priestess. It is probable that this species of oracles was uttered in a state of artificial trance, comparable to the catalepsy of the Greek pythoness, which had been induced through the chewing of laurel leaves and exposure to vapors arising from an underground stream at Delphi. Scythian priestesses went into a trance by inhaling the fumes of burnt hempseed.[250]

A similar practice is not explicitly described in any Mesopotamian document, but it is significant that all the oracles listed in a text concerning Esarhaddon[251] were uttered by women.

A very important means of communication with the deity was the dream. The Mesopotamian considered the events he experienced while asleep as being real; if he had dreamed of a god, he was convinced that the deity had really visited him during the night and given a divine revelation.

Oneiromancy was a favorite means of knowing the future at the time of Gudea; the ensi went into the temple with the intention of dreaming "in the god's abode" and of thus gaining knowledge of the divine will.[252]

Assyrian kings sometimes sent into the temple "dreamers," whose dreams were then interpreted as if experienced by the sovereign himself.[253] It is possible that the dreamer partook of a narcotic potion, before lying down to sleep, in order to be favored with a divine message.

In the Gilgamesh epic, dreams played an important role; e.g., they announced the encounter between Gilgamesh and Enkidu and fore-

---

[248] J. A. Craig, "Assyrian and Babylonian Religious Texts," Vol. I, *Assyriologische Bibliothek,* XIII (Leipzig, 1895), pl. 26–27.

[249] The text states expressly that the "vision" takes place while the "seer" is awake (H. Winckler, *Sammlung von Keilschrifttexten* [Leipzig, 1895], III, 38–48).

[250] Herodotus *History* IV. 74–75.

[251] Rawlinson, *The Cuneiform Inscriptions of Western Asia,* IV, pl. 68.

[252] Gudea Cylinder A, (de Sarzec and Heuzey, *Découvertes en Chaldée*).

[253] During the revolt of Shamash-Shum-Ukin, Ashurbanipal was granted a message from the goddess Ishtar through one of his dreamers who had replaced the King in the temple for the purpose of receiving the divine communication.

told the issue of the fight against Huwawa.[254] The "Vision" experienced by Kumma[255] furnished the prince with knowledge about the Nether World by means of a dream which the deities of the Arallu had granted him upon his own request.

Many of the dreams with which the Mesopotamian was favored needed an interpretation, since their purpose, "to reveal the god's intentions," was not always clear. The collections dealing with dream interpretations are among the most numerous and complicated in Mesopotamian divination.[256] Sometimes the basis of such an interpretation could be a pseudo-etymological similarity between the scene beheld in a dream and the event it symbolized.[257]

Divinatory practices were also based on presages connected with almost any field of natural or human activities. The appearance and position of the stars,[258] the incidents during important ceremonies,[259] the condition of a tree,[260] the shape of clouds,[261] the behavior of sick or healthy persons,[262] the movements of flames,[263] the flight of birds,[264] the features of a new-born child,[265] the formation of oil puddles on a bowl full of water, [266] and many other phenomena were considered presages and were duly interpreted by the priest.

Also significant was the inspection of the liver of an immolated animal. Hepatoscopy had developed almost into a science; there have

[254] See Part II below (II), Tablets I and V.

[255] See Part II below (VII).

[256] Oppenheim, *The Interpretation of Dreams*.

[257] E.g., in the case of Gilgamesh's dreams concerning Enkidu. Cf. A. Boissier, *Mantique babylonienne et Mantique hittite* (Paris, 1935).

[258] See the collection of astrological texts by E. F. Weidner, *Archiv für Orientforschung*, Vol. XIV (1941–44).

[259] Of particular consequence was the behavior of the king during the celebration of the New Year's festival. The shedding of tears by the monarch when the priest struck him during the re-investment scene was considered a favorable omen. H. Zimmern, *DAO*, Vol. XXV, 12.

[260] Dendromancy.

[261] Nephelomancy.

[262] Respectively iatromancy and palmomancy.

[263] Empyromancy.

[264] Ornithomancy.

[265] Teratology.

[266] Lecanomancy.

been found in Mari, on the middle Euphrates, thirty-five clay objects in the shape of an animal liver, with explications in cuneiform signs concerning malformations of the organ. Each anomaly was connected with a different presage. Other liver-shaped documents of hepatoscopy have been found in Boghaz-köi in Asia Minor, and a similar specimen was acquired in Baghdad for the British Museum.[267] The importance of hepatoscopy in ancient times was due to the concept of the liver as the seat of the soul, in particular of passions and desires.[268] The sufferer in the monologue *"Ludlul bēl nēmeqi"* exclaims in distress that, at the news of his death, the "heart" of his ill-wisher was delighted; in the Creation epic, Apsu greets his vizier with the words: "O Mummu . . . who rejoicest my 'spirit.'" The literal meaning of both "heart" and "spirit" in these texts is "liver."[269] Similarly, Hebrew word "כבד" (liver) means also "grievous" (Gen. 12:10). An Arabic parallel is the cognation of "كَبِد" (liver) with "كَبِد" (sufferer). In Greek drama, "ἧπαρ" (liver) likewise designates the seat of emotions. Sophocles, for example, makes the chorus chant: Χωρεῖ πρὸς ἧπαρ οἶδα γενναία δύη.[270] Other examples are to be found in Aeschylus.[271]

The Mesopotamians often used divination for medical prognosis, and many presages had a double interpretation; one was applicable to anybody in a general way, while the other concerned solely a sick man:

> If on the oil a circle appears in the direction of the East and remains there; for the campaign, I shall undertake it and bring back spoil; for the sick person, he will recover. If on the oil two saw-shaped figures are

---

[267] *Cuneiform Texts,* VI, pls. 1–20.

[268] Plato sees in the "liver" the organ of oneiromantic divination, since it has no share in reason but is influenced by visions and phantoms during sleep (*Timaeus* 71 a, d). The use of the liver of a sacrificial animal for divinatory practices is, however, rejected by Plato, since the dead organ "becomes blind and delivers oracles too obscure to be intelligible" (*ibid.,* 72, b).

According to the dialogue Timaeus (70 a, e), the regions of both heart and liver are seats of the mortal soul (respectively the superior and the inferior part), while the head harbors the immortal soul.

[269] See Chapter IV below, "Speculative Literature," first poem, Tablet II; and "Myths and Epics," Tablet I.

[270] *Ajax,* v. 938.

[271] *Agamemnon,* v. 432, 791 ff.; *Eumenides,* v. 135.

visible, one large and the other small, the man's wife will bear a boy; for the sick person, he will recover.[272]

Presages were often considered the equivalent of bodily symptoms in the course of a disease,[273] a view totally different from the concept of scientific prognosis. In the Neo-Assyrian period, however, the consideration of physiological symptoms prevailed, together with true medical diagnosis.

The multitude of presages brought about a great confusion which was further increased through the fact that many of them were not of absolute validity but depended on circumstances of time and space. In order to guide the common people through the labyrinth of so many presages, which sometimes seemed even to contradict each other, the priests composed hemerologies, species of calendars where day by day all possible interdictions and obligations were registered. Favorable and unfavorable days were indicated along with the actions that could or could not be exerted.[274] For instance, on the tenth day of the month Kislimmu, the wearing of a new garment was forbidden; on the thirteenth day of the same month, nobody was allowed to walk in the streets, whereas the sixteenth day was highly favorable, and psalms of repentance were not to be sung.[275] The twenty-seventh day of the month Nisan[276] was very unfavorable (as were in general all last days of a month because of the disappearance of the moon; according to Mesopotamian belief, this was caused by demons), neither physicians nor diviners attended to their tasks, and it was recommended not to utter any desire.[277] These texts show us in a particularly plain way the sensation of insecurity which reigned in the "Land of the Two Rivers" and the constraint imposed upon daily existence by devotional considerations. Religion permeated the totality of spiritual life in Mesopotamia and held sway even over political administration, reducing

---

[272] Cf. J. Hunger, *Becherwahrsagung bei den Babyloniern* (Leipzig, 1903), 39ff.

[273] See parts I and V of the Akkadian treatise on medicine mentioned above, n. 238.

[274] The number of unfavorable days could amount to 23, as in the case of the month Ab dedicated to the lamentations over the death of Tammuz (July-August).

[275] R. Labat, *Hémérologies et Ménologies d'Assur*, 131.

[276] The first month of the year, when the Akitu festival was celebrated.

[277] Labat, *Hémérologies et Ménologies d'Assur*, 55.

the king to a mere servant of his "divine lord" and ascribing military victories to the power of the deity alone.

Magic could thrive only as a means of defense against the omnipresence of demons, and the effectiveness of an exorcism was based upon the assistance of the gods.

Divination provided man with a guide to avoid the many disasters that threatened his existence, and the extraordinary extension of divinatory practices in Mesopotamia—exceeding by far the use of fortunetelling in Egypt—proves how strongly the Assyro-Babylonians felt their subjection to divine omnipotence.

# CHAPTER III

*The Testimony of Culture*

THE ANCIENT CIVILIZATION OF MESOPOTAMIA would be nothing but a legend today, reposing on Bible passages and the reports of Greek-writing authors, had not the excavations in Iraq brought to light monuments which are the direct testimony of Assyro-Babylonian culture—the thousands of clay tablets covered with the enigmatic cuneiform script, and the works of pictorial art. Both have resisted the destructive action of time and now bear witness to the accomplishments of this splendid civilization.

But while sculpture, glyptic, painting, and other crafts spoke the universally comprehensible language of art, the wedge-shaped signs covering the clay tablets remained obscure for a long time. Even now, after the puzzle of the cuneiform script has been unraveled through the patience and the skill of many scholars, the writing system of the Mesopotamians still confronts the translator with never ending problems.

### CUNEIFORM WRITING

One of the many difficulties of this system arises from the fact that while the language of Assyro-Babylonian literature was Semitic, the script had been invented for quite another idiom—that of the Sumerians, who were a non-Semitic people of the Asianic group.[1] The differences between the phonetic systems and the morphological structures of the two languages posed to the Akkadian scribes many problems which were not always solved in a satisfactory manner.

Another difficulty arose from the extreme ancientness of the writing. In the course of more than three millennia, the cuneiform system never attained the phase of alphabetic writing, nor did it, on the other hand, ever completely abandon the ideographic stage. This increased the number of signs and their ambiguity considerably and aggravated the task of the ancient scribe as well as that of the modern decipherer.

A third feature which rendered the translation of the cuneiform texts more arduous was the graphic evolution of the signs. Between the cursive characters of the earliest time and the combination of wedges and hooks used in the later writing technique lies a great variety of signs, different also because of the dialectal peculiarities of Assyria and Babylonia.

The decipherment of the cuneiform script was accomplished in a sequence exactly opposite from the chronological development of the system. The first results were obtained by G. F. Grotefend, E. Hincks, and H. C. Rawlinson, beginning with texts not written in a Mesopotamian language, nor was their system syllabic-ideographic. These first studies were based on the first parts of several trilingual inscriptions[2]

---

[1] This general term designates a wide range of various not otherwise classifiable idioms which had all died out before the beginning of the Christian era; their only common feature is that they were once spoken in the ancient Near East. Although it is possible that a relation existed between one Asianic people and another, the scanty material does not permit a conclusive statement.

[2] Cf. G. F. Grotefend, *"Praevia cuneatis, quas vocant inscriptionibus persepolitanis*

found in Persia, and the decipherers found that the cuneiform signs had been used alphabetically and that they rendered the ancient Persian language of the Achaemenides. This phase of the cuneiform script was a late variety of the Mesopotamian signs;[3] it differed from the original system in that it rendered an Indo-European language and used the cuneiform signs alphabetically.

The next step on the road of decipherment was the interpretation of the Assyro-Babylonian script, proceeding from the lowest parts of the trilingual inscriptions in Persia and from the tablets that had then begun to be excavated from the mounds of Iraq. After considerable difficulties it was ascertained that the Assyro-Babylonian language belonged to the Semitic group[4] and that the system of the relative texts was not alphabetic but syllabic[5] and partly ideographic.

A number of scholars contributed efficiently to the mastery of the Assyro-Babylonian script, especially E. Hincks, H. C. Rawlinson, H. F. Talbot, and J. Oppert. In 1857 the four Assyriologists submitted independent translations of a newly discovered Assyrian text to the Royal Asiatic Society in London. The conformity of the four renderings in all their essentials justified the assertion that the decipherment of Assyro-Babylonian texts could now be considered accomplished.[6]

---

*legendis et explicandis relatio," Archiv der Göttinger Akademie* (1802); and *Nachrichten von der Königlichen Gesellschaft der Wissenschaften zu Göttingen* (1893), No. 14; E. Hincks, "Some Passages of the Life of King Darius," *Dublin University Magazine* (Dublin, 1847), 14ff.; and H. C. Rawlinson, "Memoirs," *JRAS* (London, 1846). The other two parts of the Persepolis inscriptions followed different systems of cuneiform writing and rendered the Elamite and the Assyro-Babylonion languages.

[3] Other languages that adopted cuneiform signs are: Hurrian (2500–1000 B.C.), Cuneiform Hittite (1550–1200 B.C.), Ugaritic (fifteenth to fourteenth century B.C.), Elamite (first epoch, sixteenth to eighth century B.C.; second epoch, fifth to fourth century B.C.), and Urartean (ninth to sixth century B.C.).

[4] I. de Loewenstein was the first to make this suggestion in *Essai de déchiffrement de l'écriture assyrienne* (Paris, 1845).

[5] The syllabic character of both the second and the third parts of the Persian inscriptions was first recognized by E. Norris in "Memoir on the Scythic Version of the Behistun Inscription," *JRAS*, Vol. XV, 5.

[6] The principal contributions by the four scholars are to be found in: E. Hincks, "On the Assyrio-Babylonian Phonetic Characters," *Transactions* of the Royal Irish Academy, Vol. XXII, Part II, (1852), 293ff.; Rawlinson, "Memoir," *JRAS*, Vol. XIV (1851); H. F. Talbot, report in *JRAS*, Vol. XVIII, 150; and J. Oppert, *Report* of the Twenty-fifth Meeting of the British Association for the Advancement of Science (London, 1856), 145ff.

Among the tablets which were examined by the early Assyriologists were some that represented syllabaries and compared lists of Akkadian words with another group of signs which—although of the same shape —did not render the Assyrian or Babylonian languages. Excavations in southern Mesopotamia, especially at Telloh and Niffer, provided the decipherers with tablets written exclusively in this unknown tóngue, and it was soon established that the new idiom was non-Semitic and followed the principle of the agglutinative languages (e.g., Japanese, Turkish, Finnish, Hungarian, and Samoyed) as opposed to the inflectional tongues (e.g., the Semitic and the Indo-European families). The earlier hypothesis of E. Hincks, who supposed that the cuneiform script had not been invented by the Assyro-Babylonians,[7] was therefore confirmed, and the true creators of the wedge-shaped characters could now be identified as the Sumerians, authors of the first Mesopotamian literature.[8]

Some scholars trace the origin of Mesopotamian writing back to a pre-Sumerian prototype from which both the Sumerian script and the early Elamite pictograms[9] are supposed to have evolved.[10]

E. A. Speiser concludes that "At the beginning of the third millennium, two distinct traditions of writing were represented in Mesopotamia: the abstract signs used at Ur and at Lagash, and the semi-pictographic characters of Elam and the district of Kish. The practical contemporaneity of the two scripts precludes the possibility that the one was developed out of the other; otherwise, the presumption would be that the Sumerian writing, which grew out of earlier pictographs, owes its origin to the proto-Elamites."[11]

[7] Cf. *Report* of the Twentieth Meeting of the British Association for the Advancement of Science (London, 1850), 140.

[8] J. Halévy (in *Comptes-rendus de l'Académie des Inscriptions,* Vol. IV, série 2, 201–209–215 [1874]) affirmed that the Sumerian tongue had never been spoken by any people but was an artificial creation of the Semitic priests, who used it as a cryptic means of communication for matters of cult (*JA,* Vol. VII, série III [1874], 461 ff.). To his affirmation, which is now considered absurd, adhered for some time even so distinguished a scholar as F. Delitzsch (cf. *Assyrische Grammatik,* 1. Auflage, 25).

[9] The latter were represented to a limited extent on ancient stamp and cylinder seals of the region of Elam and on early tablets from Al-Uhaimir, the ancient Kish.

[10] See C. Frank in *OLZ* (1930), 438–47 (review of S. Langdon, "Pictographic Inscriptions from Jemdet Nasr").

[11] *Mesopotamian Origins.*

The Mesopotamian script was originally written from right to left in vertical columns, but the scribes soon found it more convenient to turn their tablets halfway and to write horizontally from left to right. Thus the signs appear to be recumbent when read horizontally.

Before assuming the form of wedge-shaped signs, the characters of Sumerian writing were pictograms, rude designs representing the objects they were to symbolize, or part of them, e.g.:  "jug," 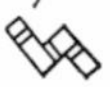 "brick,"  "date palm,"  "wild ass," etc.

The difficulty of tracing cursive lines on tablets of fresh clay was the main reason for changing the pictographs into cuneiform characters; the wedges and hooks were the natural result of the reed stylus' cutting into the clay of the tablet. The transformations were sometimes so extensive that the original pictogram was no longer recognizable, although others remained close to their prototype.

Thus the primitive sign 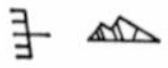 seems to have little in common with the cuneiform character , both designating "king"; but between the two signs for "mountain,"  and , a relation is clearly visible.

The Mesopotamian signs had already assumed the wedge-shaped form in the Sumerian period; after they had been adopted by the Semites, there were only slight differences between the old and new Assyrian or Babylonian characters.

But the adaptation of the cuneiform script to a language for which it had not been designed brought about a great change in the method of writing. The Sumerians had chiefly made use of ideograms, signs that expressed a whole word and its semantic derivatives; their system was completed by a small number of characters, originally also ideograms, which were used phonetically and indicated the grammatical relation or an abstract form of the word, without the word itself undergoing any change, e.g.:

 *"en"*="lord,"  *"en-me"*="lords,"  *"nam-en"*="lordship";  *"šeš"* = brother,"  *"sal-šeš"* = "sister" (literally "female brother");  "$du_3$" = "to build,"  "*mu*-$du_3$" = "he has built," etc.

The Akkadian language, however, being Semitic, not only had

other names for the same objects,[12] but, as an inflective tongue, could not content itself with adding phonetically written prefixes and suffixes to otherwise unchanged words, like the agglutinative Sumerian idiom. The Akkadian scribes therefore had to make extensive use of the syllabic method, already sparingly introduced by the Sumerians either to render grammatical particles or to spell out difficult words[13] and proper names.

The scribes derived the syllabic values from two sources: the character was either read in Sumerian or in Akkadian. Thus the sign ⊨𝕀𝕀𝕀 could be interpreted as the syllable *"e"* (Sumerian ideogram *"e₂"* = "house") or as the syllable *"bit"* (Akkadian word for "house"), and the sign ⊩𝕀𝕀 was read *"en"* (Sumerian ideogram for "lord") or *"bēl"* (Akkadian word for "lord") in syllabic use.

Since many characters expressed words of several syllables, especially in the Akkadian tongue, the whole character was used to render the first syllable only, e.g.: ▼, read in Akkadian *"šakānu"* (to put), acquired the syllabic value *"ša"* but continued also to render the Sumerian monosyllabic equivalent of "to put," which was *"gar."* The sign ⊏ meant in Akkadian *"littu"* (cow), and besides the syllabic value of *"lid,"*[14] it could also be read *"ab"* because *"ab₂"* meant "cow" in Sumerian.

It increased the confusion greatly that there existed no rule determining standard syllables; one and the same syllabic value could be written by a great many characters, each representing a word with the same beginning. On the other hand, an ideogram might have several meanings semantically or logically related to each other but of quite different pronunciation, e.g.: the ideogram ⊨⊣ originally meant *"du"* ("foot"), but it was also used to render the verbs *"gub"* (to stand), *"gin"* (to go), and *"tum₂"* (to bring). The syllabic value of the ideogram was therefore highly ambiguous, especially since the verbs could also be read in Akkadian, respectively *"nazāzu,"* *"alāku,"* and *"abālu."*

---

[12] Cf. the Latin formulae used in English: "e.g." (exempli gratia) is read "for instance"; "etc." (et cetera) is read "and so on"; "lb." (libra) is read "pound."

[13] Especially those coming from the Sumerian dialect *"eme-sal,"* which was spoken in North Sumer, and Akkadian loan words (cf. n. 140, Chapter I above).

[14] Sonant and surd consonants alternate frequently in writing.

A third difficulty derives from the fact that many Sumerian words are homonyms, with different meanings and graphic representations but the same pronunciation, e.g.: ⌷⫼ (house) and ⌷⫻ (trench) are both pronounced "*e*"; ⊐⫟ (foot), ⊐⫟ (to build), and ◁⫞ (hill) all three have the phonetic value of "*du*." The sound "*bur*" has more than eight different graphic representations with distinct semantic values, and the homonym "*uru*" may be written in twelve ways.

It may happen that one of these homonyms is represented improperly by a sign standing for another semantic value of the sound, just as if somebody should write in English "Eye by meet" instead of "I buy meat." Such a substitution of one sign by that of a homonym occurred on tablets of the Protoliterate period in the proper name "*en-lil₂-ti*," which means "The lord (en) of the air (*lil₂*) may grant life (*ti*)," but the last syllable is rendered by the sign for arrow, which is also pronounced "*ti*."[15]

A character of the cuneiform script might retain its word value instead of representing a syllable and also conserve a primitive ideographic stage without giving any clue to its pronunciation; thus the name of the city of Lagash was written in the earliest texts ─◇─ ⫤ ⫯ ; the inversion of the two phonetic components of the name into "*gaš* + *La*" was a minor irregularity, originally a habit adopted for calligraphic reasons, which had then become standard.[16] The syllable "*gaš*," however, was rendered by two signs which have the ideographic value of "*ŠIR*" and "*BUR*." The correct pronunciation of these two ideograms could be ascertained only through a much later text mentioning the phonetic values of "*gaš* + *La*."

The ideographic sign for the name of Gilgamesh is ⊐⫟, i.e., "*GIŠ*." The same sign means also "*giš*," "wood" or "tree"; in order to distinguish the personage from the material, the name of the hero, who was partly divine, was preceded by the sign ⊷⫟ which means "god," originally "star," "heaven," "high," or the sky-god Anu. This

---

[15] Other examples for the exchange of homonyms are to be found in A. Deimel, *Schultexte aus Fara* (Leipzig, 1923), nrs. 18, 20, 27, 29, 40, and 44.

[16] Another inverted sign is ⊨⫻ Akkadian "*sarru*" (king), originally composed of the signs ⫤ "*gal*" (great, tall) and ⌂ "*lu₂*" (man) to form the Sumerian word "*lugal*" = "king."

sign, however, was not read; it only served to define the association of the word that followed.[17] The same sign[18] preceded all the names of gods and goddesses, e.g., ⸱⊢⳨⧘ ⟨⊟ "Enki" and ⸱⊢⳦⧘ "Ishtar," as well as the names of minor supernatural beings and of the oldest kings.[19]

Such a sign, with an original meaning of its own but used only to classify the object which it preceded, is called a determinative. There were quite a number of these signs in use,[20] and some followed the principal word instead of preceding it. Thus the sign ⟨ⳤⳤⳤ meant "kiš," that is, "hoofed animal." But there was also a city in northern Sumer with this name, written likewise ⟨ⳤⳤⳤ. In order to distinguish the city Kish from the hoofed animal, the former was followed by the determinative ⟨⊟ , "ki," which means "place."

The Akkadian scribes also made use of phonetic complements, syllabic signs which followed polyphone ideograms and indicated the pronunciation for each case, without being pronounced themselves. If for example, the already-mentioned ideogram ⊢⳦ , which could be read "du," "gub," "gin," or "tum," was succeeded by the sign ⸱⳧ , "ba," the ideogram had to be interpreted as "gub" (to stand); if the sign ⸱⳨ "na" followed, the word meant "gin" (to go); in the case of a reading "tum" (to bring), the phonetic complement was ⊟ , "ma," while the absence of a complementary sign usually indicated that the original pronunciation of the ideogram, "du" (foot) was intended.

When an Assyrian or Babylonian text is transliterated from the cuneiform script to Roman characters, the syllables[21] are joined by hyphens; words written in capital letters represent Sumerian ideograms which have a different pronunciation. Determinatives are indicated in raised capitals, and phonetic complements in brackets or in raised small

---

17 When in 1872 the first tablets of the Gilgamesh epic had been discovered by G. Smith, the name of the hero was erroneously read "Izdubar."

18 Read in Sumerian "dingir" and abbreviated to "d" as a determinative in transliteration.

19 See n. 237, Chapter IV below.

20 ⧉⳨⳨ "lu₂" (man), ⳧ "giš" (wood), ⧘⳧ "a" (river) ⳧⧘ "uru" (town); ⳧⳦ "ḫu" (bird), ⳦⳧ "ḫa" (fish), ⳧⳦ "dug" (vessel); ⳧⳦⳦ "u₂" (plant).

21 The modern definition of "syllable" does not always apply to the segments into which the ancient scribes divided their words.

script. The sub numbers at the end of certain syllables distinguish homonyms.[22]

The following lines from the Old Babylonian version of the "Gilgamesh Epic" may do for an example of transliteration:

en- ki- du₁₀ a- na ša- šum i- sa- qa- ra- am

(Enkidu        to        him        spoke

         *DINGIR*                    *GIŠ*

a-   na      *GIŠ*   ne-      ir        *ERIN*

to   Gilgamesh:   "Slay    the   Cedar!")

The Akkadian tongue belongs to the family of Semitic languages[23] and is the only known representative of the East Semitic branch.[24] The West Semitic languages consist of two groups: the northern one (Phoenician, Hebrew, Moabite, Ugaritic,[25] and Aramaic), and the southern one (Arabic, South-Arabic,[26] and Ethiopian).[27]

There are several phases in the Akkadian language. The earliest is called Old Akkadian and is represented by inscriptions, proper names, and a few other texts dating from the time between 2500–1950 B.C.

Towards the end of this period the language began to separate into the Babylonian and the Assyrian branches.

[22] The numerical system has been adopted by A. Deimel (*Sumerisches Lexikon* [1925–37]) and several other Assyriologists, while F. Thureau-Dangin (*Syllabaire Accadien* [1926]) and W. von Soden ("*Das akkadische Syllabar*," *AO*, Vol. XXVI [Rome, 1948]) use accents as well as numbers.

[23] Member of the still larger group of the Hamito-Semitic languages, which comprises also the Egyptian, Lybico-Berber, and Kushitic idioms.

[24] A characteristic feature which distinguishes the morphology of the Akkadian language from that of other members of the Semitic group is the existence of a third tempus, the "permansive," along with the all-Semitic tempora of perfect and imperfect (called also "*telic*" and "*atelic*"). The permansive expresses a durative action in the present, past, or future, e.g. "*kašdū*" (permansive of "*kašādu*" = to conquer): "they are (have been, will be) conquering."

[25] Some philologists consider the Ugaritic language as not belonging to the Canaanite subgroup.

[26] Represented by Sabaean, Minaean, Qatabanian, and Hadrami inscriptions.

[27] The only important Semitic language that is written, like the Akkadian, from left to right.

The Babylonian dialect comprises the Old Babylonian (1950–1530 B.C., Code of Hammurabi, fragments of several epics,[28] hymns, letters, and economic texts), the Middle Babylonian (1530–1000 B.C., only sparingly represented by some historical, economic, and literary documents), the Young Babylonian (1000–500 B.C., literary language, used also in Assyria[29]), and the Neo-Babylonian (same period as the Young Babylonian, but limited to economic texts and letters).

The Assyrian dialect consists of the Old Assyrian (1950–1750 B.C., almost exclusively represented by letters and economic documents from the Assyrian colonies in Cappadocia), the Middle Assyrian (1500–1000 B.C., laws, economic texts, and some literary fragments[30]), and the Neo-Assyrian (1000–600 B.C., letters, economic documents, inscriptions, and certain texts from the library of Ashurbanipal).

Some fragments of literary texts have been preserved outside Mesopotamia, in El-Amarna[31] in Egypt (the Legend of Adapa, and the Myth of Nergal and Ereshkigal, written in a Babylonian dialect strongly influenced by Semitic idioms of the Canaanite group), and in Boghazköi[32] in Asia Minor (an Akkadian fragment of tablet IV of the Gilgamesh epic).

In the first millennium B.C., the Akkadian dialects became more and more relegated to written use, while the people—in Babylonia as well as in Assyria—spoke the Aramaic idiom. The eastern branch of Semitic languages did not survive its epoch of grandeur on the political level. The prestige of the Mesopotamian writing system, however, was so widespread that, in spite of its complications, it served as a basis for the much simplified alphabetical script of the Achaemenid empire.

## PICTORIAL ART

One of the great manifestations of Mesopotamian culture is its pictorial art. The bas-reliefs from the palace of Sargon II in Khorsabad

28 Gilgamesh, Etana, Atrahasis, Zu, Creation of Mankind by the mother-goddess.

29 Royal inscriptions of the Sargonides, wisdom literature, hymns and prayers, and the major part of the texts from the library of Ashurbanipal.

30 Parts of the Etana myth and of "Ishtar's Descent to the Nether World."

31 Together with many letters in Babylonian exchanged between the Pharaoh and Canaanite princes in the fourteenth century B.C.

32 The site of the ancient capital of the Hittite empire, Hatti.

were among the first witnesses of Assyrian civilization seen by the Western World, many years before the literary tablets could be valued.

The skill of the Mesopotamian artist is apparent already in some of the prehistoric monuments, as in certain specimens of pottery,[33] sculpture,[34] glyptic,[35] and architecture.[36]

Throughout the whole historic period we find that, apart from a number of coarsely made popular objects, there are works of art executed with painstaking care and considerable skill.

That the bas-reliefs, seal impressions, and statues nevertheless fail to conform to our post-renaissance aesthetic standards is perhaps not so much due to a lack of ability in the craftsman as to certain patterns or conventions which are often dictated by the general spiritual conceptions of the time.

We miss, for example, movement and expression in the human figures, who never betray either joy or torment, but always show a serene countenance. Yet there are many representations of animals in Mesopotamian art that abound with life and movement, like those depicted on the series of bas-reliefs showing Ashurbanipal at chase.[37] Other figurations, too, are amazingly expressive, such as the scene of a relief from Nimrud, showing a lion attacking the king's chariot and another lion being trodden down by the horses. Other examples are the famous relief, now in the British Museum, of a dying lion, and a clay relief depicting a lion about to be killed by a person who is perhaps Gilgamesh.[38]

If therefore the Assyro-Babylonian artist, when representing a human figure, concentrated all his efforts on the embroidery of the garment, the curls of hair and beard, and the exaggerated muscles of legs and

---

[33] See pp. 18–20 above, and Perkins, *Comparative Archeology.*

[34] See pp. 23 and 25 above; cf. also A. Moortgat, *Frühe Bildkunst in Sumer.*

[35] See pp. 21 and 25 above and—for stone vases—p. 22; cf. also L. Delaporte, *Catalogue des Cylindres Orientaux du Musée du Louvre* and L. Legain, *Ur Excavations. III Archaic Seal Impressions* (London, 1936.)

[36] See pp. 16–17, 21, and 24–25 above; cf. also H. J. Lenzen, *Mesopotamische Tempelanlagen von der Frühzeit bis zum zweiten Jahrtausend," ZA* (1955), 1–36.

[37] Cf. V. Place, *Ninive et l'Assyrie* (Paris, 1867–70), III, pls. 48–57.

[38] Relief found at Niffer, now on display in the Museum of Istanbul.

arms, instead of conferring movement and expression, he did so quite intentionally, not because his capacity was limited.

Except for animal representation, Mesopotamian art is not realistic. This feature, however, proves to be of value for the scholar of today, because art reveals best the peculiarities of its creators where it deviates from an exact imitation of nature.

The conventions of Assyro-Babylonian art are of two kinds. One is the specific Mesopotamian solution of the problem of technique and has therefore rather an objective character; the other results from the spiritual background of the epoch and is therefore subjective.

Concerning technique, the Mesopotamian relief-sculptor was confronted—as every artist is—with the task of representing the three dimensions of the human figure on a flat surface which allowed only two dimensions. The Assyro-Babylonian solved this problem much in the same way as the Egyptian or the Cretan: he represented the personage with face, pelvis, and legs in profile, but shoulders, eyes, and beard in front view. Only in the Neo-Assyrian time was the human figure portrayed in a more normal posture.

As for perspective, the ancient artist never tried to create the illusion of foreground and background. If he had to depict a scene of several plans, he divided the relief into as many registers, as on the exorcism plate described earlier.

How poorly the Mesopotamian could conceive superposed plans is apparent from the curious fact that archers were often represented with a stringless bow or with an incomplete arrow only because the respective lines would have barred the archer's face or his upper body.

In a scene showing an Assyrian holding several horses by their reins, the number of animals is not clear because the artist has designed four superposed heads, while the legs correspond to only two horses. An Assyrian relief shows two servants carrying a sort of chariot, but their hands do not grasp the bars. Another minor inconsistency can be noted in several Assyrian reliefs preserved in the Louvre, where the hands are folded in an unnatural way.[39]

---

[39] Concerning similar inconsistencies in Greek art cf. A. Philadelpheus, "Bases archaïques trouvées dans le mur de Thémistocle à Athènes," Bulletin de Correspondance Hellénique (1922), 1 ff.

The artist's respect for symmetry, obvious throughout the Assyro-Babylonian time and even in prehistory, often went so far that he depicted a person twice, as on a bas-relief from the palace of Ashurnazirpal in Nimrud, which shows the king doubled, on either side of a tree, with a protecting genius behind him in each position. On a cylinder seal in the Louvre we see a person with a two-faced head, looking simultaneously towards the deity ahead of him and towards another person following him.

King before Sacred Tree, a Sculpture from Palace of Ashurnazirpal III, in Calah—British Museum

A. H. Layard, *Monuments of Nineveh*

To another sphere of conventions belongs the disproportion of personages of different ranks represented together, as on the fragment of a mural painting from Tell-Hariri, dating from the beginning of the second millennium B.C. Especially in the first part of the historic period, we notice that a god, although on the same plan as his adorants, has a giant figure. This might be explained by a creed that deities were physically of superhuman size, but on an Assyrian relief hewn in the rock at Malatia, the statues of the seven gods carried in procession are of exactly the same size as the king standing—for the sake of symmetry —before and behind the row of deities.

Moreover, a similar disproportion is also found in figurations of a king, very tall, and his subjects, quite tiny. It is therefore the superior rank alone that accounts for these differences in size.

Such a convention is based on the Mesopotamian conception of religion: the omnipotent god exceeded in importance, and therefore in size, all his human subjects, as illustrated by a stone relief found at Abu-Habba, in which the god is two and one-half times the size of his adorants, including a king.

Double-Faced Personage on a Cylinder Seal, "Le Dieu Šamaš et l'Homme-oiseau"—British Museum
The god Shamash is sitting while a person half-man and half-bird is brought to him. The two-faced head of the official looks simultaneously towards the deity and towards the prisoner.

M. Jastrow, *Bildermappe zur Religion Babyloniens und Assyriens*

A similar disproportion, owing to a difference in hierarchy or in potency, exists between Ur-Nanshe, the king of Lagash, and the members of his family[40] and between the gigantic image of King Esarhaddon and the tiny figures of two vanquished enemies, who are less than one-fourth the king's size.[41]

[40] Votive tablet of the third millennium B.C.
[41] Diorite stela of Esarhaddon, now in the Museum of Berlin.

From a purely archaeological point of view, the Mesopotamian works of art are of the highest value, because they supplement very efficaciously the written documents of the corresponding epoch.

The stelae and the reliefs hewn in the rock are often the only reports of a historic event that occurred in the dim past, as, for example, the famous Stela of the Vultures, erected by Eannatum, ensi of Lagash, about 2650 B.C. in commemoration of his victorious campaign against the city of Umma. The representations of fighting warriors, impaled enemies, and the victorious monarch provide rich information on ancient warfare and show us the costumes, weapons, and accompanying animals of the protagonists.[42]

The pictorial arts bear important witness concerning the problem of the ethnic situation of early Mesopotamia. In the representation of human figures we find principally two types: one is brachycephalous, low browed, with flat occiput and a strongly curved nose;[43] the other type, less frequent in the early period, is dolicocephalous, high browed, with prominent occiput and a slightly aquiline nose.[44] The latter type probably represents the Semitic part of the population in ancient Mesopotamia. But it is doubtful that the personages with the globular heads represent Sumerians. The measurements of skulls found in southern Iraq dating from the beginning of the third millennium B.C. indicate, on the contrary, that the brachycephalous type was extremely rare in Mesopotamia during that period. Archaeological evidence then would favor the assumption that the Sumerians belonged to the dolicocephalous type attested largely all over the Mediterranean area. But the consistency of pictorial representations, almost invariably showing personages with globular heads and strongly curved noses during the Pre-Babylonian period, speaks against such a deduction. It seems plausible to the writer

[42] The horse as battle animal was introduced definitely by the Kassites, but it had been known also in an earlier historic period. Cf. A. Falkenstein, *"Ein Šulgi-Lied,"* ZA (1952), 64, verse 17: *"anše-ḳur-ra-ḥar-ra-an-na ḳun sù-sù-me-en"* = I am the horse on the caravan trail, with outstretched tail. See also A. Salonen, *"Hippologica Accadica,"* *Annales Academiae Scientiarum Fennicae,* Vol. 100 (Helsinki, 1956). In the Old Babylonian period, the onager was the battle animal.

[43] E.g., the personages of the scene on a chest from the Royal Cemetery of Ur (about 2750 B.C.), and the votive tablet of Ur-Nanshe and his family (first Dynasty of Ur).

[44] E.g., the mural paintings of Tell-Hariri (A. Parrot, *Mari* [Neuchâtel-Paris, 1953]), and the figure of Hammurabi on the diorite stela of the Codex (the Louvre).

that the Sumerians were indeed brachycephalous but that their number was relatively small. Politically and culturally they dominated a larger group of people, probably belonging to the dolicocephalous Mediterranean group. Evidently the artists depicted the leading class of the population, even though it was numerically the minority.

That the ethnic type of the prehistoric Sumerian was not general in the country might be inferred also from the current designation in Sumerian myths: "the blackheaded people."[45] The term is an equivalent for "Sumerians"; yet it is striking that such a physical feature was chosen by the Sumerians to characterize themselves. One cannot help but associate this term with the opposite word *"namruti,"* which, in connection with highly esteemed slaves coming from mountain regions populated by Asianics, appears in two texts dating from about the middle of the third millennium[46] and is generally interpreted as "fair-complexioned." It is quite probable that the term "blackheaded" was used by the Sumerians to distinguish themselves from fellow inhabitants of their country of a different ethnic type and perhaps of a socially inferior status. But the *"namruti"* people can hardly be identified with Indo-Europeans since the migration of these latter tribes did not reach the Land of Sumer prior to the second millennium.[47]

Pictorial art often provides the archaeologist with important evidence about religious life in Assyro-Babylonia. Most cylinder seals, bas-reliefs, and mural paintings depict religious scenes; the gods and their emblems[48] are the themata most frequently represented in early Mesopotamian glyptic. Also of religious meaning is the relief decoration on the famous stone vase (pp. 119–20) found at Warka,[49] which shows

[45] Cf. "The Deluge," translated by N. S. Kramer (*ANET*, 43, verse 48). Reference to the "blackheaded people" (*uku₃ sag-gi₆-ga*) is made also in the "Hymn of Shulgi," verses 5 and 47 (A. Falkenstein, *ZA* [1952], 64 and 66).

[46] Cf. E. A. Speiser, *Mesopotamian Origins,* 101–108 (here the interpretation of the term as "fair-skinned" is rejected).

[47] Concerning the problem of the ethnic composition in Mesopotamia, see pp. 26–27 and 28 above.

[48] The most important emblems are: horned tiara (Anu or Enlil), antelope with fish body and fishtail (Ea), crescent (Sin), four-pointed star (Shamash), star with seven or eight rays (Ishtar as goddess of love), scorpion (Ishtar as queen of battle), winged disk (Ashur), spade (Marduk), stylus (Nabu), and lightning (Adad).

[49] About forty inches high, now in the Museum of Baghdad.

on three registers of unequal heights, each separated by a narrow blank band, a very significant religious ceremony. The scene apparently represents a cult-offering to the goddess of fertility by a group of shepherds. The principal personage, the goddess herself or a priestess in her stead, appears on the upper register, with the strange symbols usually ascribed to Ishtar behind her. To the right of these symbols are jars and bowls which were probably filled with food offerings, two theriomorphic vessels, and a sheep carrying on its back two tiny robed figures, perhaps idols. Before the goddess (or priestess) stands a man offering her a brimming bowl; he is presumably followed by a personage of high rank, unfortunately not preserved. Only a part of the richly embroidered garment of the latter is visible, and a figure dressed in a short skirt stands behind him holding the train of the embroidered robe. The middle register is occupied by a row of men carrying filled bowls and jars. All the figures except the goddess, the high-ranking personage, and the train-bearer are nude (ten men). The lowest register represents a row of animals, alternatively a calf and a sheep, over another row consisting of grain stalks.

This cult scene, the earliest of its kind, reveals among other details the feature that in prehistoric times the adorant, while presenting his offerings to the deity, was nude. The reason for this was a ritual precaution, since the type of a garment might have caused offense—against the god of cattle, if the robe were made of wool or skins; against the god of vegetation, if it were of linen, cotton, or another vegetable fiber. By wearing no clothing at all, the worshiper escaped these dangers.

Besides the sacrificers of the archaic period,[50] the only nude figures in Mesopotamian art are the idols of the ancient fertility cult. In general, gods and goddesses, kings, warriors, and servants are clothed.[51] The fact that the nude females are often adorned with jewels seems to indicate that these ornaments are not simply objects of vanity but have a religious significance. Certain passages of the Ishtar myths corroborate this supposition, as, for example, the episode of the progressive removal

[50] Nude sacrificers appear also on a votive tablet (see p. 121) of Ur-Enlil, "ensi" of Nippur at the beginning of the third millennium, and on a libation scene engraved on white limestone, found in Telloh.

[51] The so-called "nude Ishtar" figurines are not representations of the goddess herself but idols connected with her cult.

Stone Vase of Warka—
Museum of Baghdad

G. Contenau, *La Civilisation d'Assur
et de Babylone*

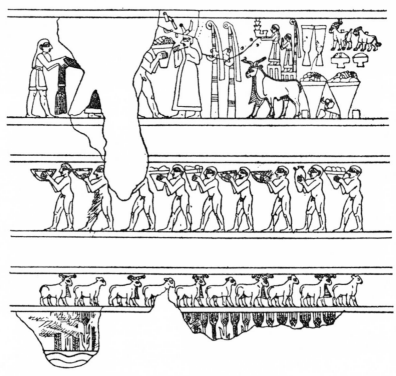

Stone Vase of Warka (details)

of Ishtar's adornments[52] at each of the seven gates of the Nether World. When she arrives before Ereshkigal, she is nude and stripped of her powers. It is probable that the obscure allusion—at the end of the Akkadian version of "Ishtar's Descent to the Nether World"—to the jewelry which the goddess is stringing has a ritual background; most likely, such ornaments were supposed to be endowed with a mysterious power conjuring fertility.

Certain categories of pictorial art not only describe religious scenes but have themselves a talismanic significance. The numerous statues of Gudea, ensi of Lagash about 2250 B.C., are meant to substitute for the ruler in his religious role; Gudea is almost always represented in an

[52] One of them has the significant designation "girdle of birthstones."

Votive Tablet of Ur-Enlil, Excavated in Nippur— Museum of Istanbul

John P. Peters, *Nippur; or, Explorations and Adventures on the Euphrates*

attitude of prayer, with his hands folded at his breast.[53] The act of putting the statue (sometimes with a prayer inscribed on the robe) in front of the god in a temple, is equivalent to a prayer perpetually uttered by the ruler himself. In this sense we have to understand also the statue of "Ebih-il" (about 2600 B.C.) in sitting posture and with folded hands.

Other monuments serve as protective genii, such as the colossal limestone statues of winged anthropocephalous bulls[54] that guarded the

[53] Another attitude of adoration is expressed by showing one arm raised halfway; the fingers seem to render sometimes the gesture of snapping, as a means to attract the god's attention.

[54] A curious detail of these gigantic creatures (they are fourteen feet high) is the

entrance to the royal palaces of Sargon II in Khorsabad and of Ashurna-zirpal in Nimrud. They were not mere decorative elements but, in the opinion of the Assyro-Babylonians, actually repelled malign influences. The bronze plate described in Chapter II had the supposed virtue of chasing away the demons that plagued the sick man; other figurines of evil spirits, such as the one showing the wind-demon Pazuzu—now to be seen in the Louvre—served as amulets against being possessed by demons.

To this group of talismanic objects belongs also the great quantity[55] of beads and other personal ornaments found in prehistoric tombs, made of all kinds of stone, clay, crystal, bone, shell, gold, copper, and other material. It is possible that even the decoration on pottery destined for graves had a ritual significance,[56] as for instance the scenes of plants, animals, and humans on the "scarlet ware" found in the Diyala region, dating from the beginning of the historic era.

While gods and kings are always closely associated on the works of art attributed to the older periods, in scenes of adoration, presentation,[57] or sacrifice the Middle and Neo-Assyrian epochs provide us with abundant documents describing the secular aspect of kingship.[58] The palaces of Ashurnazirpal, Sargon II, Ashurbanipal and other Assyrian dignitaries were decorated on the inside with bas-reliefs depicting in great detail the occupations of the ruler. There are, for example, scenes where the king is surrounded by his officials, approached by his servants,

---

fact that, since they are part of the wall and exposed to view on three sides, they appear to have five paws, because the artist sculptured in the round only the front, using for the two sides the bas-relief technique.

[55] A single tomb of Tepe Gawra (level X) yielded the astonishing quantity of 25,192 beads.

[56] Cf. also the ornithomorphic vessels found in Warka, Arpachiyyah, Khafajah, and the pisciform amulets of Warka, Telloh, and Khafajah.

[57] See, e.g., the fragment of a bas-relief showing Gudea, ensi of Lagash, presented by his patron deity Ningishzida to the principal god Ningirsu: M. Rutten, *Art en Styles du Moyen-Orient Ancien* (Paris, 1950), pl. 15. See also numerous seals in the collection of E. Porada, *Corpus of Ancient Near Eastern Seals in North American Collections;* and of A. Moortgat, *Vorderasiatische Rollsiegel.*

[58] As far as secularization is possible in a time when religion dominated every action of man. Cf. the collection of Assyrian and Neo-Babylonian bas-reliefs at the British Museum. H. R. Hall, *La sculpture Babylonienne et Assyrienne au British Museum.*

or offered gifts by tributaries; the army is represented while resting from a campaign, during a battle, and in the act of plundering the property of the enemy. Assyrian cruelty is apparent in the scenes depicting the massacres of vanquished warriors and showing the impaled heads of the slain. Among the chase reliefs, the most frequent representations are the hunting of lions, sometimes of birds. To the descriptions of the royal chase we owe the finest specimens of animal designs in Mesopotamia.

By far the greater part of Assyro-Babylonian art, such as has come to us, is represented by bas-reliefs. It is mostly to be found in Assyria, where the reliefs are sculptured on alabaster plinths; but there are also bas-reliefs, often made of clay, coming from Babylonia. There is a certain progress to be detected in their execution since the time of Ashurnazirpal, where the figures are not as well proportioned as in the later specimens. Under Ashurbanipal the technique of the bas-relief arrived at its zenith. Not only are the figures much better designed, but also the landscape is depicted in a more natural way; edifices and various kinds of trees appear in the background. A relief from Khorsabad, describing the transportation of cedar wood, shows the boats on the waves of the sea animated by a number of marine creatures, such as crabs, fish, snakes, and turtles.

In the beginning the bas-reliefs are covered with writing, but in the later periods the script is separated from the picture and appears under or above the relief.

The stelae also are decorated with relief work. Among the finest are the Victory stela of Naram-Sin (dynasty of Akkad, about 2400 B.C.) and the Code of Hammurabi (1700 B.C.). Other stones showing relief decoration are the so-called "*kudurru*," documents of land investiture, about twenty inches high, on which, besides the details of the contract, the symbols of various gods are represented. Most of the *kudurru* date from the period of the Kassites (second half of the second millennium). Remarkable works of art also are the alabaster vase of Warka and other stone vases from the same site, decorated with friezes of bulls and lions or rows of petals or barley ears.

Another kind of relief decoration is to be found in Babylon, where bulls, lions, dragons, and griffins are represented by means of enameled bricks on the walls of the Ishtar Gate and the Via Sacra that led to the

Esagil, the temple of Marduk. Also in Assyria, enameled brick is sometimes used for wall decoration, as can be seen from a representation of Assyrian warriors which is now preserved in the Museum of Berlin.

The main difference between the wall decorations in Assyria and Babylonia is that the alabaster plinths of the North are for interior use and of narrative character, while the brick reliefs of the city of Babylon are for exterior use and appear as single figures which are probably of talismanic significance.[59]

A very important branch of Mesopotamian craftsmanship is constituted by the art of glyptic. It is limited to stone seals,[60] which have been used since prehistoric times as a mark of ownership with simultaneous talismanic efficiency. There are two different kinds of seals; the most current type, the cylinder, appears after the Warka period (fourth millennium B.C.) and lasts until the beginning of the Neo-Babylonian epoch. It is a form characteristic of Mesopotamia, and cylinder seals existing in other regions of the Near East go back to Assyro-Babylonian influence.

Another type of seal, the stamp seal, is to be found in the North since the period of Ubaid, and a certain number of this kind occurs also in the South, a short time before the first appearance of cylinders, but recedes very soon before this more popular type of seal. Only in the Neo-Babylonian period did the use of the stamp seal become general, probably because of influence from other countries.

The cylinder seals are small sticks engraved with a hollow design on their circumference; by rolling the cylinder over fresh clay and thus producing a relief, the owner of the seal legalized a contract, marked his property, or sealed his abode. A seal impression not only served as a kind of signature, as in the first case, but also assured a supernatural protection by the gods, especially in the latter case: the offender who broke the seal impression while trying to enter the house in the proprietor's absence would be punished by the gods depicted on the seal.

---

[59] Protective genii were often represented under the form of bulls and lions (cf. also the stone vase decoration mentioned in the previous page).

[60] In some rare cases the seals are made of ivory (*BASOR*, No. 42, p. 13), bone (M. E. L. Mallowan, "Excavations at Brak and Chagar Bazar," *Iraq*, Vol. IX, pl. VIII) or shell (*ibid.*, pl. XXI).

By far the greater part of the seals represent religious scenes, often combined with dedicatory inscriptions; in the Kassite period some are long enough to contain a whole prayer. Some cylinder seals depict scenes of heroic tales, for example, episodes of the Gilgamesh legend or the Etana myth. One of the most beautiful cylinders, dating from the dynasty of Akkad (about 2400 B.C.), shows Gilgamesh in kneeling position, watering a bull from an overflowing vase.[61] Stamp seals almost invariably represent the figure of an adorant praying before an altar of Marduk or Nabu.

The role of painting was probably important in the decoration of Mesopotamian royal palaces. Unfortunately, only relatively few mural paintings have been preserved. This is due in part to the unfavorable atmospheric conditions which have exercised their devastating action during the millennia separating the ancient epoch from the modern era of excavations. The lower part of the inner walls was usually decorated with bas-reliefs; these have suffered little damage in the course of time, since they are imbedded in the remains of the fallen-down brick walls. But the paintings which often ornamented the upper part of the walls were mostly destroyed if the palace caved in.

Many paintings, however, have doubtless been ruined unwittingly by early archaeologists, whose interest was directed towards objects in very good condition which could be transported.

More recent excavations, such as those executed at Tell-Hariri (1933–39), have brought to light numerous paintings which had decorated the inner walls of the royal palace and date from the period preceding the reign of Hammurabi. Also in Khorsabad fragments of mural paintings have been found. The largest group of paintings was discovered by F. Thureau-Dangin and other archaeologists between 1929 and 1931 in Tell-Ahmar, on the left bank of the upper Euphrates. These paintings

[61] The motif of the overflowing vase was extremely popular in Mesopotamia in ancient times. In the palace of Tell Hariri a hollow statue of Ishtar has been found, showing the goddess in the attitude of pressing against her breast a vase that could be filled with water. From the Kassite period dates a wall decoration of molded bricks on a temple at Uruk, where a row of gods and goddesses, each with an overflowing vase against the breast, is represented. In Khorsabad several statues have been found which were part of a larger decoration showing the same motif of the overflowing vase.

covered the walls of a palace which had served as a residence for several Assyrian kings, from Shalmaneser III to Ashurbanipal.

The Mesopotamian paintings represent about the same scenes as the bas-reliefs; they, too, are narrative in character. The colors used are those of the enameled bricks (black, green, purple, yellow, blue, and white) with the addition of red, which had been used only rarely on bricks.

The Assyro-Babylonian artist excelled in the working of metal. The execution of the bronze bands which decorated the two wings of a door found at Balawat[62] very nearly equals that of the best alabaster reliefs. Also statues, human or animal heads,[63] and medical talismans[64] made of gold, copper, or bronze[65] attest the quality of Mesopotamian craftsmanship. A beautiful silver vase with a copper base comes from the period of Entemena, one of Eannatum's successors as ruler of Lagash (about 2600 B.C.); it is decorated with lion-headed eagles, rams, bulls, and other animals.

When fabricating the statue of a deity or the head of an animal, the ancient artist often fashioned a figure of wood and then nailed to it thin metal plates, mostly of bronze, which were sometimes covered by another layer of gold fillets. Such a technique was also employed for gilding palm-trees in the palace of Khorsabad.[66]

Mesopotamian architecture, though not as conspicuous and durable as the Egyptian pyramids, was nevertheless monumental and massive. The building material being almost exclusively mud bricks, sun dried or kiln burnt, the edifices had only a short life, and the temples and palaces continually needed repair and reconstruction. But this draw-

---

[62] A small tell between Mosul and Nimrud; no palace to which the doors may have belonged has been discovered at the site. Fragments of the bands are now in the British Museum, the Louvre, and the Museum of Istanbul.

[63] See, for example, the head of a bull, made of gold, that adorned the harp of the queen (Royal cemetery of Al-Mughair).

[64] For example, the bronze plate described in Chapter II.

[65] The passage from copper to bronze is accomplished very slowly and gradually in Mesopotamia; most objects of the ancient periods are made of a very high percentage of copper and only insignificant parts of other metals such as antimony and tin.

[66] Another procedure has been employed for the fabrication of the statue of the Elamite queen Napir Asu. Executed in cast bronze, the figure—although mutilated—weighs about 4,000 lbs.

Servant with Folded Hands, an Assyrian Relief Dating from the
Eighth Century B.C.—the Louvre

Bompiani, *Dizionario delle Opere*

Boundary Stone from Abu Habba, Found in an Old Temple
of Sippar, Ruins of Abu Habba—British Museum

L. W. King, *Babylonian Boundary Stones and Memorial
Tablets in the British Museum*

Esarhaddon with
Vanquished Kings, a
Stela Found in Syria—
Berliner Museum

Felix von Luschan,
*Ausgrabungen in Sendschirli*

Stela of the Vultures, Excavated in Telloh—the Louvre

Heuzey and Thureau-Dangin, *Restitution materielle de la Stele de Vautours*

Chest from the Royal Cemetery of Ur—British Museum

Leonard Woolley, *Ur Excavations*

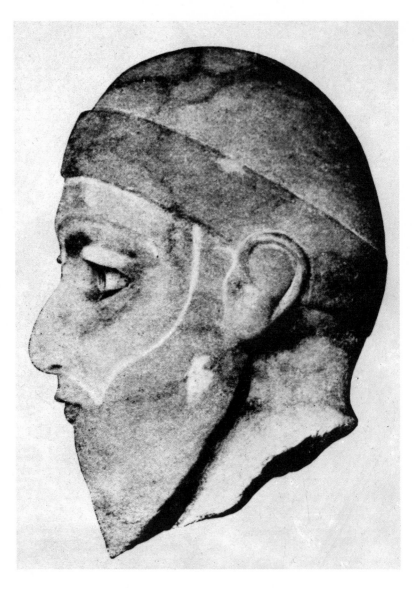

Old-Assyrian Type, Excavated in Bismaya by E. J. Banks—
Private Collection

M. Jastrow, *Bildermappe zur Religion Babyloniens und Assyriens*

Statue of Ebih-il—
the Louvre

S. Moscati, *Le Antiche
civilta semitiche*

The Demon Pazuzu, Lord of the Wicked "lile," the Wind-Demons—
the Louvre

Georges Perrot, *Histoire de l'Art*

back represents, on the other hand, an advantage for the excavator of today: the tumbling clay walls preserved intact the tracing of their foundations, even when different levels of civilization were superposed.[67]

So we know at least the foundation plans of the ancient structures, and the lower part of the walls, having been covered up by the mass of fallen-in ruins, are usually in a fair state of preservation.

The greater part of Mesopotamian architecture consists of temples. Their plan is more or less tripartite, as in prehistoric times. There were two ways of beginning the construction of a temple; it was either built directly on the ground or on a large terrace of mud bricks. It is possible that the latter form was the prototype of the famous *ziqqurat* or step-tower so important in Mesopotamian religion.

The *ziqqurat* was a very old place of worship and is probably of Sumerian origin. It always accompanied the principal temple but was much taller. Ruins of steptowers, of more or less square plan and consisting of two to seven platforms, have been found in Niffer, Al-Mughair, Al-Uhaimir, Birs-Nimrud, Abu-Shahrain, and many other southern sites;[68] traces of later *ziqqurats* have been discovered in Assyria, especially in Nimrud, Khorsabad, Qalat Shergat, and Tell-Hariri.

The *ziqqurats* were constructed of colored bricks. The seven platforms of the steptower of Birs-Nimrud, of which the four lower ones have been preserved, were of the following colors: black, white, orange, blue, scarlet, silver, and gold.[69]

The exact purpose of the *ziqqurat* is not known. Probably the most important part of it was the upper platform, which has in none of the

[67] E.g., the superposition of temple foundations in Abu Shahrain, Warka, and Tepe Gawra. In Abu Shahrain the bases of thirteen directly superimposed temples were found in the stratum of the Ubaid period; under the two layers of the "Mosaic temple" in Warka four earlier building foundations could be identified. The excavations in Tepe-Gawra showed the succession of two temples and a tholos, all erected on the same site, in levels XIX–XVII.

[68] The *ziqqurat E-temen-an-ki* ("House of the foundation of Heaven and Earth") in Babylon reached the height of 279 feet. The passage Gen. 11:4 probably refers to the Babylonian steptower rather than to the E-ur-imin-an-ki ("House of the seven guides of Heaven and Earth") in Borsippa, which underlies the legend of the confusion of languages in Arabic and Talmudic traditions.

[69] The seven platforms of the *ziqqurat* in Dur-Sharrukin seem to have been of the following colors: white, black, pink, blue, vermilion, silver, and gold.

cases been preserved. Referring allegedly to the sanctuary of Marduk, Herodotus reports[70] that the top of the steptower contained the bridal chamber of the Babylonian god.

The statement of Strabo,[71] according to which the *ziqqurat* of Babylon was the symbolic tomb of Marduk, seemed to have found support some time ago in a text pertaining to the ritual of the Babylonian Akitu festival, which H. Zimmern[72] interpreted as describing the celebration of Marduk's death and resurrection. Recently, however, W. von Soden[73] proved the incorrectness of Zimmern's translation,[74] pointing out that the text was no Babylonian *Kultkommentar*[75] but an Assyrian composition of strongly tendentious character; probably written under the auspices of Sennacherib, a fanatical enemy of Babylon, the text had the purpose of humiliating Marduk in the eyes of the people. The Babylonian god was described as undergoing an ordeal; his enemies beat and arrested him. Finally Shamash, Sin, and probably also Ashur passed judgment on him.[76] No mention is made of Marduk's death or his resurrection. The idea of a divine tomb in connection with the *ziqqurat* of the Marduk-temple is therefore without substantiation.[77]

[70] History I. 181. It is possible that Herodotus confused the *ziqqurat* of Babylon with the one of Borsippa (see note 68 above).

[71] Strabo *Geography* XVI. I.

[72] *"Zum babylonischen Neujahrsfest—Zweiter Beitrag"* (*BSGW*, Phil.-hist. Klasse, vol. 70, fasc. 5, 1918).

[73] *"Gibt es ein Zeugnis, dass die Babylonier an Marduks Wiederauferstehung glaubten?"* *ZA* (1955), 130–166.

[74] For the three errors on which Zimmern's assumption was based, see *ibid.,* 158.

[75] At the end of the text a curse is directed against those who, after having learnt the contents of the tablet, do not help in the propagation of the message. This fact, overlooked by Zimmern, who assumed a meaning exactly opposite, is another proof that the text could not be part of Babylonian cult literature, since writings dealing with rituals were, on the contrary, to be kept secret from all uninitiated.

[76] The text has many obscure passages, and the outcome of both the ordeal and the judgment is not known.

[77] It is not excluded, however, that in the earliest times *ziqqurats* did contain a symbolic tomb of a dead and resurrecting fertility deity; the steptowers are sometimes called "House of the Gigunu," and "Gigunu" has among other meanings that of "tomb," as is apparent from an inscription of Sennacherib. For this text see D. Luckenbill, "Annals of Sennacherib," *Ancient Records of Assyria and Babylonia* (Chicago, 1927), 163. This would indicate a relationship between the Mesopotamian *ziqqurat* and the Egyptian pyramid, which were perhaps both replicas of the primeval hill still apparent in Egyptian mythology,

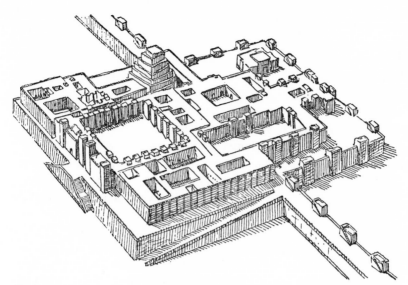

Restoration Drawing of the Palace of Khorsabad, Old Residence of
Sargon II

Luckenback Adami, *Arte e storia del mondo antico*

Besides religious structures, there have been found important traces
of secular dwellings, especially royal palaces. They are all erected on
a high platform and have massive walls without windows. The gateway,
of particular importance in oriental architecture,[78] led towards several
courtyards with adjoining chambers. A part of each palace seems to
have been set aside for religious use.

When we examine the expression of Mesopotamian pictorial art,
we see that it is characterized by a search for symmetry rather than

though not attested in Mesopotamia. G. Contenau, *La Tour de Babel* (Paris, 1941), 249ff.,
supposes that the Mesopotamian *ziqqurat* goes back to the type of the square pyramid
erected at Saqqarah in Egypt by Zoser, first monarch of the third dynasty, and that a still
older prototype is the stepped tomb of Nebetka, equally in Saqqarah, dating from the
first dynasty.

[78] Cf. the "Puerta del Sol" in Toledo, dating from the Arabic occupation, and the
designation "Sublime Porte" for the Turkish government; see also Esther 2:21, and
Dan. 2:49. A study about the mythological significance of the temple doors has been
made by A. S. Kapelrud, "The Gates of Hell and the Guardian Angels of Paradise," *JAOS*
(1950), 151 ff.

harmony. A tendency for stylization is apparent, and decoration of abstract geometrical design is often used. While the elaboration of detail is extensive, the vision of the whole is generally poor.

Mesopotamian art impresses the observer through the skillful craftsmanship it displays but fails—with the exception of the scenes showing animals—to raise any deeper sensation than admiration.

The world which is depicted throughout the periods represents the official one of gods and kings, overshadowed by a solemnity which leaves no room for emotions or individuality. The latter features, however, break through in poetry, and it is for this reason that the poetry gives us a more vivid idea of the Assyro-Babylonian soul than does the pictorial art.

# PART TWO

*The Poetry*

*"Litteras semper arbitror Assyriis fuisse"*—
Caius Plinius Secundus, *Naturalis historia VII*

# THE POETRY

الماخوذ غير كله ترك لا غير الماخوذ

A FTER HAVING EXAMINED in the preceding pages the historical, spiritual, and iconographic elements that compose the setting of Assyro-Babylonian literature, we will now turn to the poems themselves. Our guide will be the Arabic saying above, "If the 'whole' cannot be obtained, let not the greater part of it be left unmentioned."

We know indeed only a fraction of the literary production of Mesopotamia, and it may well be that whole classes of poetry have flourished, the very existence of which we ignore.

We must bear in mind that only the literature which was written by the scribes has come to us. Therefore only the officially recognized poems were recorded, to the exclusion of whatever may have been judged vulgar, formally imperfect, or of no relevance for the contemporary society.

It must be assumed, then, that a considerable part of the oral literature has perished, together with the civilization by which it was created.

No line of any popular song has been preserved, although the existence of such a genre may be inferred from a document[1] which seems to be an enumeration of titles[2] of sacred and profane songs.

The difficulty of the cuneiform script may be one of the chief reasons why no Edubba[3] pupil, has on any of his tablets, recorded a scrap of non-official poetry, granting thus an unconscious boon to posterity, as did much later, in the Latin Middle Ages, the anonymous Franconian friar who saved from oblivion the commencement of the *Hildebrandslied*.

The greater and most important part of Assyro-Babylonian poetry consists of myths and epics. They owe their preservation not only to their popularity but also—and chiefly—to the fact that they were almost without exception included in the cult literature. Many of these—the Creation epic, the legends of Atrahasis and of Adapa, and the myth of Ishtar's descent to the Nether World—are cosmological introductions to incantations; "The Epic of Era" and "Kumma's Vision of the Nether World" serve as amulets.

The only other important body of poetry which the Assyro-Babylonians have transmitted to us is the speculative literature, which dates almost entirely from the later period. It is possible that these monologues and dialogues have likewise evolved out of cult poetry, namely the hymns and prayers, as will be shown below.

Lyric poetry, as we have understood the term since the Greeks, seems not to have existed as a genre in Babylonia.[4] Those compositions

[1] See G. Contenau, *La vie quotidienne à Babylone et en Assyrie* (Paris, 1950), 106ff.

[2] In Mesopotamian literature the title of a poem consists of its initial line.

[3] "The House of Tablets," i.e., the Mesopotamian school of writing.

[4] Certain passages of the epic and speculative literature equal in beauty and pathos the lyrical expressions of later civilizations.

called psalms, prayers, or lamentations are to a great extent written in Sumerian, sometimes with an interlinear Akkadian translation; in construction they follow Sumerian models, in which rhythm, repetitions, and invocations are dictated solely by considerations of a religious, not aesthetic, nature.

The Mesopotamian proverbs, too, are a Sumerian, not Akkadian, genre and occur on the tablets almost always in Sumerian, with defective Akkadian adaptations.

The importance of poems like the "Dispute between the Date-Palm and the Tamarisk" lies more in their structure than in their mythological or spiritual implications; they have been taken into consideration in the concluding chapter on formal aspects of Akkadian literature.

In this chapter and the next we shall treat each single important poem, beginning with the epic tales and ending with the speculative literature.

The text has been followed passage by passage; for obscure lines we have offered an interpretation which might help to clarify dubious instances; in some cases an altered arrangement of the text has been proposed. The comment is intended to acquaint the reader with the mythological background of each episode and calls attention to similar passages in other Semitic literatures.

# CHAPTER IV
*Myths and Epics*

## The Creation Epic

THIS POEM,[1] also called the Babylonian Genesis because of its parallels with passages of the Old Testament, consists of seven tablets which have been excavated in Nineveh, Ashur, and Kish. None of them were written before the first millennium B.C., but the date of composition is certainly much older and is to be placed at the beginning of the second millennium B.C. The cuneiform text has been published by L. W. King, *The Seven Tablets of Creation* (London, 1902).

[1] Another title of the poem is *"Enuma elish,"* after the Akkadian words which initiate the first tablet and mean "When on high."

TABLET I

*Before heaven and earth had been named, the world was a chaotic mixture of sweet and salty waters personified by Apsu and Tiamat, the father and mother of all the gods.*

The creation of the world is conceived in the first lines as being the result of a verbal action. Such a concept would constitute important progress over that of a purely material creation, apparent in most cosmogonies; however, Marduk does not, in tablet IV, call heaven and earth into existence by magical words, and there is no *creatio ex nihilo.* An allusion to the final separation of the salty and the sweet-water seas by God is to be found in Sura XXV of the Qur'ān[2]: "It is He who has made the two seas to flow freely, one sweet and fresh, the other salty and bitter, and has put between them a barrier and an insurmountable obstruction." (Cf. also XXXV, 12, and LV, 19–20.)

*Within the watery chaos the first gods are brought forth: Lahmu and Lahamu, Anshar[3] and Kishar, Anu, and Ea.[4] Each of these gods surpasses his forefathers, and the wisest of all is Ea, prominent by strength as well as by his understanding.*

It seems that Anu was the begetter of Ea, who is called "Anu's first-born."[5] No mention is made of younger sons of Anu, and the term "first-born" is rather to be understood as designating a specific rank. The first-born son had special privileges in Mesopotamian society, and we know that only the first son of a king had the right of succession to the throne. If it happened that the first son died before his father (as was the case of Sin-iddina-apla, eldest son of Esarhaddon), the succession was open to any of his brothers indiscriminately, the second son having no priority over his younger brothers. It never occurred in Mesopotamian history that a younger son ascended to the throne while the

---

[2] Qur'ān XXV:

وهو الذي مرج البحرين هذا عذب فرات وهذا ملح أجاج وجعل بينهما
برزخاً وحجراً محجوراً

[3] The Assyrian version equates Anshar with the "national" god Ashur, who, throughout the Creation epic, takes the place of Marduk, Babylonian national god.

[4] One of the many names of Ea is Nudimmud, mentioned in these first passages.

[5] For the interpretation of the passage on the gods' birth, see W. F. Albright, *JAOS*, Vol. LXXI (July, 1951), 264.

oldest brother was still living; if there was jealousy on the part of the former, it might happen that the older brother was slain. But no legal succession was possible during the lifetime of the crown prince. There was no illegality in the fact that Ashurbanipal was assigned the Assyrian empire, while his older brother Shamash-shum-ukin received Babylonia as his portion; the latter had no priority over Ashurbanipal, since the death of Sin-iddina-apla had allotted equal chances of succession to the surviving brothers.

*The divine brothers disturb Tiamat by their noisy ways and raise profound discontent in Apsu and Tiamat, who try in vain to restore calm. Apsu at last calls his vizier Mummu and goes with him before Tiamat. He proposes to destroy the gods so that he may have rest again. Tiamat disagrees and reproaches Apsu for his wicked intention. She proposes instead to have patience with their sons. But Mummu gives evil advice to Apsu, strengthening him in his original purpose, and Apsu no longer heeds the opinion of Tiamat, but plots the destruction of the gods.*

Tiamat is evidently the principal personage; Apsu, her husband, instead of asking her to appear before him, goes to her abode and sits down before her. This conception of the supremacy of the female reflects a primitive form of matriarchate originating in the importance attributed to the motherly functions of womanhood. A similar preference for the female deity is to be found in Egypt, where, for example, the goddess Nut is superior to her consort Nu.

Turning now to the relationship between Apsu and Mummu, we wonder at the degree of influence exercised by the vizier. Apsu does not execute his destructive project as long as he is the only one to desire it; but as soon as Mummu advocates his wish, he makes up his mind, even though Tiamat is against it. His reaction to Mummu's advice— he kisses the vizier and embraces him joyfully—shows the entire dependence of the god on his counselor.

*The gods are informed of the evil which Apsu and Mummu have plotted against them. Ea, the wisest among the gods, brings a magic sleep upon Apsu and reduces Mummu to impotence. He then removes the tiara and halo of Apsu and puts them on his own head; finally Ea slays Apsu and makes Mummu a prisoner. After his victory, Ea establishes*

138

*a dwelling for himself upon the body of Apsu and founds his cult chamber for himself and his spouse Damkina. This is where Marduk, the wisest of all the gods, is born.*

It is to be noted that Ea subdues Apsu by magic instead of overpowering him by physical strength or strategic skill.

The erection of Ea's new dwelling is particularly stressed; in all the Semitic literatures emerges the prime importance of a god's abode, as a shelter and a home. Its construction may be ordered by the deity, or offered to him by his inferiors. The *Anunnaki* express their gratitude to Marduk by building the temple Esagila for him; Huwawa offers, in exchange for sparing his life, to construct a house for Gilgamesh; the Ugaritic god Baal strives hard to win from his father El the privilege of a dwelling of his own.[6]

Even in the non-idolatrous religions of the later periods there are traces of such concepts of the necessity of a god's having an abode: Yahweh demands that a tabernacle be erected for him, "that I may dwell among them";[7] Simon Peter offers to build three houses for Jesus, Moses, and Elias, when Christ is transfigured;[8] according to an Arabic legend, Allah ordered the construction of the Ka'ba and himself revealed—through the shadow of a cloud—its plan to Abraham, who, with his son Ismael, built the divine abode.[9]

*Ea looks in admiration at his son and endows him with a double godhead. Marduk is sharp of eyes and of ears, and the perfection of his members places him above all the other gods. He is clad with the halos of ten gods.*

*Anu then creates the fourfold wind to disturb Tiamat. Those gods who are on the latter's side incite Tiamat to avenge Apsu, her husband. Tiamat consents gladly and prepares for battle against her adversaries. Her principal preparation is the bringing forth of monsters who are to help her in the fight. She crowns these monsters with halos so that they become equal to the gods. There are eleven species of monsters, includ-*

[6] Text in "Ugaritic Myths, Epics, and Legends," H. L. Ginsberg, *ANET*, 137 (fragment E).

[7] Exod. 25:8.

[8] Matt. 17:4.

[9] Account of the legend by A. Bausani, *Il Corano* (Florence, 1955), 509.

*ing the Viper, the Dragon, the Sphinx, the Great Lion, the Mad Dog, the Scorpion Man, the Dragonfly, the Centaur, and the Lion Demons.*

*The gods who are on her side form an assembly, and Tiamat chooses Kingu to be commander-in-chief of her fearful army.*

The halo with which every god is endowed is supposed to lend its bearer special strength and power; it seems to consist of rays of light but sometimes appears to be also of material substance. In the Gilgamesh epic, the monstrous watchman of the Holy Cedar, Huwawa, wears a halo on his head, and Enkidu tells Gilgamesh that when Huwawa is slain, the pieces of his halo will remain scattered on the ground and continue to illuminate the forest.

We encounter once more the influence exercised by another person or a group of persons on the sovereign; as Apsu needed the counsel of his vizier, so Tiamat is incited by the gods on her side to act against her foes. This is in accordance with the social structure of Mesopotamia as it appears in contemporary documents.[10]

*Tiamat sets Kingu above all the other gods, exalts him in the assembly, endows him with full power, and bequeaths to him the Tablets of Fate. She thus elevates Kingu to the rank of Anu. Kingu's first action is to decree the fate of his fellow gods: they will vanquish the fire and the power weapon.*

Here is apparent the extraordinary importance accorded to the Tablets of Fate: to possess them is to be master of the universe. They alone give the supreme power; with their possession the fate of all the other gods can be decreed. We shall see the consequences of a transfer of these tablets in the myth of Zu. The fire mentioned by Tiamat and Kingu is perhaps the element which Anu and his sons incarnate, just as Tiamat and her monsters incarnate the water.

## TABLET II

*Tiamat's preparations are divulged to Ea, Marduk's father. His preoccupation is expressed in his utter silence. After a while he resolves to acquaint Anshar with the danger that threatens the gods. He reports that all the gods, even those whom Anshar begat, are on Tiamat's side.* [The following thirty-four lines repeat word for word the statement con-

[10] Cf. Chapter II above, p. 82ff.

cerning Tiamat's activity related at the end of the first tablet.] *Anshar, on hearing such news, reacts violently, smiting his loins, biting his lips, and stifling an outcry with his hand. He commands Ea to slay Kingu, as before he had slain Apsu and Mummu.* [Ea's reply, which seems to have been negative, is lost in a break of about fourteen lines.]

*Anshar then turns to Anu and asks him to go before Tiamat and calm her anger. Anu sets out on his mission, but on seeing Tiamat's preparations, he is seized by fear and goes back to Anshar. When the latter sees that nobody is able to resist Tiamat, he lapses into silence, and all the other gods with him.*

Ea is unable to fight Tiamat successfully; his magic power, which had been strong enough to wrap Apsu and Mummu in sleep, is supposed to be inefficient against the superior Tiamat. The fact that she possesses, together with Kingu, the Tablets of Fate, probably makes her invulnerable.

*Finally Anshar has the idea of making Marduk avenge the gods. Ea calls his son and instructs him how to appear before Anshar. The latter regains confidence on beholding Marduk. The young god encourages Anshar and promises to be the champion of the gods. He tells Anshar to open wide his lips[11] because he, Marduk, is going to slay Tiamat, who is only a woman and therefore not to be feared. Anshar advises Marduk to use his potent spell against Tiamat and to mount the storm chariot. In return, however, Marduk asks for special privileges: Anshar is to set up the assembly and proclaim supreme the young god's destiny; he wants to have the right of determining the fates instead of Anshar.*

The fact that Marduk considers Tiamat's being a woman a mark of inferiority may indicate a shift in primitive adoration: the mother worshipers have retreated before the father worshipers.

Marduk claims the privilege of decreeing the fates: this is equal to the power which Tiamat has conferred on Kingu, except that no tablets are mentioned as belonging to Anshar. It is to be noted that only the Assembly is able to bestow special rights on Marduk; Anshar alone has insufficient authority.

11 There seems to be a special significance in the gesture of closing or opening one's lips; the first one expresses preoccupation at the highest degree, while the latter indicates relief and joy.

## TABLET III

*Anshar makes haste to do as Marduk wishes. He calls for his vizier, Gaga, and sends him to Lahmu and Lahamu, the primeval pair brought forth by Tiamat and Apsu in the watery Chaos. Gaga is to make a full report to them and ask for their presence at the Assembly. All the gods are to participate in a banquet, eat bread and drink wine, and proclaim Marduk's destiny. Anshar instructs Gaga to utter the same words already pronounced by Ea* [the thirty-four lines mentioned above are once more repeated] *and to add the report on the failure of Ea and Anu to make Tiamat change her mind. Gaga's report is to close with a statement of Marduk's request and an invitation to come to the Assembly. Gaga does Anshar's bidding, goes to Lahmu and Lahamu, greets them respectfully, kissing the ground at their feet, and makes his report, exactly as Anshar has told him. The two deities, as well as all the other gods,[12] are deeply concerned with Tiamat's evil intention and go at once to the assembly hall, where they kiss each other. They eat and drink, and the effect of the strong drink makes their spirits rise high. So they fix Marduk's fate.*

The inebriating effect of strong drink was well known to the Mesopotamians, but they did not consider it an evil influence. The elation provoked by wine was a mood which befitted the gods on such an occasion. In the Gilgamesh epic the imbibing of strong drink is even considered a sign of higher civilization; when Enkidu, who in his primitive life knew only the milk of wild beasts, partakes of the beverage offered him by the shepherds, he feels that the new elevation of his mind signals a further step away from his former existence.

A different opinion about the consequences of imbibing of strong drink is to be found, however, in later Semitic literatures. Solomon says in a proverb: "Wine is a mocker, strong drink is raging: and whosoever is deceived thereby is not wise."[13] Muhammad condemns wine as an instrument of Satan: "Indeed Satan wants, through wine . . . [to] cast enmity and hatred among you, and deter you from mentioning the name of God and from praying."[14]

---

[12] They are called sometimes *"Igigi,"* sometimes also *"Anunnaki,"* without distinction.

[13] Prov. 20:1.            [14] Sura V. 91.

## Tablet IV

*The gods erect a throne for Marduk and confer the highest honors upon him; his rank is now equal to that of the sky-god Anu. His words are never to be changed, his command will be followed by all the gods. The supremacy of Marduk shall be expressed by the fact that all the gods will have shrines in the temple belonging to him. In order to furnish a proof of the new power bestowed on Marduk, the gods propose that, through the force of his word, he cause a garment, which they place before him, to be destroyed, and afterwards by a second word, to be recreated. Marduk follows this proposal: the garment vanishes and reappears at his command.*

The basis for this singular test of Marduk's omnipotence is a pun which has its origin in the two syllables composing the name of the god. *"Mar"* has among many other meanings those of "to destroy" and "to create," while *"duk"* is phonetically the same as the Sumerian *"tug,"* which means "garment."[15]

*Marduk is proclaimed king and is given throne, scepter, and weapons. He then proceeds to arm himself for his battle with Tiamat. He fashions a bow, hangs it at his side together with the quiver, and grasps a mace in his right hand. Lightning is in front of him, his whole body is filled with fire. He carries a net with him and gathers a group of four winds (the South, North, East, and West wind) and another of seven winds (the Evil, the Fourfold, the Sevenfold, the Matchless, the Whirlwind, the Hurricane, and the Cyclone) by his side. He raises the floodstorm, his mighty weapon, and mounts the storm chariot, to which are yoked the Killer, the Relentless, the Trampler, and the Swift. To his right he posts the Smiter, to his left the Combat. In his mouth he holds a spell, in his hand he carries a plant against poison.*

Marduk's outfit consists of three groups: material weapons (bow and arrows, mace, net), natural elements (the two groups of winds, the lightning, the floodstorm, the fire which fills his body), and magical arms (the spell in his mouth and the miraculous plant). The animals which are yoked to his chariot are not defined; they may be horses, but an interpretation seeing in them only the incarnation of some natural

---

[15] For puns in Mesopotamian documents, see G. Dossin, *"Brg'yh, roi de KTK," Museon,* Vol. LVII (1944), 147ff. and *"Le vêtement de Marduk," Museon,* Vol. LXI (1947), 1.

power is possible, too. The same stands for the creatures posted at his sides.

Similar stylistic devices are still used in later Semitic poetry, as, for example, in the famous "Lamiyyat al-Arab," by the pre-Islamic poet Shanfara,[16] who calls the panther "the Spotted One,"[17] and the Hyena "the Highcrested One";[18] in the expressions "the White Unsheathed One" and "the Yellow Long One" we have to recognize respectively the sword and the bow.[19]

*On seeing Marduk, Kingu becomes confused; the other gods on his side are likewise blinded by Marduk's splendor, and Tiamat utters a cry. She greets Marduk with defiance. The latter raises his weapon, the floodstorm, and challenges her. He stresses the wickedness of her intentions and asks her to meet him in single combat. Tiamat enters into a terrible fury and shakes with wrath. She recites a spell and meets Marduk. The god sends one of the seven winds against her, which enters Tiamat's mouth and inflates her body. Marduk catches her in his net and splits her heart with one arrow that tears her insides open. Having thus killed the monster, he stands upon her carcass. After Tiamat's death, all her helpers flee, but Marduk captures them and casts them in fetters. As for Kingu, Marduk delivers him to the god of death and takes away from him the Tablets of Fate, which he fastens on his own breast.*

What strikes one in this passage is the extremely succinct account of the duel between Marduk and Tiamat. The monster succumbs at once, and the immediacy of Marduk's victory almost seems to imply that she was, after all, only a weak adversary. The intention of the epic is certainly quite different. The lack of drama in the description of the battle is perhaps due to the fact that the recital of the poem was an important part of the ritual on the New Year's festival and had a magical rather than an edifying aim; the supremacy of Marduk had to be overwhelming, his victory immediate and complete. It is possible that an older, not preserved, version of this cosmic combat offered a fuller

[16] See F. Gabrieli, *Shanfara* (Florence, 1947).

[17] The adjective أُرْقَط is now currently used to designate the panther, also called نمر "the Speckled One."

[18] The adjective عرفاء (highcrested) stands for the word ضبع (hyaena).

[19] الإ بيض , الاصلت "the White Unsheathed One" instead of السـيف (sword) and الصفرآء العيطل "The Yellow Long one" instead of القوس (bow).

description. We miss here the opportunities for the god to make use of his formidable weapons: only one of the eleven winds, the net, and an arrow are mentioned. The terrifying monsters filled with venom, whom Tiamat had brought forth, are without any consequence in the entire passage. In Marduk's combat against Tiamat we have an example of a battle in which physical strength is of little importance. Just as in the Gilgamesh epic Huwawa, the guardian of the Holy Cedar, is vanquished by virtue of a strong wind which Gilgamesh sends against him, so Tiamat is overcome by a cosmic force, not by magic, as was her murdered husband Apsu, nor by physical strength, as is, for example, Enkidu by the strong Gilgamesh. It is possible that the myth of the combat between the watery Chaos (of the marshlands in Sumer perhaps) and the life-giving fire was much older than the dynasty of Babylon and the effort of the clergy to glorify Marduk. In all probability it was Enlil (who has as yet not been mentioned in the epic, although he was of prime importance in Sumerian religion) who fought the female monster in a primitive version, the existence of which we can only surmise.

*Marduk approaches his dead enemy; he treads on Tiamat's legs and crushes her skull. The great gods rejoice at Marduk's victory and bring him gifts. Marduk splits Tiamat's body into two halves; one of them he makes into the sky, where he posts guards so that her waters may not escape; from the other half he fashions the "Esharra," the earth, pictured as placed above the Apsu—the abode of Ea—like a canopy. Then Marduk assigns Anu, Enlil,[20] and Ea their places.*

It is to be noted that, although Tiamat has been pictured as a being with legs, belly, heart, mouth, and skull, she now reappears under the form of a cosmic element: she is once more identical with the primeval water. The half of her body which Marduk sets up for the sky overflows with water and needs guards to prevent the water from escaping.

It is needless to emphasize that this myth of the Creation of the Universe has nothing in common with the *creatio ex nihilo* of Genesis.

## Tablet V

*Marduk builds the stations for each of the great gods and forms constellations with their astral likenesses. He fixes the course of the year,*

[20] This is the first time Enlil is mentioned in the poem.

*the twelve months, and the days. The station of Nebiru (Jove) sep-*
*arates the northern band, domain of Enlil, and the southern band, realm*
*of Ea. He opens the gates on both sides for the rising and the setting of*
*the sun, and fixes the zenith in Tiamat's belly. He decrees the course*
*of the moon with all the changes of shape during its monthly way.*

This tablet, which probably contained the sum of astronomical
knowledge during the Old Babylonian period, is unfortunately broken
away, after a few lines which show us the conception of astral movements as being the result of an order imposed by a god.

### TABLET VI

*Marduk sets his mind on creating mankind. He informs Ea, his*
*father, of his plan to create a savage man to perform the service of the*
*gods; Marduk proposes to divide the gods into two groups. Ea offers a*
*counter proposal: one of the gods shall perish, so that out of his blood*
*mankind can be fashioned. Following the advice of his father, Marduk*
*calls the Assembly; the great gods have to decide who from among them*
*shall be put to death. Marduk asks the gods to declare on oath who was*
*responsible for Tiamat's uprising.*

*Kingu is found to be guilty of it, and so he is killed; out of his blood*
*mankind is fashioned. On the latter is imposed the service of the gods.*
*Afterwards Marduk executes his plan to divide the gods into two groups:*
*three hundred gods he assigns to the earth, three hundred gods to the*
*heaven; to all of them he assigns a position.*

In Mesopotamian tradition it was Ea who created mankind. The
purpose of the present poem being the glorification of Marduk, it seemed
necessary for the Babylonian clergy to assign a decisive role to Ea's son
in the creation of mankind. Thus Ea merely executes Marduk's supreme
idea. The statements concerning the gods are rather confused in this
passage; it is possible that the Assembly comprises also the gods who
had formerly rallied to Tiamat and who were afterwards charged with
the service of the victorious gods. Their common guilt is then imposed
on Kingu, their leader (apparently on Ea's advice), and the other gods
go free: it is mankind now who is charged with the service of the gods.

The terms *"Igigi"* and *"Anunnaki"* are used indifferently for all the
gods without distinction between lower and higher, vanquished and

victorious deities, and Marduk states expressly that both groups are to be alike revered.

The condemnation of Kingu is not a personal decision of the highest god, but the verdict of the whole Assembly, who utter their accusation under oath. The omnipotence of Marduk is therefore limited by the decision of the assembly. However, since the present poem has been devised for the glorification of Marduk, the assembly is always described as in perfect accordance with Marduk's decrees.

*The gods propose to show Marduk their gratitude for their deliverance by building a sanctuary for him. Marduk chooses Babylon as the site of his abode, and thus the gods set to work.*

*In two years they build the* Esagila[21] *with shrines for Marduk, Enlil, and Ea, and for each of the Anunnaki. When the construction of the temple is finished, the gods celebrate the event with a festive banquet. The fifty great gods take their seats, and the seven gods of destiny assign their stations to the three hundred celestial gods.*

In this passage we encounter different groups of gods, corresponding to the sacred numbers 3, 7, and 50. The "three great gods" here are Marduk, Enlil, and Ea. Enlil is now at Marduk's side, but he has displaced Anu, whose name is not mentioned in this episode: there can be only three, not four, gods at the head of the pantheon. The "seven great gods" are not individually named; they are probably identical with the "seven gods" of the Etana myth (see below).

Equally unnamed are the "fifty great gods." The number 50 is the symbol of Enlil,[22] who was probably the hero of the combat against Tiamat in an older, perhaps Sumerian, version. The same number becomes now the symbol of Marduk, virtually the successor of the pre-Babylonian national god.

*Enlil shows to the other gods his bow and his net. Anu praises the bow, kissing it and proclaiming it his daughter, and he gives it three names. The bow is assigned a place among the gods in the Assembly, and Anu decrees the fate of the weapon.*

[21] The name signifies in Sumerian: "Temple of the High Head."

[22] In Mesopotamian mythology, all deities had a sacred number, the motivation for which is obscure (only the number of Sin, which is 30, finds its explanation in the thirty days of the month). To Anu is attributed the supreme number 60, to Ea 40, to Ishtar 15, etc.

This short episode of Enlil's bow seems wholly out of place; it does not contain the name of Marduk and is most probably a remnant of the older, still unexcavated, version in which Enlil was the principal hero.

The bow plays a role also in other Semitic mythologies; in the Ugaritic tale of Aqhat,[23] the goddess Anath slays the youth because he refused to give her his bow, which she coveted. Elohim places his bow (the Hebrew word קשת means the natural phenomenon as well as the weapon) into the sky as the sign of his covenant with Noah.

*The gods assemble and, pronouncing a solemn oath, they accept Marduk's hegemony. Anshar declares the young god's name supreme. He praises Marduk for having caused the blackheaded people to support the gods with food and incense offerings, to tend their sanctuaries, and to improve the cultivation of the lands.*

As already stated at the beginning of the tablet, mankind is created for the sole purpose of serving the gods. The latter are in need of food, as human beings, and of incense, sign of veneration. The "blackheaded people"[24] are the slaves of the gods and have no right to expect any benefit in return.

*The gods pronounce the fifty names of their king:[25] Anshar calls him Marduk, Marukka, and Marutukku; Lahmu calls him Barashakushu, Lugaldimmerankia, and Nari-Lugaldimmerankia; Lahamu calls him Asaruludu, Namtillaku, and Namru. After the "fathers of the gods" have pronounced these nine names, they invite the other deities to do the same, and the latter comply joyfully.*

## Tablet VII

*The gods continue to pronounce the names of Marduk, praising his strength, wisdom, justice, grace, supremacy in battle and in counsel, and his quality of irrigator and provider of crops and pastures; they exalt him as their saviour and sustainer, as the god who vanquished Tiamat and created mankind and the universe.*

The names, which are almost exclusively Sumerian, celebrate more

[23] Text by H. L. Ginsberg, "Ugaritic Myths, Epics, and Legends," *ANET*, 151 ff.

[24] Concerning the adjective "blackheaded," cf. p. 117.

[25] For the interpretation of the fifty names, see F. M. T. Böhl, *Archiv für Orientforschung*, 191.

or less the same qualities, and their meaning is mostly cabalistic and symbolic. Apart from the merits exalted in the poem, Marduk's primitive function as a chthonian deity reappears in the praise, and the functions of irrigator and fertility god are equally attributed to him.

### Epilogue

*May the wise leaders of the congregation recite and explain Marduk's fifty names and pass them on from father to son. May everybody praise Marduk, the "Enlil of the Gods," so that the fields be prosperous. He is almighty and wise, his justice will punish the evildoer.* [The poem ends after a few unintelligible lines.]

The name of Enlil, the original hero of the battle against the primeval monster, is here reduced to a mere title conferred upon Marduk.

The Creation epic centers around Marduk's successful combat against Tiamat; the creation of the universe is only a consequence of this victory, and, contrary to the account in the first chapter of Genesis, there is no *creatio ex nihilo;* Marduk, instead of calling into existence heaven and earth, fashions them from Tiamat's body. Mankind is made from the blood of a slain god; but while in the Old Testament man is the lord of the earth, in Mesopotamian mythology he is merely the slave of the gods.

Besides the poem *"Enuma elish,"* there were other accounts of how the Mesopotamians imagined the origin of the world. They are not complete cosmogonies like the present epic but introductions to incantations, temple rituals, etc. The creation of mankind is attributed to various deities: In a fragment excavated in Abu Habba,[26] Marduk and the goddess Aruru create mankind, before animals and plants. In another fragment, found at Nineveh,[27] mankind is fashioned after the creation of the animals, and the creator is Ea.

In a tablet from Babylon[28] the same god is credited with forming mankind out of clay following the creation of several minor deities. According to a text from the epoch of Hammurabi,[29] Ea makes man-

---

[26] Text published by L. W. King, *Cuneiform Texts,* XIII, pls. 35–38.

[27] *Ibid.,* pls. 34.

[28] R. Campbell Thompson, *Cuneiform Texts* (London, 1903), XVII, pl. 50.

[29] T. G. Pinches, *Cuneiform Texts* (London, 1898), VI, pl. 5.

kind, with the help of the goddess Mami, from the flesh and blood of a slain god mixed with clay. The blood of slain gods is the starting point also in a fragment excavated at Qalat Shergat,[30] in which the creation of mankind is attributed to a group of gods (Anu, Enlil, Ea, and Shamash).

In almost all these texts, even in *"Enuma elish,"* it is Ea who appears as the creator of mankind, either alone or with other deities. The only exception is the fragment of Abu Habba, in which Marduk is said to have fashioned mankind. This is probably due to a simple substitution of the new Babylonian deity for the original Sumerian god Enki or Ea, who is frequently associated with the mother-goddess.

All the Mesopotamian texts coincide in considering man the slave of the gods, created for the sole purpose of tending the sanctuaries and providing food and incense offerings for the deities.

As for the combat between Marduk and Tiamat, there seems to have existed an anterior tradition according to which Enlil was the hero of the fight. But no fragments of such an older version have been preserved. Allusions to a battle between a god and a dragon exist also in other Semitic literatures, as, for example, in the Old Testament,[31] in which Yahweh is several times praised as the victor over Rahab or Leviathan, both mythical animals resembling a serpent or a crocodile. In a Ras Shamra text we find the following verses in a message from Mot to Baal: *"If thou smite Lotan, the serpent slant, Destroy the serpent tortuous, Shalyat of the seven heads . . ."* and Anath, Baal's sister, boasts: "Did I not muzzle the dragon? I did crush the crooked serpent, Shalyat the seven-headed."[32]

The only trace that is to be found in Mesopotamian literature of the combat between a dragon and a god, apart from and perhaps anterior to the poem *"Enuma elish,"* is a text about the slaying of a marine monster called "Labbu"[33] by one of the gods, who in recompense for this deed is awarded the rank of king over the pantheon.

The name of the deity who, after the fruitless attempt of at least one other god,[34] succeeds in slaying the monster[35] is not recognizable

[30] E. Ebeling, *Keilschrifttexte aus Assur religiösen Inhalts,* 4.

[31] Ps. 74:13–14 and 89:10; Isa 27:1 and 51:9; and Job 26:13.

[32] Ginsberg, "Ugaritic Myths, and Legends," *ANET,* 137–38.

[33] King, *Cuneiform Texts,* XIII, pls. 33ff.

in the rather fragmentary text; but since the weapons of the victor are thunder and storm, it may well be Adad, or perhaps even Enlil, the supposed original hero of the Creation epic.

Enlil, who is mentioned at the beginning of the Labbu text as drawing a picture of the dragon in the sky, does not appear as the highest god; the head of the pantheon is here Sin, the moon-god, whose cult is one of the most ancient ones in Mesopotamia.

### The Gilgamesh Epic

This poem[36] is a heroic tale containing, among other episodes, the account of a great Flood which resembles in many respects the Biblical Deluge.

The Gilgamesh epic was highly popular in the ancient Near East, as shown by the existence of translations into Hurrian and Hittite, besides an Old Babylonian and a Neo-Assyrian version, as well as an Akkadian rendering of the tale, current in the Hittite kingdom.[37] The most complete account is the text found in Nineveh;[38] it consists of twelve tablets, the last of which is, however, an almost literal translation from an earlier Sumerian text; apart from the central figure, Gilgamesh, and that of his friend, Enkidu, this last tablet does not appear to have any connection with the Akkadian version. It has therefore been omitted in the discussion of the Semitic text and will be considered at the end of the comment along with other Sumerian fragments of the Gilgamesh story.

From the four Old Babylonian fragments[39] it is apparent that the first composition of the Semitic text is anterior to the turn of the second

34 "Tishpak," main god of Eshnunna.

35 The battle does not precede the Creation of the world, as in *"Enuma elish,"* but takes place after the Labbu has terrorized the cities and their inhabitants.

36 Another title of the epic is according to the first words in Akkadian, *"Sha nagba imuru,"* or "He who saw everything."

37 A portion of this Akkadian version as well as Hurrite and Hittite fragments have been excavated in Boghazköi, the site of the ancient capital of the Hittite empire, Hattusas.

38 In the library of King Ashurbanipal and in the temple of the god Nabu.

39 Fragments 1 and 2, respectively the Pennsylvania and the Yale tablets, have been published by A. Jastrow and A. T. Clay; fragment 3, the Chicago tablet, by T. Bauer, and fragment 4 by B. Meissner.

millennium. The cuneiform text of the different Akkadian versions has been published by:

R. Campbell Thompson, *The Epic of Gilgamish* (Oxford, 1930) (Assyrian version).

M. Jastrow and A. T. Clay, *An Old Babylonian Version of the Gilgamesh Epic* (Yale Oriental Series, Vol. IV), 3 (Old Babylonian version, fragments 1 and 2).

T. Bauer, *"Ein viertes altbabylonisches Fragment des Gilgameš-Epos," JNES* (1957) (Old Babylonian version, fragment 3).

B. Meissner, *"Mitteilungen der Vorderasiatisch-Aegyptischen Gesellschaft,"* VII (1902) (Old Babylonian version, fragment 4).

E. F. Weidner in *"Keilschrifturkunden aus Boghazköi,"* IV (1922) (Akkadian version of Hattusas).

A. Heidel, "A Neo-Babylonian Gilgamesh Fragment," *JNES* (1952).

Since the extant Sumerian portions of the Gilgamesh tale differ considerably from the Akkadian versions,[40] the latter cannot be considered mere translations or adaptations of a Sumerian text but represent an independent poetic creation having little more than the names of the principal protagonists in common with the Sumerian fragments.

## TABLET I

*Gilgamesh acquired supreme wisdom through his journeys from one end of the earth to the other, learned hidden secrets, and brought to his country the report on the great Flood. He engraved his deeds on a stela; he erected the ramparts of Uruk and built the walls of the Eanna temple,[41] works of incomparable beauty and solidity; they are constructed from burnt bricks, and their foundations have been laid by the Seven Sages themselves.[42]*

[40] See S. N. Kramer, "The Epic of Gilgamesh and its Sumerian Sources," *JAOS* Vol. LXIV (January, 1944), 7ff.

[41] The Eanna temple, sanctuary of Anu and Ishtar, held a place of prime importance in Uruk. Eanna ("The House of Heaven") was even the older name of Uruk. The city was, according to the Sumerian king list, built by Enmekar, second king of the dynasty of Eanna and predecessor of Lugalbanda.

[42] See the study about the Seven Sages by Zimmern, *"Die sieben Weisen Babyloniens," ZA,* Vol. XXXV (1923), 151 ff.

Except for an allusion to the journey towards the abode of Utnapishtim—the Babylonian prototype of the Biblical Noah—the achievements of Gilgamesh[43] mentioned in the introductory lines are not illustrated in the poem. The walls of Uruk and of the Eanna temple are supposed to have already been erected before the story begins, and there is no further indication concerning a stela throughout the poem.

The four lines that conclude the short introduction are repeated verbatim at the end of the eleventh tablet, in which Gilgamesh invites Utnapishtim's boatman, Urshanabi, to admire the solid brickwork of the walls that surround Uruk. (The following lines are destroyed, but a Hittite fragment fits in, which acquaints us with the creation of Gilgamesh at the hands of the great gods and with his arrival at Uruk.)

*Gilgamesh is of partly divine (two-thirds) and partly human (one-third) nature. He is endowed with exceptional strength and prowess in battle.*

*Gilgamesh imposes an unbearable burden on the inhabitants of Uruk, day and night, by summoning all the young men and taking possession of maidens and wives, so that the nobles of the city bring their complaint before the gods.*

As in almost all heroic tales, the superior strength and wisdom of the principal personage are attributed to a divine parentage. Here it is the mother of Gilgamesh, Ninsun (first named in a later passage), who is supposed to be a goddess.

Gilgamesh's father is not mentioned in the poem. According to an inscription of the Sumerian King Utu-Hegal (end of the third millennium B.C.), Ninsun's husband was the god Lugalbanda. But nowhere in the present epic does Lugalbanda appear as father of Gilgamesh or as Ninsun's consort; instead, the god is considered the tutelary deity of Gilgamesh.

[43] See, concerning the name of the hero, R. Campbell Thompson, "The Epic of Gilgamish," *Cuneiform Texts*, 8ff.; the only classical writer mentioning the name of Gilgamesh is the Roman polygraph Claudius Aelianus, who, towards the end of the second century A.D., cites the Babylonian hero under the Greek form of Gilgamos in his treatise *The Nature of Animals*: book XII, chapter XXI. After this legend, Gilgamos is the grandson of the Babylonian king Seuechorus (Enemekar, king of Uruk). According to a prophecy, Seuechorus was to lose his kingdom by the hand of his daughter's son; he therefore confined his daughter in the citadel. In spite of this measure, the king's daughter bore a son by an obscure father, and the child, whose name was Gilgamos, grew up to be king of Uruk.

In the Sumerian king list,[44] Lugalbanda is mentioned as a divine shepherd ruling over Uruk before Gilgamesh's immediate predecessor, the god Dumuzi. The same list indicates as father of Gilgamesh a high priest of Kullab, a district of Uruk.

As appears from the discontent of the nobles, there seems to be no means for the elders to exercise any degree of authority in order to bridle the arrogance of the king. Although in the course of the poem[45] a kind of assembly is mentioned several times, its influence seems to be very limited; if the elders express a negative opinion regarding an enterprise planned by Gilgamesh, the King does not heed their advice but does as he pleases. The Mesopotamian assembly at the time of Gilgamesh therefore appears completely destitute of power.

The lament of the nobles probably refers to the recruiting of the young men for labor on the city walls, as well as to Gilgamesh's arrogation of a variant of the *ius primae noctis*.[46] Because of the King's behavior, the elders doubt his quality of "shepherd" over the people of Uruk, but dare not express their opinion to the ruler himself.

*The gods heed the complaint of the city and recount Gilgamesh's ways before Anu. Anu then summons the goddess Aruru, the presumed creatress of Gilgamesh, and asks her to create a counterpart to the King of Uruk, so that the latter may be occupied with fighting against the new creature.*

*Aruru cleans her hands and casts a piece of clay on the steppe:*[47] *thus Enkidu is born. The future companion of Gilgamesh resembles a savage: his body is covered with hair, and the hair on his head sprouts like grain; his garb is that of Sumuqan, the god of cattle; as a wild animal, he subsists on grass and water, and the beasts of the steppe are his companions.*

There seems to be neither a political enemy nor an ambitious neigh-

---

[44] Cf. A. L. Oppenheim, "Babylonian and Assyrian Historical Texts," *ANET*, 266.

[45] As well as in the Sumerian fragment "Gilgamesh and Agga" (text: S. N. Kramer, "Sumerian Myths and Epic Tales," *ANET*, 44ff.)

[46] The Greek hero Heracles, who resembles in many respects his Babylonian ancestor, is likewise described as sexually prodigious. Cf. Brundage, "Herakles the Levantine," *JNES*, Vol. XVII (October, 1958), 225–36.

[47] According to E. A. Speiser, the passage may also be interpreted as "she drew a design on it" or "she spat on it."

bor of Gilgamesh desirous of battling the powerful King of Uruk; therefore the gods plan the creation of a savage man of great strength who is to challenge Gilgamesh.

Although Enkidu is said to be Gilgamesh's image, their likeness is limited to strength alone, for Gilgamesh certainly has neither long hair like a woman, nor a hairy body.

It is possible that Enkidu is quite an independent figure who has not always been connected with Gilgamesh. The indications concerning Enkidu's hair, which "sprouts like Nisaba" (the goddess of grain), and his garb, which is that of Sumuqan (the god of cattle), may be traces of an old tradition that held Enkidu to be a fertility god.

There is perfect concord between Enkidu and the wild beasts; however, it will last only as long as he is in the state of innocence, as we shall see later.

The indication that Enkidu knows neither people nor land is in contrast to a later passage in which it is stated that Enkidu knows the way to Huwawa: "He has seen the way, has trodden the road."

*A hunter meets Enkidu at the watering place and is frightened by the appearance of the savage. The hunter hurries to his father and reports his experience. He complains that Enkidu has hindered him from catching animals: the hunter had found that the traps which he had set were destroyed and that the pits previously dug had been filled in.*

*According to his father's advice, the hunter is to go to Uruk, where the powerful Gilgamesh rules; he shall ask the king to give him a harlot, and with her he is to return to the steppe where the savage man lives. Enkidu, meeting her, will lose his innocence, and his friendly relations with the beasts of the steppe will change immediately.*

Enkidu is here depicted not so much as an ignorant primitive as a friend of the animals. He is not only their playmate but appears as their benefactor by protecting them from the traps and pits of the hunter. It is this intimacy with the wild beasts of the steppe which the latter is to infringe with the help of a woman.

*The hunter acts according to his father's advice. He reports his experience to Gilgamesh* [an exact replica of what he had previously told his father], *and the king reacts in the expected manner: he gives the hunter a harlot to go with him to the place where Enkidu lives.*

155

*After three days of travel, the hunter and the woman arrive in the steppe and wait for Enkidu at the watering place. On the third day he appears; the hunter retires after having given his instructions to the harlot. The woman attracts Enkidu immediately with her charms, and they remain together for six days and seven nights. Then Enkidu experiences the consequences of his new state: the animals flee from him and reject their old companion. His strength is no longer as before; but he has acquired in its stead wisdom and broader understanding,[48] and the woman tells him that he has now become like a god. Enkidu listens attentively to the harlot's proposal of conducting him towards Uruk. When she speaks to him about Gilgamesh, Enkidu is ready to make the king's acquaintance, eager to win a friend.*

The loss of innocence on the part of Enkidu is not considered a downfall from a paradisaical state of grace to the miserable condition of sin but as a progress on the road from primitiveness towards civilization; through the new knowledge the savage becomes godlike.[49]

*Enkidu accepts the invitation to meet Gilgamesh. But though he yearns for a friend, his intentions are all but amicable: he wants to challenge the King and show his superior strength.*

*The harlot then praises Uruk and the Eanna temple,[50] the people clad in festive attire, and the mighty Gilgamesh, resplendent with beauty and vigor. She warns Enkidu that the King of Uruk is stronger than he: Gilgamesh possesses the favor of Shamash, and has been endowed with wisdom by the great gods Anu, Ea, and Enlil.*

*The woman tells Enkidu that, before his arrival in Uruk, Gilgamesh will see him in a dream.*

The brief description of Gilgamesh, as given by the harlot, is limited to the glorification of his radiant youth and exceptional vigor. These features seem to be the only ones that distinguish the King from the other inhabitants of Uruk; no mention is made of further individual details.

The representations of the hero in Mesopotamian pictorial art are

---

[48] The Old Babylonian version does not allude to any of these consequences.
[49] Cf. Gen. 3:22.
[50] In the Old Babylonian version the Eanna is the temple only of Anu, not also of Ishtar.

not similar to each other but always correspond to the racially prominent type of the respective periods.

A wall-relief of the eighth century B.C., excavated in Khorsabad, shows the ruler of Uruk with the beard-dress and costume character-istic of the Neo-Assyrian kings.

A bas-relief of the Old Babylonian time, found at Telloh, depicts Gilgamesh's features as those of the late Sumerian type contaminated by the increasing Semitic preponderance.

On a cylinder seal dating from the third millennium B.C., Gilgamesh appears beardless, in conformity with the Sumerian custom of the early period.[51]

In consideration of the fact that Shamash appears in Mesopotamian mythology as the patron of justice, it is surprising that the god has granted his favor to Gilgamesh, whose tyrannical rule, as mentioned at the beginning of the tablet, exasperates his subjects. It is true that Shamash, throughout the poem, holds the role of Gilgamesh's tutelary deity[52] rather than that of god of justice.

It is to be noted that nowhere in the poem is the name of Marduk mentioned; this fact confirms the assumption that the composition of the epic goes back to a time preceding the epoch of the first dynasty of Babylon.

*Gilgamesh tells his mother two dreams: In the first one he saw a star descending upon him, so heavy that he could not remove it. All the people were gathered about it, and Gilgamesh himself felt an attraction towards the star as if it were a woman; he brought it to his mother. Ninsun interprets the dream at once, predicting her son's encounter with a future comrade. In the second dream Gilgamesh beheld an axe of singular shape in the street of Uruk, and he loved it as if it were a woman. Once more Ninsun foresees that Gilgamesh will meet a comrade.*

The episode of the two dreams is incorporated into the scene be-tween Enkidu and the harlot as a juxtaposition in the Old Babylonian version, as a digression in the Assyrian version. The detail that Gilga-

[51] Cf. the stone vase of Warka, the chest from the royal tomb of Ur, etc.

[52] As such might be considered also, though in a much lesser degree, the god Lugal-banda.

mesh feels, towards the object representing Enkidu, an attraction as if the latter were a woman, is perhaps an allusion to a particular aspect of the relationship which will arise between the two friends,[53] paralleling I Sam. 20:30, concerning the friendship between David and Jonathan.

## TABLET II[54]

*The harlot clothes Enkidu with a part of her garment and leads him to a group of shepherds. Here Enkidu is fed with bread[55] and the men give him strong drink. At first he stares at these aliments which he has never tasted; the harlot encourages him to partake of bread and strong drink,[56] as is the custom of the land, and Enkidu follows her suggestion. He eats bread until he is sated and drinks seven[57] goblets of strong drink. He becomes cheerful and merry, and the process of civilization continues: he anoints himself with oil and puts on proper clothing. Enkidu then takes his weapon and chases the wild beasts that threaten the sheepfold, thus allowing the herdsmen to rest.* [Break of about 13 lines.]

One might infer from the first lines that the garb which Enkidu wore before he met the harlot, and which was like that of Sumuqan, did not consist of skins (he obviously did not kill the animals who were his companions) but was simply the shaggy growth on his body. Clothing appears, therefore, as another step towards humanization. The taking of strong drink apparently does not provoke inebriation in Enkidu; he only feels in high spirits and wishes to go on with his transformation

---

[53] Cf. also Enkidu's words in the Sumerian fragment incorporated into the Akkadian text as tablet "XII "My body . . . which thou didst touch as thy heart rejoiced, vermin devour as though an old garment" (Speiser, *ANET*, 99).

[54] The Assyrian version of this tablet is very fragmentary, but the narration can be restored from an Old Babylonian fragment (the Pennsylvania tablet) that repeats in the beginning the two dreams of Gilgamesh and then the six days and seven nights which Enkidu passes with the harlot.

[55] It is dubious whether the Mesopotamians used, at the beginning of history, bread in the form of cakes; since this particular food was measured according to capacity instead of weight or number, it is to be supposed that it resembled a kind of polenta. Cf. G. Contenau, *La vie quotidienne à Babylone et en Assyrie*, 77.

[56] G. Contenau interprets the term as "beer."

[57] The figure seven is meant to express a great quantity, rather than the exact number (cf. Matt. 18:22: "Seventy times seven").

into a human being. The act of anointing himself seems to be the final step towards civilization.

Enkidu's attitude respecting the animals has radically changed: while he had been their ally, helping them to escape the hunter, he now meets them with a weapon, chasing them away from the sheepfold. He thus performs a primitive duty incumbent on kings, who had to protect the flock against the attacks of wild beasts.[58]

*Enkidu, while on his way to Uruk, sees a man, and the harlot asks the man where he is going. The man answers with another complaint about the arrogant Gilgamesh, who has penetrated into the community house and imposed on the unfortunate city the* ius primae noctis. *The man says that this right of Gilgamesh's derives from the decree of the gods, who accorded him this privilege on the day of his birth. Enkidu turns white at such news.*[59] [Break of about 9 lines.]

The privileges of the king are incontestable because they have been allotted by divine decree. Therefore Gilgamesh's authority is absolute, and his subjects, though discontented with his conduct, do not rebel against the king's decisions.

As is apparent from the account of the man, the Mesopotamians believed that the destiny of a mortal was decreed on the day of his birth, precisely at the moment when the child was severed definitely from its mother.

*Enkidu enters Uruk with the harlot behind him. The people gather around him, as Gilgamesh had foreseen in his dreams. They compare the stranger, who had been wont to suck the milk of wild beasts, with their king and expect that a continuing combat will ensue after the encounter between Enkidu and Gilgamesh. When the latter approaches the community house*[60] *where the nuptial feast has been prepared, Enkidu bars the street that leads to the entrance. Both fight so hard that the doorpost is shattered and the walls shaken. Gilgamesh eventually subdues Enkidu, and his anger gives way. Enkidu praises Gilgamesh because of his superiority, hailing him as the only son of Ninsun, the wild cow, and the two heroes become friends.*

[58] See Chapter II above.

[59] Cf. G. Dossin, *La pâleur d'Enkidu* (Louvain, 1931).

[60] Cf. the relative study of Thorkild Jacobsen in *Acta Orientalia*, Vol. VIII (1929), 70 ff.

While admiring Enkidu's strength, the inhabitants stress the fact that the savage had fed on the milk of wild beasts. The creed that animal milk endowed a child with superhuman strength is still apparent in the myths of Remus and Romulus and the Germanic Sigurd.

Enkidu addresses Gilgamesh as the only son of Ninsun,[61] not mentioning the father of the king. It is possible that the importance given to the mother of Gilgamesh throughout the poem—in the Old Babylonian as well as in the Assyrian version—points to a remnant of matriarchate.[62] The derivation of Gilgamesh's divine nature from his maternal, instead of paternal, parentage also speaks for such an assumption.[63]

As the mother of the king, Ninsun occupies an elevated position in the kingdom of Uruk, and to her alone Gilgamesh pays respect and reverence. She lives in a palace of her own, and Gilgamesh—as we shall see—humbly begs admission when wishing to enter the abode of his mother.

## TABLET III

[The beginning of this tablet is destroyed; it probably introduces Gilgamesh's project to slay Huwawa, "the guardian of the Holy Cedar."]

*Enkidu is afraid of Huwawa; his eyes fill with tears, and he feels as if all strength had left him. But Gilgamesh insists on his plan to kill Huwawa. He wants his friend to accompany him and help him with the slaying of the monstrous guardian[64] so that all evil may be banished from the land. Enkidu warns him against the dreadful Huwawa, de-*

---

[61] The frequent comparison of Ninsun with a cow and of Gilgamesh with a wild ox in the poem derives from a mythical background of ancient religious conceptions centering around bovine deities. Parallels are to be found in Ugaritic myths, in which the god El is called "bull El"; the maiden Anath announces to Baal that a wild ox has been born to him. In Exod. 32:4, the apostate Hebrews adore an idol in the form of a calf. Examples of bovine deities are to be found also in Egyptian and Greek mythology.

[62] Another trace of matriarchate may be seen in the Sumerian admonition: "To the word of your mother, as to the word of your God, pay heed." Text in J. J. A. van Dijk, *La sagesse suméro-accadienne* (Leyden, 1953).

[63] For traditions of matriarchate in other Semitic people, see W. R. Smith, *Kinship and Marriage in Early Arabia* (London, 1903).

[64] The guardian's name is Huwawa in the Old Babylonian, Hittite, and also in the Sumerian versions; "Humbaba" in the Assyrian text.

*scribing the terrible risk of such an enterprise; he knows by experience the forest where Huwawa resides; he cautions Gilgamesh against the monster's deadly power and against his hypersensitive ear, which perceives the slightest noise at a distance of many leagues. Huwawa has been appointed by the god Enlil to guard the Holy Cedar, and everybody approaching the forest will be bereaved of his strength.*

It is generally assumed that the region of the "Forest of the Cedar" is identical with the Anti-Lebanon west of Babylonia. However, there are also reasons for believing that the original residence of Huwawa was situated in Elam, east of Mesopotamia.

Nowhere does the text warrant the assumption that the forest consisted only of cedars (see also below); such a fact would have justified the interpretation that Gilgamesh was guided in his campaign by the rather practical purpose of obtaining a quantity of precious cedarwood for his country. The cedars of the Lebanon and the Anti-Lebanon were indeed in great demand throughout the Near East and highly esteemed in the countries where the only trees were palms, which furnished wood of much inferior quality. But in the case of Gilgamesh there is only one cedar mentioned,[65] and its sacred character is stressed to such a degree that the enterprise seems to have a mythical rather than a practical purpose. It is possible that the forest included all kinds of trees and that there was only one cedar which was considered sacred; Huwawa had expressly been stationed in the forest to be the guardian of the Cedar.

The cuneiform sign ▜🏳 renders the name of Susa, capital of Elam. The sign, pronounced *SUH-erin*ki ("the Land of the Foundation of the Cedar"), stands also for the tree-god "Shushinak," chief deity of Elam.

It is therefore not certain that Gilgamesh's journey was to the west; there are many reasons favoring the hypothesis that the original abode of Huwawa was located in the mountainous region of Elam, oldest adversary of Sumer.[66]

The noble reason which Gilgamesh mentions as motivation of his project, namely to banish all evil from the land, seems without foun-

---

[65] Speiser assumes for the singular a collective sense: Heidel and other Assyriologists prefer the literal meaning of the singular.

[66] Cf. Chapter I above, p. 31.

dation, at least according to the extant text. No destructive activity is signalized on the part of Huwawa, and in all probability he does not exercise oppression over the land of Uruk. Moreover, the slaying of Huwawa and the felling of the Cedar will later be considered a grave offense, and the gods decree a severe punishment for Gilgamesh and Enkidu.

It is possible that Shamash, the personal god of Gilgamesh, is an adversary of Enlil, the master of Huwawa. Gilgamesh therefore justifies his combat against the monster by alluding to an obscure wrong on Huwawa's part, which demands reparation in order to satisfy Shamash, god of justice.

*Gilgamesh encourages Enkidu to overcome his fear of Huwawa. He expresses his disdain of death and his desire to make a name for himself. Human life is bound to be of limited duration; only the gods are immortal; but the glory of a heroic deed will last far beyond the lifespan of his own offspring. Enkidu, impressed by Gilgamesh's words, agrees to accompany the king and fell the Holy Cedar.*

*The two heroes therefore proceed to prepare heavy weapons for their enterprise. Skillful artisans cast axes weighing three talents, swords with blades of two talents, knobs of thirty minas, and golden sheaths of thirty minas. All in all, Gilgamesh and Enkidu carry weapons of ten talents' weight.*[67]

Gilgamesh's view of death in this passage stands in sharp contrast to the tragic despair expressed later at the death of his friend. Here he does not care for his life; only the glory of his name is important. Gilgamesh accepts as a matter of fact that the gods allotted mortality to mankind and is satisfied with the eternal duration of his fame.

Since the weapons of the two heroes are "cast," they probably are made of bronze: the story was set down long before iron was used for armaments.

*Gilgamesh and Enkidu present themselves to the populace of Uruk and proclaim their desire to vanquish Hawawa and fell the Holy Cedar.*

---

[67] Each talent consisted of sixty minas, one mina being about the equivalent of a pound. The sum of the indicated measures is inferior to the total mentioned in the poem; the heroes probably carried still other weapons, or there were more than one axe or sword to each of them.

*The elders advise against such a dangerous enterprise. But since Gilgamesh insists, the elders recommend Gilgamesh to his god and express their wish for his safe return. Gilgamesh prays to Shamash asking him for his protection.*

The role of the elders is without moment; Gilgamesh does not heed their advice. The relationship between the king and the assembly of Uruk resembles that between the king and the "old men's" counsel in I Kings 12:13; but, unlike Rehoboam, Gilgamesh shows a filial respect for the elders, even while he decides not to take their advice.

In the Assyrian version, it is not Gilgamesh who prays to Shamash, but Ninsun, the king's divine mother. Gilgamesh and Enkidu enter the queen's palace, and Gilgamesh explains his enterprise to his mother, asking her to pray to Shamash in his behalf. The queen thereupon clothes herself in a special garment and dons her tiara. Then she mounts to the parapet of the temple[68] and offers incense to Shamash. Her prayer begins with a reproach to the god for having incited Gilgamesh to undertake the dangerous enterprise; then she asks Shamash to assist her son during his campaign.[69] After the prayer, Ninsun calls Enkidu and adopts him with the priestesses and hierodules of Gilgamesh,[70] placing an object around his neck; this probably signifies the elevation of Enkidu to a superior rank.

[There is a small break in the text, probably with the interpretation of an omen which seems to be unfavorable.]

*Gilgamesh is seized with fear; his heart fails him, and tears run down his face. He considers that he does not know the road and that the issue of his combat against Huwawa is all but certain. But he recovers quickly from his dejection and dons his arms.*

*The people gather around the two heroes, wishing the king a safe return. The elders warn Gilgamesh once more and counsel him to let his friend go before him, so that he be shielded. They wish him good*

---

[68] See the indications concerning the *ziqqurat*, pp. 127–28.

[69] During the nocturnal absence of the sun-god, Ninsun invokes the help of Aya, Shamash's bride. For Shamash's absence during the night, cf. also "Prayer to the Gods of the Night." Text published by V. K. Shileiko, *Izvestija Rossijskoj Akademii Istorii Material'noj Kul'tury*, III (Leningrad, 1924), 147.

[70] See note 53 above.

*luck and recommend that he wash his feet after having slain Huwawa,
dig a well each night, and pray to Shamash and Lugalbanda.*[71]

*Enkidu then speaks to Gilgamesh, encouraging the king to follow
him without fear, since he, Enkidu, knows the road towards Huwawa.
The elders confide Gilgamesh to Enkidu, asking him to deliver the
king back to the assembly after his adventure. Thus Gilgamesh sets out
with his companion for his combat against Huwawa.*

The recommendation of the elders regarding the washing of the
feet seems to refer to some ritual act of purification, perhaps an atonement for the planned slaying of Huwawa. The digging of a well is
meant for an offering of fresh water to Shamash.

## TABLET IV[72]

*In three days the two heroes, walking fifty leagues every day, traverse
the distance which would take an ordinary traveler one and one-half
months. Towards noon they eat a light meal, and during the night they
rest. Following the counsel of the elders in Uruk, they dig a well for
Shamash. Gilgamesh then offers flour to the mountain, asking the latter
for a favorable dream.*

This part of the text is known through two small Babylonian fragments found in Warka, where the account of the journey is apparently
repeated three times, perhaps to illustrate the duration of the three days.

The mountain to which Gilgamesh offers the flour is probably considered divine; this may be the remnant of an ancient religious conception that included the cult of stones, or there may be a connection
between the mountain of the Cedar and the Primeval Hill of Egyptian
mythology.[73] The contents of the dream is not known, since the fragment breaks off.

*Gilgamesh appears to be in a state of despondency, having seen
Huwawa's watchman who guards the gate of entrance. But Enkidu encourages his friend by reminding him of his words to the people of Uruk
before the departure. Thereupon Gilgamesh is inspired once more with*

[71] Oppenheim, "Babylonian and Assyrian Historical Texts," *ANET*, 266.

[72] There are only fragments of this and the following tablets, partly in Assyrian,
partly in Babylonian, and also in Hittite. The sequence of these fragments is not certain.

[73] Cf. Chapter III above, n. 77.

*courage. He decides to attack the watchman, who has just clothed him-*
*self with the first of his seven cloaks.* [A break follows, and in the missing
portion it was probably stated that the two heroes kill Huwawa's watchman and open the gate which leads to the forest of the Cedar.]

As already noted in the Creation epic, the advice of the king's friend
is of decisive importance in Mesopotamian hierarchy.[74] The seven cloaks
of the watchman are probably garments of magical efficacy that confer
on their wearer an invulnerability which decreases progressively with
each cloak he takes off.

*On touching the gate that opens Huwawa's realm, Enkidu's hand*
*becomes limp, his strength forsakes him. Now it is Enkidu who wants*
*to turn back, but Gilgamesh encourages his friend to pursue. He ad-*
*monishes Enkidu to touch his garment, and the fear of death will vanish.*
*Enkidu shall forget death; even if they fall, they will have made a*
*glorious name for themselves. So they continue and arrive at the green*
*mountain, where Huwawa resides.*

Gilgamesh's garment, like the seven cloaks of the watchman, seems
to possess a talismanic power, since on touching it, Enkidu regains
strength and confidence. We encounter once more Gilgamesh's view of
death—he considers death a matter of little importance. There is, in the
whole episode, no trace of the despair shown later by Gilgamesh when
confronted with the idea of death. In tablets III–IV he accepts death as
a necessity of human existence, but in tablets VII–XI, after the decease
of Enkidu, he never ceases to rebel against the decree of the gods who
retained immortality in their own hands.

### Tablet V[75]

*Gilgamesh and Enkidu arrive in front of the forest; they gaze at*
*the Cedar which stands on a mountain that is the dwelling place of the*
*gods, the throne-seat of Ishtar;[76] they admire the beauty and abundant*
*shade of the lofty tree.* [The text breaks off.]

[74] Cf. Chapter II above, pp. 82–83.

[75] See note 72 above.

[76] The cuneiform sign ⟨sign⟩ corresponding to the name of the goddess, is identical
with another spelling of Susa, the capital of Elam: *nin₂ ERIN-ki* (the Land of the Gate of
the Cedar).

165

It is clear from the passage that the Cedar had a sacred character[77] and that the mountain where it grew was an important place of worship. Perhaps the cult of the cedar[78] is a reminiscence of an ancient antagonism between the lands of Sumer and of Elam[79] with a religious background.

The Cedar Mountain is here expressly described as a sanctuary of the gods, and Gilgamesh's pretext for slaying Huwawa ("to banish all evil from the land") seems to lack all foundation. Mesopotamian religion does not mention a pronounced enmity between Shamash, tutelary god of Gilgamesh, and Enlil, master of the forest of the Cedar. It is possible that in an older version it was Shushinak, tree-god of Elam,[80] who was the lord of the Cedar and the rival of the Sumerian sun-god Utu.[81]

*Gilgamesh dreams[82] that a mountain falls upon him but that a man full of grace saves and refreshes him. Enkidu interprets the dream favorably, as a token that the two heroes will vanquish Huwawa. A third dream comes upon Gilgamesh, showing him a frightful thunderstorm with flames and lightning; at last the fire is extinguished, and everything turns to ashes.*

The "man full of grace" is obviously Shamash, who, in fact, will assist Gilgamesh in his combat against Huwawa and save him from the monster. (The account of the battle between Huwawa and the two friends has not been preserved in the Assyrian version; only the last line of a mutilated fragment informs us that the two heroes cut down Huwawa's head.)

*According to a fragment of the Hittite version, Gilgamesh fells the*

---

[77] Traces of such a conception are still to be found in the Arabic language, where the Cedar, in some regions, is called "Tree of Allah" الله‎ شجرة‎ .

[78] See Chapter II above, p. 60; note also the role of cedarwood in the New Year's festival, where a statue holding in its hand a serpent of cedarwood is solemnly decapitated on the third day of the Akitu. A bundle of cedarwood is an important instrument in Mesopotamian divination.

[79] Cf. Chapter I above, p. 31.

[80] Cf. p. 161 above, concerning the cuneiform equivalent of the god's name.

[81] In the Sumerian version, Utu, is the tutelary god of Gilgamesh as well as the caretaker of the forest. The role of Enlil, whose name appears only at the end of the fragment, is not clear.

[82] The text implies that the dream was preceded by another one, the contents of which is not preserved in the extant fragments.

*trees of the grove, and then the holy Cedar, thereby attracting Huwawa's attention. Offended by Gilgamesh's act, Huwawa approaches the hero and presses him so hard that the latter calls to Shamash[83] for help. The god sends eight winds to Gilgamesh's rescue, and Huwawa is now unable to move. He asks his conqueror to spare his life and offers to become Gilgamesh's servant; he will build houses for the king from the trees of the forest. But Enkidu advises against any gesture of generosity, and, as the last line of the Assyrian fragment implies, both the heroes proceed to cut Huwawa's head.*

*In an Old Babylonian fragment belonging to the Oriental Institute of Chicago, the facts are related in a different sequence. The heroes try first of all to slay the dangerous Huwawa, who is provided with a crown of rays, probably of magical efficacy. Before beginning his combat with Huwawa, Gilgamesh worries that the rays will be extinguished as soon at Huwawa is killed, and then the forest will be wrapped in utter darkness. Enkidu tells Gilgamesh not to bother, the rays will continue to glow after Huwawa is slain. The two friends then kill Huwawa (the first blow is dealt by Gilgamesh, the second by Enkidu; the author of the third blow, the decisive one, is not recognizable, but it seems that the major responsibility for the act reverts to Enkidu). Thereupon the Cedar, who is considered a living creature, sets up a lament, and the whole forest trembles with horror at the sacrilegious action of the two heroes.[84] Gilgamesh and Enkidu then proceed to "open the abode of the Anunnaki," obviously a sacred grove, in the center of which stands the Cedar. Gilgamesh fells the trees of the grove, while Enkidu digs out the roots.[85] At last the Holy Cedar is "slain,"[86] and presumably carried to Uruk.*

Therewith ends the episode of the combat against Huwawa. There is no further allusion to the fate of the Cedar in the whole poem. Per-

---

[83] In the Hittite version, Shamash has throughout the epithet "heavenly," perhaps in contrast to another solar deity, belonging to the Nether World, such as Nergal.

[84] The text contains here a mutilated allusion to seven beings or objects which Gilgamesh slays, apparently with his sword.

[85] This detail seems to confirm that the purpose of the felling of the trees was purely mythical. Enkidu takes the precaution of rooting out completely the grove that surrounded the Cedar.

[86] Cf. Chapter II above, note 51.

haps there was once a connection between the episode of Gilgamesh's combat against the guardian of the Cedar and the Sumerian legend "Gilgamesh and the Huluppu Tree,"[87] in which a certain tree is mentioned which, while floating on the Euphrates, is seized by Ishtar, who plants it in her garden in Uruk; Gilgamesh obliges the goddess by freeing the tree from a serpent and the grateful Ishtar offers him two objects made of the wood of this tree.[88]

## TABLET VI

*Gilgamesh, having washed his hair and changed his soiled clothes, appears in all his beauty; the goddess Ishtar falls in love with him and offers to become his wife. She promises him gifts, honors, and abundance of flocks. But Gilgamesh has only disdain for Ishtar's offer. The advantages outlined by the goddess are nothing in comparison with the obligations which a husband has towards his wife: food and drink, clothing, and oil for ointment he has to provide for her. Then Gilgamesh reproaches the goddess for her well-known inconstancy and wickedness; he names, one after the other, her lovers, all of whom met an ill fate after she abandoned them:*

*For Tammuz, the young shepherd, Ishtar decreed annual wailings; of the shepherd bird, her next lover, the goddess broke a wing; Ishtar then loved a lion, but afterwards dug pits for him; she loved a horse, but made it suffer by whip and spur; another shepherd was turned into a wolf, though he offered Ishtar cakes and meat day after day; finally, the goddess had set her eyes on her father's gardener, Ishullanu. He, however, refused to accept Ishtar's love, so the angry goddess turned him into a mole.*

*Gilgamesh, remembering all these deeds, does not want to be another victim of Ishtar's volatility and rejects her offer.*

This last passage seems to be a summary of several legends connected with Ishtar. According to the present account, the goddess ap-

---

[87] See the monograph by S. N. Kramer (Philadelphia, 1938). The second part of the Sumerian legend had been translated into Akkadian and forms the twelfth tablet of the Gilgamesh epic.

[88] A *"pukku"* and a *"mikku,"* probably a drum and a drumstick of magical potencies, which later fell into the Nether World (see below).

parently did not bemoan Tammuz, but provoked in some way the yearly wailings over the dead god. This attitude, while in contradiction to legends such as "Inanna and Bilulu,"[89] coincides with the behavior of the goddess in the myth of her "Descent to the Nether World," in which she hands Tammuz pitilessly over to the demons of the *Arallu* as her own ransom price.[90]

The second legend, concerning the shepherd bird, is based on a word play: the plaintive cry of the bird is rendered as *"ḳappi,"* which means in Akkadian "my wing."

The last instance lacks a logical connection with the taunt intended for Ishtar. Ishullanu had been transformed, not after the goddess had abandoned him, but after he had refused to accept Ishtar's love. A similar misfortune would have been likely to happen to Gilgamesh, since he reacts to Ishtar's proposal in much the same way as had done Ishullanu.

*Enraged at Gilgamesh's refusal, Ishtar asks her father, Anu, to create the Bull of Heaven to smite the insolent Gilgamesh. Anu, instead of showing indignation at Gilgamesh's disdain, reproves his daughter for her behavior and hesitates to do her bidding. He warns Ishtar that if the Bull of Heaven descends, there will be seven years of famine. Ishtar assures her father that she has provided grain for the people and grass for the beasts to last over the barren period.* [Anu seems to have agreed at last to create the Bull of Heaven; the account of the god's decision is lost in a break.] *The animal descends and ḳills a hundred men at every snort. Enḳidu, who is attacked by the third snort of the Bull, seizes the animal by its horns.* [The details of the ensuing battle are unknown, since this part of the text is badly mutilated. The Bull seems to have been slain by both the heroes.] *They tear out the animal's heart and place it before Shamash.*

Ishtar does not cut a good figure in this episode. Although she is one of the deities in the Eanna temple, her role in the epic is decidedly negative. The reason for such a description of the principal Mesopotamian goddess may be some religious rivalry between Ishtar

[89] Text and comment by Kramer and Jacobsen, *JNES*, Vol. XII (July, 1953), 160–87.

[90] See S. N. Kramer, *ANET*, 52, n. 6; cf. also the obscure lines at the end of the Akkadian myth "Ishtar's Descent to the Nether World" (see below), in which the goddess expresses a kind of fear at the hearing of Tammuz' flute announcing the god's return to the upper world.

and Shamash. The latter is, except for Lugalbanda, the only deity whom Gilgamesh worships in his prayers,[91] although Uruk's greatest sanctuary is dedicated to Anu and, later on, to Ishtar.[92] The singular position of Shamash has been seen already in the Huwawa episode, in which Gilgamesh, by executing Shamash's command, mortally offends Enlil. The fact that Gilgamesh has plain contempt for Ishtar but offers the Bull's heart on Shamash's altar[93] seems to indicate another instance of religious rivalry.

*Ishtar curses Gilgamesh for what has happened to the Bull of Heaven. Thereupon Enkidu tears out the animal's right thigh and flings it into the goddess' face, shouting that he would gladly do to her what he has done to the Bull. Ishtar assembles all the women belonging to the temple[94] and sets up a lamentation over the right thigh of the Bull. Gilgamesh calls his craftsmen, who admire the animal's horns cast from thirty minas[95] of lapis lazuli. The king hangs both horns in his bedchamber after having offered to his god Lugalbanda a quantity of oil corresponding to their capacity.*

*The two heroes wash their hands in the Euphrates and ride together through the street of Uruk. Gilgamesh asks the lyre maids for the name of the most splendid hero, and the girls answer that it is Gilgamesh. After a banquet in the royal palace, the two friends go to sleep. Enkidu dreams that in heaven the great gods have assembled, and, frightened by the vision, he asks Gilgamesh the reason for the divine council.*

The act of washing their hands is most probably a symbolical gesture meant as a propitiation for the slaying of the Bull of Heaven.[96] The ride through the town of Uruk[97] is a kind of triumphal procession glorifying only Gilgamesh, without any allusion to Enkidu. It seems

[91] In tablet IX he prays to Sin, the moon-god, during the night.

[92] See p. 156 above, n. 50.

[93] In several Sumerian myths, Utu (Shamash) is the brother of Inanna (Ishtar).

[94] The Ishtar women consisted of both prostitutes and votaries; actually, such a distinction between the personnel of a temple is visible also in Assyrian and Babylonian laws, which imply that there was a class of virgin priestesses who concluded only formal marriages and provided their husbands with other women to bear them children.

[95] See n. 67 above for the equivalent of this measure.

[96] The Assyrian King Ashburbanipal pours a libation over the lions which he has slain as an atonement for having taken their lives.

[97] Cf. Luke 19:35–38.

that in ancient times panegyric was the task of women only. Another example of women's proclaiming a hero's glory by their chants is to be found in I Sam. 18:6–7, which tells of the women of Israel celebrating in song the exploits of David.

## TABLET VII[98]

*Enkidu relates his dream to Gilgamesh: the great gods hold council, in consideration of the deeds of the two heroes. Anu decides that the feller of the Holy Cedar must die as an atonement for the slaying of the Bull of Heaven and of Huwawa.[99] Enlil proposes that Enkidu be the one who shall suffer death, while Gilgamesh is to be spared. Shamash, however, defends both heroes, who did but execute his own command, and remonstrates against the decree of the great gods. Enlil reproves Shamash for his familiarity with the mortals, and Enkidu is condemned to death.*

We meet once more an example of discord among the gods. Enlil, national god of Sumer, stands against Shamash, tutelary deity of Gilgamesh. The sun-god is not connected with Uruk, since the great temple of the city is dedicated exclusively to Anu and Ishtar. The Semitic name of the deity might suggest that Shamash was a usurper in the country of Sumer, as Gilgamesh was a usurper of the throne of Uruk. Although it is by no means established that Gilgamesh was a Semite, it may be supposed that the worship of Shamash had been introduced in Uruk by Gilgamesh.

The decree of the gods follows the ancient custom of the royal substitute: whenever a danger or an unfavorable presage threatened the king, he was temporarily replaced by the person next to him in rank; if the menace persisted or the oracle predicted the king's death, the substitute was immolated in order to save the sovereign's life.

It is to be noted that, of all the deeds committed by the two friends and judged as offenses, the worst crime seems to have been the "slaying" of the Cedar.

*Gilgamesh bemoans his friend, whom he calls his brother. The*

---

98 The first part of this tablet, dealing with Enkidu's dream, has been preserved only in a Hittite rendering.

99 Note the inversion of the two exploits.

*thought of the fatal separation which Enkidu's death would bring causes anguish and dismay in Gilgamesh's heart.*

Here, before the cruel prospect of losing his friend, Gilgamesh changes his view of death. As yet, he is concerned only with Enkidu's imminent death and the consequent solitude for himself. Only after Enkidu has really left him will Gilgamesh be seized by the idea of the ineluctability of man's destiny and by a desperate anxiety for his own life.

[The narration is resumed here by the Assyrian fragment of the tablet.]

*Enkidu, prostrate on his deathbed, recalls with bitterness the events that have led to his present sad condition. He remembers the beauty of the gate at the entrance to the forest of Huwawa, made of choice wood by a craftsman of Nippur.*[100] *If he had known the sequel of their adventure, he would have shattered*[101] *the door.* [Here occurs a gap of about fifty lines.]

*Enkidu asks Shamash to bring misfortune upon the hunter who first beheld Enkidu on the steppe. Continuing his survey, he curses the harlot who introduced him to civilization. He decrees it her fate to dwell in the road, in the shadow of a wall, and the passers-by shall smite her cheek. But Shamash, patron of justice, reproves Enkidu for his rash curse, reminding him of the benefits of his encounter with the woman: she had made him eat bread and drink wine and had clothed him and given him Gilgamesh for a companion. The god recalls the honors conferred upon Enkidu by Gilgamesh; the king made him lie on a splendid couch and assigned to him the seat at his own left. Gilgamesh will have all Uruk weep for Enkidu, and will himself don the garb of mourning.*

The curse against the harlot implies the importance of a sheltered abode in the ancient Near East, where nomadism was a frequent mode of existence. The malediction does not refer to the harlot's particular profession, but is a general ill wish which may be directed against any

---

[100] City where the god Enlil is worshiped. In the cult of Nippur an important role was held by the Holy Cedar. Cf. the *"Kult-Kalender"* of B. Landsberger in *Der kultische Kalender* (*Leipziger Semitistische Studien*, Vol. VI, Leipzig, 1915), 28.

[101] The translation of this verb is not certain; it seems in fact surprising that Enkidu should have considered such a measure as preventive of the final disaster.

person. The same curse, for example, is uttered against Asushunamir by Ereshkigal, in "Ishtar's Descent to the Nether World."[102]

The essence of Shamash's exhortation is that Enkidu should not regret having abandoned his primitive existence and not bemoan the premature end of his life but, rather, consider the honors that have been conferred upon him by Gilgamesh, and will still be conferred upon him after his death. Honor and glory are esteemed more than mere physical existence. The spirit of Shamash's argument is the same as that of Gilgamesh's challenge when he sets out to slay Huwawa: the glory of a heroic deed will last far longer than life itself.[103]

*Enkidu admits Shamash's arguments and changes his curse against the harlot into a blessing: he wishes that she may win the love of princes and be preferred to legitimate wives who have borne many children. Upon the man who had defiled her shall descend poverty and misery. May the priest let her enter the temple and admit her to the presence of the gods.*

The woman who brought Enkidu to Uruk apparently does not belong to the class of hierodules attached to the Ishtar temples in Mesopotamia, since there is no allusion to any sacred function of the harlot in the whole epic. The last part of Enkidu's benediction seems to imply rather that an ordinary prostitute was not allowed to appear before the divine statues of the temples. Her encounter with Enkidu on the steppe is purely secular and has nothing to do with the ritual background of the ἱερὸς γάμος [104] which was extensively practiced in many temples of the ancient Near East. The fact that Enkidu curses the man who had defiled the harlot is a further argument against the assumption that the woman in question was a temple prostitute.[105]

*Enkidu has a dream and relates it to Gilgamesh: He was taken away by a creature with the face of the Zu bird and the claws of an*

---

[102] For the importance of an abode, cf. the observations on p. 139 concerning instances in Babylonian (Marduk, Huwawa), Ugaritic (Baal), Hebrew (Yahweh's tabernacle), and Arabic (the Ka'ba) mythology.

[103] See tablet III above.

[104] Concerning this ancient fertility cult, see the first part of this book, Chapter II, p. 63.

[105] In a text published by S. Langdon in *Proceedings of the Society of Biblical Archaeology* (1916), 105ff., distinctions are made between ordinary harlots, sacred prostitutes, and votaries in Mesopotamian society.

*eagle. The demon submerged Enkidu, then transformed him into a bird and conducted him to the abode of Ereshkigal, where the dead lead a miserable existence without light, feeding on dust and clay. Here kings and nobles, priests and heroes are alike, those who once wore crowns are now servants. The queen over them all is Ereshkigal; before her kneels Belit-Seri, the lady scribe of the Nether World. She beholds Enkidu and asks the reason for his presence in the* Arallu. [Here the fragment ends.]

This dream, evidently a foreboding of Enkidu's imminent death, represents a vision of the Nether World. According to it, the Mesopotamians imagined life after death as a desolate existence in the House of Dust, without light, water, or food. There is, in this passage, no allusion whatever to a difference between the condition of one dead or another. In the twelfth tablet,[106] however, there is a different account by Enkidu on the conditions of life after death: the more sons a man has, the better is his situation in the *Arallu;* those who die a heroic death lead an almost comfortable existence; they repose on couches and drink pure water, their parents and wives are with them. On the other hand, those who are left unburied and for whom nobody cares have no rest in the underworld, and feed on the offal that has been thrown into the street.

Enkidu's being submerged refers to a Mesopotamian creed according to which the dead, on leaving the upper world, had to traverse the waters of the *Apsu,* situated under the firm soil, before they arrived in the realm of Ereshkigal. The boundary of water surrounding the Nether World was also called the "River Hubur."[107]

*After the dream, Enkidu's suffering increases from day to day.[108] At the end of the twelfth day, he calls Gilgamesh and expresses his sorrow that he is to die on his bed. He would have preferred to fall in battle and count among the blessed; but since he dies from sickness, he is among the cursed.*

This passage seems to indicate that, while the ordinary mortal leads

106 For the role of this tablet see the introduction to the Gilgamesh epic earlier in this chapter.

107 Cf. B. Landsberger, *"Die babylonische Theodizee,"* ZA, Vol. XLIII (1936), 46.

108 This last part of tablet VII has been preserved on a small Assyrian fragment.

a miserable existence after death, the hero killed in battle enjoys pleasant conditions, since he is "blessed." This is in agreement with the account in tablet XII.

### TABLET VIII[109]

*Gilgamesh, steeped in sorrow, demands that all those involved in Enkidu's life now weep for him: the elders and warriors of Uruk, the harlot who anointed him, all those who provided him with grain, ale, and salve. Gilgamesh asks also the rivers Ula and Euphrates to weep for Enkidu, as well as all the beasts of the steppe. Even the tracks of Enkidu in the forest of the Cedar and the countryside are to participate in the mourning.*

Gilgamesh's funeral oration shows how intrinsically the human, animal, vegetable, and mineral worlds were interwoven in the imagination of ancient man; even the landscape is conceived as a living creature capable of mourning. It is very probable that this passage, singularly pathetic in its appearance, reposes on a basis of obscure ritual customs; the more a dead person is bemoaned, the better will be his condition in the afterlife. The weeping and wailing on the occasion of a death is, as a rule, not the expression of sincere grief, but the discharge of a ceremony necessary for the peace of the dead; the lack of wailing would be as grave a negligence as, for example, the omission of funeral oblations, and the spirit of the deceased would relentlessly haunt the survivors. The hiring of wailing women was therefore in no way considered a sign of heartlessness.[110]

*Gilgamesh[111] apprises the elders of his grief for Enkidu, who has been his faithful companion in all his enterprises. He calls in vain for his friend; Enkidu cannot hear him any more, his heart has ceased to beat. Thereupon Gilgamesh veils him like a bride and gives vent to a vehement lamentation, pulling out his hair and tearing his garments.*

---

[109] The beginning of this tablet has been preserved on a fragment found in Sultantepe, published by O. R. Gurney, *Journal of Cuneiform Studies*, Vol. VIII (1954).

[110] It seems that there was a ritual obligation for wailing at the time of the sowing of grain; the corns represented the god Tammuz, who was put into his grave; the newly sprouting ears were, as the image of his resurrection, hailed with joy (see Ps. 126:6).

[111] Here sets in the Assyrian version, extant only in fragments.

*When the sun rises the next day,*[112] *Gilgamesh calls the craftsmen to help him fashion a statue of his friend. He prepares a carnelian bowl filled with honey and a lapis lazuli bowl filled with curds.*

This passage shows Gilgamesh's grief for his dead friend at the height of a pure and humane feeling; no ritual necessity seems to dictate his behavior. The purpose of his activity at the end of the tablet does not appear from the fragmentary state of the text; honey and curds may be meant as a funeral oblation, but the verbs "to decorate" and "to expose (to the sun)," recognizable in the last mutilated lines, might well allude to some technique of painting in which casein is used.

## TABLET IX

*Gilgamesh roams over the steppe, weeping for his friend. The fear of death has come upon him; he is afraid that he will some day be obliged to go the same way as Enkidu. He sets out upon a long voyage to meet Utnapishtim.*[113] *While he proceeds on his road, he is menaced by wild beasts, and he prays to Sin, the moon-god, for protection.*[114]

Gilgamesh has been seized with the fear of his own death. In this tablet begins his desperate struggle for immortality. The grief caused by Enkidu's loss has now been surpassed by the consideration that the latter's fate will one day also be the fate of Gilgamesh himself: Enkidu has become an exemplification of human mortality.

*Gilgamesh arrives at the foot of the mountain Mashu, which reaches from the vault of heaven to the depths of the Nether World. The gate of entrance is guarded by the awesome scorpion-men, whose glances provoke death.*[115] *Gilgamesh is terror stricken, but he approaches them nevertheless. They recognize his partly divine nature and ask him the purpose of this long and difficult journey. Gilgamesh answers that he seeks his forefather Utnapishtim to learn from him the secret of immortality. The scorpion-man advises the hero not to persist in his design:*

[112] The fragmentary account of this passage does not permit a definite assertion concerning the interval between Enkidu's death and the fashioning of the statue.

[113] The Babylonian name of the hero of the Flood corresponding to the Sumerian Ziusudra, the Greek Xisouthros, and the Hebrew Noah.

[114] See n. 91 above concerning this isolated invocation by Gilgamesh of another deity than Shamash.

[115] Cf. the medieval bestiaries, in which the same creed is expressed.

*the way through the mountain is so hard that no mortal has ever dared
carry out such an enterprise.*

*But Gilgamesh has set his mind and asks the scorpion-man to open
the gate of the mountain. The latter complies and wishes the hero good
luck. Gilgamesh travels the road of the sun, walking league after league
in utter darkness. After eight leagues he cries out; but after one more
league the end of the tunnel seems near, since he feels the north wind
blowing into his face. At last, after eleven leagues, a faint light appears,
and at the end of the twelfth league the light shines fully.*

The Mesopotamians imagined that every evening the sun entered
the gate of the west, then pursued a mysterious voyage underground,
and finally appeared in the morning at the gate of the east. Apparently
Gilgamesh is supposed to travel the sun-god's nocturnal road; the direction of the journey would then be from west to east.[116]

*Gilgamesh beholds a garden of precious stones that have the shape
of fruit and flowers. [Here the text breaks off.]*

The mysterious garden, the description of which seems to be extended in the next mutilated lines of the tablet, is probably connected
with a very ancient cult of the adoration of stones.[117]

## TABLET X[118]

*Gilgamesh meets Shamash and pours forth his despair at the ter-
rifying prospect of death. Shamash counsels him not to pursue his search
for immortality, but Gilgamesh wants at least to have his fill of the
light of the sun, even after he is dead.*

Once again Gilgamesh expresses his anguish at the thought of death.
He desires above all the light of the sun; being surrounded by its bril-
liance, he might yet have the illusion of not sojourning in the darkness
of the *Arallu*.

*Gilgamesh encounters Siduri, the alewife who lives near the border*

---

[116] E. A. Speiser supposes the contrary (*ANET*, 89, n. 152).

[117] Cf. Chapter II above, p. 61–62; see also the episode of the trees bearing precious
stones in *"Alf leila wa leila,"* story of Aladdin and the magic lamp. Note, too, the origin
of the cult around the Black Stone in Mecca.

[118] The text of this tablet is extant partly in Old Babylonian (fragment of B. Meissner),
partly in Assyrian; there are also small fragments of a Hittite and of a Hurrian version
of tablet X.

*of the sea. The gods have provided her with a jug and a golden mashing-bowl; a veil covers her face.*[119] *When she beholds Gilgamesh, clothed in the skins of the animals he has killed, his features worn out, Siduri is seized with fear, and she locks her abode against the wayfarer.*

*Gilgamesh threatens to shatter door and gate, and enumerates his slayings: the watchman of the forest, fierce Huwawa, the lions he encountered in the mountains, and the Bull of Heaven. Siduri asks him the reason for his weary appearance and the purpose of his travel. Gilgamesh relates the death of Enkidu, whom he calls his younger brother; six days and seven nights did he mourn for Enkidu, refusing to give him up for burial. After he has witnessed his friend's death, Gilgamesh is unable to find peace because he is tormented by the thought of his own death.*

*He then asks the alewife the way to Utnapishtim, declaring that no obstacle—neither sea nor steppe—will be hard enough to prevent him from reaching his goal. Siduri advises the hero to enjoy his present life*[120] *instead of striving for an impossible objective. May he make a feast of each day, bathe in clean water, don a fresh garment, and rejoice in the company of his spouse and offspring.*

To the spiritual torment of Gilgamesh, who rebels with all his soul against the terrifying idea that his life will one day come to an end, is opposed the hedonistic counsel of the alewife; to meet the tragic prospect of death by rejoicing each day in the material pleasures which the present life affords. There is no allusion to the consolation that might be found in the certainty of glory; "having made a name" is of no importance here.

The speech of the alewife recalls the Egyptian "Songs of the Harper," in which the pleasures of the present are preferred to the glory of heroic exploits or to the exercise of virtue, since such an attitude does not lead to eternal bliss but only to the loss of the earthly joy allotted to mankind.[121]

*Gilgamesh does not heed the counsel of Siduri but beseeches her*

[119] This detail indicates that she belongs to the higher class of women (see paragraphs 40 and 41 of the Middle Assyrian laws, *ANET*, 183).

[120] This passage is not contained in the Assyrian version.

[121] Cf. the tragical background of the *Decameron*.

*to indicate the way to Utnapishtim, the only human to have gained immortality. The alewife confronts the hero with the insurmountable difficulties of the road to Utnapishtim: he will have to cross the sea, barred by the Waters of Death. She finally recommends that Gilgamesh meet Urshanabi,[122] Utnapishtim's boatman, and follow his advice. Gilgamesh approaches the place[123] of the "Stone Things,"[124] where Urshanabi resides, and wrathfully shatters the idols.[125] He meets Urshanabi and explains his desire to gain immortality. He asks the boatman to show him how he might cross the waters that separate him from Utnapishtim. Urshanabi complains that Gilgamesh has himself destroyed the means of traversing the sea, since he has shattered the stone images and picked the* urnu-snakes[126] *of the forest.*

The stone images are probably objects of magical properties which, together with the *urnu*-snakes, enable Urshanabi to cross the Waters of Death. Gilgamesh having destroyed these idols, the talismanic protection of them has ceased, and Gilgamesh and Urshanabi are now exposed to the danger of the lethal waters.

Here we have another discrepancy between Gilgamesh's actions and the exigencies of religion: when he and Enkidu felled the Holy Cedar, he provoked the malediction of the great gods and caused the expiatory death of his friend.

Now he shatters idols of stone and kills the sacred snakes, which would have been necessary for the pursuit of his voyage. We are probably confronted with a conflict between different forms of worship, indicating a rivalry between two parts of the population: one may have adhered to the more ancient cult of trees, stones, and animals, connected perhaps with Elam, while the other part, in conformity with Gilgamesh, addressed their worship to the stars (Shamash and Sin), possibly a Semitic feature.[127]

---

122 *"Sursunabu"* in the Babylonian version.

123 Perhaps Urshanabi's boat; cf. below.

124 Apparently idols. For the adoration of stones in Mesopotamia, see Chapter II above, p. 61–62.

125 From the sequel of the episode it may be guessed that this passage was preceded by an allusion, no longer preserved, to the *urnu*-snakes mentioned later.

126 Supposedly a reptile propitious for navigation, see *ANET,* 91, n. 174.

127 See Chapter II above, p. 156, for the Semitic names of these deities.

*Urshanabi proposes to cut 120 punting poles so that Gilgamesh and he may cross the Waters of Death unharmed. Gilgamesh does Urshanabi's bidding and prepares the punting poles. The two men sail through the sea until they arrive at the Waters of Death. Urshanabi recommends taking a fresh pole for each thrust, lest the fatal water touch his hand. Gilgamesh follows the boatman's advice; but when the last pole has been used, he has not arrived at Utnapishtim's abode. He therefore takes off his garment and holds it with his hands as a sail.*

*Utnapishtim*[128] *sees the boat approach, but he notices at once that the stone images are broken*[129] *and that there is a stranger with Urshanabi.*

The Waters of Death, which reappear in Greek mythology, do not play a conspicuous role in the Mesopotamian legends of the afterlife. It was generally believed that the *Arallu* was situated below the earth: it was the place which the dead reached after having traversed the grave.[130] In certain texts, however, an older creed emerges. A Babylonian incantation sends a restless spirit back to his home in the *Arallu*, "to the setting of the sun."[131] The gifts enumerated in the text as allotted to the deceased are about the same as the current offerings to the demoness Lamashtu when she is conjured to return to her abode in the west.[132] To accomplish this voyage, she is provided with a boat enabling her to cross the waters that separate the country of man from the habitation of the demons.[133]

The case of Gilgamesh is obviously unique, since, by crossing the Waters of Death, he does not attain the *Arallu* but the abode of the immortal Utnapishtim.

*Gilgamesh meets Utnapishtim and describes the hardships of his voyage.* [A gap in the text probably corresponds to Gilgamesh's enun-

---

[128] In the Babylonian version, Utnapishtim is regularly called the "Faraway."

[129] See n. 123 above.

[130] See also tablet XII, in which Gilgamesh complains that his drum and drumstick fell into the Nether World.

[131] Cf. E. Ebeling, *Tod und Leben nach den Vorstellungen der Babylonier* (Berlin, 1931), 140 ff.

[132] See Chapter II above, pp. 91–92.

[133] The ancient supposition that the dead have to cross the river Ḫubur (see Landsberger, *ZA*, Vol. XLIII [1936], 46) derives apparently from an assumption that the earth is divided into three layers, of which the central one is constituted by the watery abyss of Ea, while the lowest corresponds to the Nether World.

ciation of his desire to gain immortality.] *Utnapishtim answers the hero that there is no permanence in this world: every creature, every institution, every phenomenon will end one day. The gods alone determine death and life.*

## Tablet XI

*Gilgamesh looks at Utnapishtim and wonders why the latter's appearance is in no wise different from that of any other man. He asks the Flood hero why the extraordinary privilege of immortality was allotted to him, and Utnapishtim reveals the story of the Deluge.[134] In recompense for his exceptional piety, eternal life was decreed for him and his wife, and they were transferred to the "mouth of the rivers."[135]*

*For Gilgamesh, however, it would be necessary to cause all the gods to assemble so that they might decree for him the fate of immortality. Utnapishtim then invites the traveler to stay with him for six days and seven nights without sleep.*

According to the creed expressed in this poem, death is not considered the natural issue of life, but as one of two alternatives: the gods may decree either life or death for a mortal. In order to fix a destiny of immortality, all the gods have to assemble. Yet, in the case of Utnapishtim himself, it was Enlil alone who allotted eternal life to the survivor of the Flood.

Utnapishtim proposes the test of sleep to Gilgamesh because in the ancient mind death was only a form of sleep.[136] The idea of resurrection is quite common in Mesopotamian myths,[137] in which the possibility of an awakening from death as from sleep is frequently taken into consideration.

*If Gilgamesh is able to resist sleep, he might resist death also. Gilgamesh tries to overcome the temptation of falling asleep but yields on the first day. Utnapishtim's wife prays her husband to wake Gilgamesh so that he may be able to return home. But the Flood hero exhorts his spouse to bake each day a fresh wafer for their guest and to put it near*

---

134 The Flood episode will be treated separately after the Gilgamesh epic.
135 The interpretation of this term will be given below.
136 Cf. the burial customs of the prehistoric period, Chapter I above.
137 Cf. the Tammuz festivals, etc.

*his head. Furthermore, she is to mark on the wall each day that passes. Through these devices, it will be impossible for Gilgamesh to pretend that he had not slept for the whole week. On the seventh day, Utnapishtim touches Gilgamesh to rouse him from his slumber.*

Sleep is considered, like death, an affliction coming from the outside, not a consequence of bodily fatigue. The sleep that befalls Gilgamesh is a likeness of death: he never rises in the morning, and Utnapishtim's wife is afraid that the hero will not wake up by himself.

*As Utnapishtim had foreseen, Gilgamesh pretends not to have succumbed to sleep. His host then shows him the wafers, each in a successive stage of decomposition, and Gilgamesh is unable to protest. But he does not give up his search for a way of escape from death.*

*Utnapishtim recommends his guest to Urshanabi but at the same time banishes the boatman from the shore. Urshanabi is to take Gilgamesh to the washing place and provide him with a new garment and a new band for his head. The boatman carries out his master's behest, and Gilgamesh washes off his grime and casts off his skins in water clean as snow, then puts on a new cloak and a new headband. At last both Urshanabi and Gilgamesh board the boat that will take them back to Uruk, and leave the washing place.*

Gilgamesh's refusal to recognize that he has fallen asleep is but a manifestation of his inflexible will to defy death. Undaunted by the proof of the wafers, he continues to seek immortality.

Utnapishtim's offer of a bath and a fresh garment to Gilgamesh is the customary treatment required by ancient oriental hospitality. Urshanabi is banished from the coast where he had received the weary traveler apparently because the stone idols are destroyed and the crossing of the Waters of Death is no longer possible for the boatman, who, in all probability, does not share the immortality of his master.

The washing place is apparently the *"pī nārāti"* itself ("Mouth of the Rivers," i.e., of the Euphrates and the Tigris), where Utnapishtim and his wife had been transferred after the Flood. "Mouth" in Sumerian is equal to "source," not to "estuary"; it indicates the opening through which the river ascends from the *Apsu,* the sweet underground waters, to the upper world. Utnapishtim's abode was therefore situated, not at the estuary, but at the source of the two rivers.[138]

A special purifying virtue is, in Mesopotamian incantations, ascribed to the water of the sources of the two rivers, as in a text published by H. Zimmern (*Beiträge zur Kenntnis der babylonischen Religion,* Pl. LXXIX), in which a purification is performed with "water which the Lord Ea . . . down the pure Euphrates had guided, the product of the Apsu, for the purpose of lustration."

The location of the *pī nārāti* is still recorded in the various Muslim adaptations of the Alexander legend [139]: the Hero " of the two horns" ذو القرنين accomplishes a voyage which recalls that of Gilgamesh,[140] crossing Mount Masius (identical with the mountain Mashu, "the Twins," where Gilgamesh encounters the scorpion men[141]) and entering the "cave of darkness" كهف الظلمات at the source of the Tigris[142] before he reaches, in the East,[143] Paradise.

*Utnapishtim's wife exhorts her spouse to give a present to their guest since he accomplished a very toilsome voyage. So Utnapishtim reveals to Gilgamesh, who has, in Urshanabi's boat, reapproached the shore, as a hospitable gift the secret of the Plant of Life.*

*As soon as Gilgamesh hears this, he opens the water pipe, ties stones to his feet, and dives[144] to the ground of the sea, where he finds the plant, which pricks his hands with its thorns. Then he cuts the stones from his feet and emerges once more. He tells Urshanabi that he wants*

---

138 In the Sumerian version the Flood hero is said to reside in Dilmun, which is identified by some scholars with the isle of Bahrein, near the estuary of the Euphrates and the Tigris. On this assumption, cf. the different opinions of S. N. Kramer ("Dilmun, the Land of the Living," *BASOR,* Vol. XCVI [January, 1944], 18ff.) and P. B. Cornwall ("Dilmun," *BASOR,* Vol. CIII [January, 1946], 3ff.).

139 See also *"Ahsan at-taqasim fi marifat alaqalim,"* by al-Muqaddasi (about A.D. 980), in which reference is made to the legend.

140 Cf. *Alexandri Magni iter ad Paradisum,* ed. by L. P. Peckham and M. S. La Du (Princeton, 1935).

141 Cf. the سـدان ("Two barriers") of Sura XVIII in the Qur'ān.

142 M. Hartman supposes that the مجمع البحرين "Confluence of the two seas" mentioned in the Sura indicated under n. 141 is in reality the source of the Tigris (see *ZDMG,* Vol. LXVII, p. 749ff.).

143 Cf. n. 116 above concerning Gilgamesh's west-east direction.

144 The mysterious water pipe is perhaps a cane which Gilgamesh used for breathing under water, as do still certain primitive people today, when diving or swimming under water.

*to take the plant to Uruk,*[145] *and confers on it the name "Man becomes young in old age."*

The secret of life is revealed to Gilgamesh not as an answer to his supplication or as the objective of his toilsome voyage but simply as a hospitable gift.[146] The thorny submarine plant, in reality, does not have the power of conferring immortality, but only that of rejuvenating the aged. Immortality can be acquired, as Utnapishtim had affirmed, only through a decree of the gods. The marvelous plant produces only an ephemeral prolongation of life and as such may be included in the group of medicinal herbs known in the ancient world[147] and supposed to possess magical properties. Utnapishtim himself, the same as all the Mesopotamian deities,[148] needs not consume special food or drink to remain eternally alive, as the Greek gods had to do.

Another mortal, Adapa, had been offered food and drink of life; but, as Gilgamesh (see below), he misses the occasion of tasting it. In neither case is there a mention of immortality; the plant, as well as the bread and water offered to Adapa, are apparently endowed only with the temporary potency of rejuvenation.

There may have been in remote times a connection between the myth of the Plant of Life and the legend of Gilgamesh's felling of the Holy Cedar. In ancient incantation literature, mention is made of Mount Ḫašur, which coincides with the region of the sources of the Tigris and Euphrates. This mountain is also called *"shad erini"* ("the Cedar Mountain").[149]

*Gilgamesh and Urshanabi proceed on their voyage towards Uruk.*

[145] A fragmentary line seems to express Gilgamesh's intention to share the plant of life with some or all the inhabitants of Uruk.

[146] The ancient custom seems to have obliged a host to provide the guest with a gift on the occasion of his departure; cf. the epic of Adapa, in which Anu offers bread and water of life to the mortal who visits him in heaven.

[147] A Sumero-Akkadian text of the British Museum (XVI, 46, 183ff.) contains a passage in which a miraculous plant called *"kishkanu"* is said to grow in the sweet-water sea, between the mouths of the two rivers: *"ri-ba-an-na id-ka-min-a-ta."*

[148] The water of life is once mentioned in connection with the goddess Ishtar, but she does not partake of it as of a drink; her body is sprinkled with it, as with a kind of antidote against the spell of death that keeps the goddess imprisoned in the Nether World.

[149] In a passage from the Tammuz liturgy the god calls his mother "a sacred Cedar, a Cedar of Hashur."

*After one day, the King spies a cool well and bathes in the water; mean-*
*while a serpent approaches the plant and carries it off. The magical effect*
*of the herb is visible at once; the reptile sheds its skin. Gilgamesh sits*
*down and weeps over the loss of the precious plant. He abandons the*
*boat on the shore and continues his journey by land, together with*
*Urshanabi. After a second day the two men arrive in Uruk, and Gilga-*
*mesh shows Urshanabi the ramparts of the city, praising the quality*
*of the brickwork and the extension of the domain of the Eanna.*

The loss of the Plant of Life as the negative issue of the Gilgamesh
epic is characteristic of Mesopotamian literature: The boon of new life
is denied to Gilgamesh, as well as to Adapa, for a futile reason; likewise,
Etana, the king who tried to attain the heaven of Ishtar in order to obtain
the Plant of Birth, probably failed in his enterprise. But these heroes had
set their minds on objectives which are generally not within the reach
of mankind.

The attitude of the Mesopotamian poet is therefore an expression not
so much of pessimism[150] as of plain realism: man has to accept life as it is
and must renounce superhuman exploits. Such a view stands in singular
contrast to the history of Mesopotamia, so rich in ambitious kings who
conquered all the known world; in contrast also to the achievements of
architecture, the splendor of which provoked admiration and envy
among all the neighboring people of the epoch.

The central theme of the epic of Gilgamesh as it appears in the
Akkadian version, is not, as has often been sustained, the anxiety of
death. In the greater part of the poem (tablets I–VI), the danger of
losing life is envisaged almost with indifference, as an inevitable necessity of human existence. To gain glory and make oneself a name is
judged much more important than death: to be afraid of death connotes
cowardice. Gilgamesh's principal preoccupation in this part of the poem
is with the accomplishment of heroic deeds in the service of his god
Shamash. He rejoices in his strength and in the exercise of his kingship over Uruk.

It is not until tablet VII that his tragical apprehension of death
begins. Enkidu's dying has filled him with horror at the idea of a final

---

[150] Imbued with genuine pessimism is, however, the "Dialogue between Master and
Servant" (see below) of the later period, which ends with the gloomy prospect of suicide.

annihilation. During his long vigil over the corpse of his friend, he has been seized with nausea at the sight of physical decay. But he is, above all, shaken by metaphysical anguish; the indomitable hero cannot resign himself to the certainty that his existence will one day come to an end. Gilgamesh's fear of death, as expressed in this second part of the poem, has nothing to do with cowardice. During his desperate search for immortality, he faces the dangers of his journey with the same steadfastness he showed in his previous exploits and does not hesitate to cross the Waters of Death in spite of the risk he incurs.

The central point of the epic is the person of Gilgamesh himself, who shows throughout the poem a remarkable unity of character; the only change is the natural evolution from early youth to ripe age. The exuberance and carelessness of the first tablets give way to weariness and despair at the end, hardly brightened by the final proud presentation of the city ramparts, probably nothing but an exigence of style.[151] But it is the same impetuosity and tenacity with which he persuaded Enkidu to join him in his expedition against Huwawa that pushes him onward in his search for immortality.

Gilgamesh is depicted with a truly human countenance: manifestations of genuine heroism alternate with moments of weakness and discouragement. Unlike Marduk, the protagonist of the Creation epic, Gilgamesh nearly succumbs to his adversary in his combat with Huwawa and overpowers his enemy only with the help of Shamash. It is principally because of this human description of the hero that the epic has lost nothing of its timeless appeal over the ages.

Enkidu, on the other hand, is less uniform than Gilgamesh. Between the ignorant savage of the steppe and the expert counselor of the king, there is only a slight connection; the allusion to Enkidu's previous knowledge concerning Huwawa confirms the supposition that Gilgamesh's companion was originally not identical with the hairy primitive who knew neither land nor people.

There seems to have existed a Sumerian version of the Gilgamesh epic, of which a few fragments are extant. It is, however, not certain that they were parts of a connected story, as is the case of the Akkadian

---

[151] The last lines of tablet XI are identical with the concluding lines of the introduction on tablet I.

version. Some of the fragments have no counterpart in the Semitic text,[152] but one of the principal episodes, the combat against Huwawa, is represented by the Sumerian story "Gilgamesh and the Land of the Living."[153]

Gilgamesh wants to go to the "Land," which belongs to Utu[154] (Shamash), in order to "set up a name" for himself and for the gods. The enterprise seems to culminate in a rite connected with the felling of the Cedar; the obscure lines following the passage in which the hero is said to have felled the sacred tree appear to indicate that, immediately afterwards, Gilgamesh "set up (his name)," perhaps by burning the wood of the Cedar or by accomplishing some other rite aimed at gaining immortality.

The Sumerian text does not mention the particular hardships which Gilgamesh had to overcome in order to accomplish the purpose of his journey. Huwawa, who in the Akkadian version is the frightful guardian of the Cedar who must be fought with, is in the Sumerian fragment not even mentioned in the course of the episode concerning the Cedar. Gilgamesh apparently had the possibility of returning to Uruk right after having "set up his name" in the Land, without being obliged to face Huwawa. The monster's role in the epic is not clear; although he lives in a cedar house, he certainly is not the guardian of the sacred tree.[155]

In the Akkadian version Gilgamesh wants to make a name for himself through the glory of a dangerous enterprise so that long after his death, people will remember his heroic deed.

In the Sumerian version, however, it is not the admiration of posterity which Gilgamesh seeks; he accomplishes a quite concrete ritual activity in a particular place, where "the names have been raised up." The Sumerian Gilgamesh intends to gain immortality, not through the glory of his enterprise, but through the effect of the rite.[156]

---

[152] E.g., "Gilgamesh and Agga" and "The Death of Gilgamesh."

[153] Text published by S. N. Kramer, *Journal of Cuneiform Studies,* Vol. I (1947), 3–46.

[154] Utu is also said to have reared Huwawa.

[155] It is possible that the seven objects mentioned in the text are trees, which perhaps compose a grove. But nothing warrants the assumption that the "felling of the Cedar" occurs only in this passage.

[156] The lines which follow Enkidu's description of Huwawa in the Sumerian text

The connection between eternal life and the Cedar, which is no longer recognizable in the Akkadian version[157] but exists in the Sumerian text, is evident also in other points of ancient oriental mythology. The name of the tree-god Ningishzida, in many respects a counterpart of Tammuz,[158] signifies "Lord of the tree of life"; in a hymn addressed to this deity,[159] the god is called "the cedar borne by his mother."

The "tree of life" mentioned in Gen. 3:22 stands, like the cedar of the Babylonian myth,[160] in the midst of a grove (Gen.3:3): The flaming sword "which turned every way," placed by Yahweh at the east of Eden to safeguard the "tree of life," recalls the terrifying rays that emanate from Huwawa, guardian of the Cedar.

Cedarwood was, in the ancient Near East, supposed to be imperishable. Its use for sarcophagi is probably a survival of the creed of the life-giving potency of the cedar.

Another Sumerian fragment, "Gilgamesh and the Huluppu-Tree,"[161] informs us of the facts that preceded Enkidu's death.[162] Here the Sumerian account differs widely from the Akkadian text: Enkidu descends to the Nether World while still in life, with the intention of retrieving two magic objects that belong to Gilgamesh, a *pukku* and a *mikku* (probably a drum and a drumstick), which had fallen into the realm of the dead. Since Enkidu does not follow the instructions of his master during his stay in the Nether World,[163] he is seized by the powers of the *Arallu* and can no longer ascend to the upper world. Through the intercession of the god Ea, the servant's spirit is allowed to issue

---

allude to funeral rites that shall not be accomplished in Gilgamesh's behalf; perhaps the passage is meant to express the hero's confidence in his newly gained immortality.

[157] See p. 184 above.

[158] For the connection of Tammuz with the Cedar, see n. 149 above.

[159] Text published by S. Langdon, *Sumerian and Babylonian Psalms* (Paris, 1909), 332.

[160] See especially the Old Babylonian fragment of the Oriental Institute of Chicago.

[161] The first part of the legend has been published by S. N. Kramer, *Gilgamesh and the Huluppu-Tree* (Chicago, 1938); for the second part, which underlies the Akkadian translation, cf. Kramer, *Sumerian Mythology*.

[162] This same epic gives also, in its first part, quite a different account of the relationship between Gilgamesh and Ishtar; while in the Semitic text the hero insults the goddess, in the Sumerian story he renders her a service for which she compensates him.

[163] In the Sumerian version, Enkidu is Gilgamesh's servant, not his friend.

forth through a hole which Nergal, king of the *Arallu,* has opened in the earth for this special purpose, so that through the voice of Enkidu, Gilgamesh might learn "the ways of the Nether World." After the desolate description of the conditions of the dead, the text ends without further indications concerning either hero.

In the Akkadian epic, however, Enkidu's death is considered an atonement for offenses against the great gods and is preceded by an illness of fourteen days.

The difference in the account of Enkidu's catabasis is the principal discrepancy between the first eleven tablets and the last tablet of the Akkadian epic. The second part of the Sumerian legend "Gilgamesh and the Ḫuluppu Tree," starting with the hero's lament at the loss of his *pukku* and *mikku,* has in fact been added, in an almost literal translation, to the eleven tablets of the Akkadian epic.[164] The reason for incorporating this Sumerian episode into the seemingly already complete Akkadian version[165] probably lies in the fact that Enkidu's report about the Nether World was judged to be of particular interest for the auditors of the poem.

### THE MESOPOTAMIAN DELUGE

The story of the Flood has come to us as an episode of the Gilgamesh epic and is recorded on the eleventh tablet of this poem. The account of the Deluge is placed in the mouth of Utnapishtim, who therewith explains to Gilgamesh the reason the gods allotted immortality to himself and his wife. The King of Uruk is supposed to be the first man to learn the secret of the Deluge. He is to divulge the story to the people of his city after his return from Utnapishtim's abode.

*The gods decide to produce a great flood in the land. Ea,*[166] *the god of the sweet underground waters, who has attended the divine assembly, confides the disastrous project to Utnapishtim, Ubar-Tutu's*

---

164 The eleventh tablet records, as "catch-line," the first verse of the twelfth tablet, and the colophon of this last one indicates that it is "Tablet XII of *Sha nagba imuru.*"

165 The praise of "ramparted Uruk," already proclaimed in the introduction of the poem, is repeated verbatim at the end of tablet XI.

166 The god does not give a reason for such a decree, nor are there in the whole poem any allusions to some fault incurred by mankind; thus the Deluge appears more as a caprice of the gods than as a divine punishment.

*son and ruling king of Shuruppak. To avoid a direct communication with a mortal, the shrewd god addresses the wall of the reed hut where Utnapishtim lives.*[167] *The King of Shuruppak is to tear down his house and build a ship, for only through the abandonment of his worldly goods will he be able to save his life.*[168] *The ship, which has to be loaded with "the seed of all living things," shall be a cubelike structure, with a ceiling that has a hatch.*

*Utnapishtim is willing to do as Ea advises, but he is at a loss about what to tell the elders of his city to justify his unusual activity. Ea proposes a pretext: the King is to pretend that an enmity has arisen between himself and the god Enlil and that he is therefore going to stay in the waters of the god Ea. The people of Shuruppak shall then be told that a rain of abundance and rich crops is in store for them.*[169]

*The next morning Utnapishtim sets to work, with children and grownups helping in the preparation. He builds six decks so that the ship will have seven stories. The floor plan is divided into nine parts.*[170] *Bitumen, asphalt, and oil are used to make the ship seaworthy. The King provides all the workmen abundantly with meat and drink. The construction lasts seven days. Then the ark is launched and loaded with all the King's possessions, including his cattle. All the members of his family and kin enter the ship; then Utnapishtim forces the tame and the wild animals of the field to go aboard, as well as all the craftsmen.*[171] *Shamash*[172] *had foretold that the time for boarding the boat would come when a rain of misery and destruction would fall.*[173] *At the ap-*

[167] Later on, Ea justifies his behavior before the gods by insisting that he did not reveal the divine secret to Utnapishtim but only made the king see a dream.

[168] This seems to concern only the immovable property of the king, since a later passage indicates that the boat is loaded with Utnapishtim's possessions.

[169] The prophesy reposes on a word play, in that *"kukku"* and *"kibati"* have the double significance of bran and wheat or "misfortune and sorrow." Cf. C. Frank, *"Zu den Wortspielen kukku and kibati in Gilgamesch Ep. XI," ZA,* Vol. XXXVI (1925).

[170] Utnapishtim thus had sixty-three compartments in his ark.

[171] A craft was considered in Mesopotamia not as a mere dexterity but as an art revealed by a divine being (see Chapter II above, p. 61).

[172] The mentioning of Shamash in this connection is surprising, since this deity is not otherwise named in the Deluge episode.

[173] The pun of *"kukku"* and *"kibati"* is taken up once more and used as a formula to indicate the day of the impending disaster (cf. Gen. 19:24, in which Sodom and Gomorrah are destroyed by a "rain of brimstone and fire").

Transportation of Cedarwood, a Relief Dating from the Eighth
Century B.C.—the Louvre

Bompiana, *Il volto delle Epoche*

Stela of Naram-Sin, Excavated in Susa—the Louvre

John de Morgan, *Délégation en Perse*

Kudurru from the
Kassite Period, Excavated
in Susa—the Louvre

John de Morgan,
*Délégation en Perse*

Lion of Molded Enameled Bricks, Reconstituted from Many Fragments
Excavated in Kasr—Berliner Museum
It was probably a wall decoration of the "Via Sacra" in Babylon.

R. Koldewey, *Mitteilungen der deutschen Orient-gesellschaft zu Berlin*

Gilgamesh Watering a Bull

L. de Clercq, *Catalogue de Clercq*

Mural Painting from Tell Hariri, Excavated in the Ruins of Mari—
the Louvre

A. Parrot, *Mari, une ville perdue*

Silver Vase of Entemena, Excavated in Telloh—
the Louvre

Ernest de Salzec and Léon Heuzey, *Découvertes en Chaldée*

Spiral-Shaped Stylization—British Museum

L. W. King, *Babylonian Boundary Stones and Memorial Tablets in the British Museum*

*proach of the fateful weather, Utnapishtim enters the ship and puts it in charge of Puzur-Amurri, the boatman.*

*The flood begins with a fearful thunderstorm, caused by Adad; other gods break down the world dam and the dikes, and darkness settles over the land. The south wind blows at a fearful speed, submerging everything, carrying the flood into the land for six days and six nights.*[174] *During the raging of the storm, gods and goddesses flee to the heaven of Anu, afraid of the disastrous flood which they themselves have caused.*

*Ishtar, the creatress of mankind,*[175] *repents of having approved the fatal decree of the divine assembly, since all human beings have been entirely destroyed; the other gods join her mourning.*

*On the seventh day the storm abates, and the flood recedes. Thereupon Utnapishtim opens the hatch of his ark and beholds daylight. He sees the landscape leveled by the flood and all mankind turned to clay. The ark comes to a standstill on Mount Nisir*[176] *and remains there for seven days. Then Utnapishtim sends forth successively a dove, a swallow, and a raven; but only the third bird finds a resting place and does not return to the ship. Thereupon the King leaves the ark to offer a sacrifice and pour out a libation and makes sweet incense rise to heaven. The gods, attracted by the savor, cluster around the sacrificer. Ishtar swears never to forget the awful days of the catastrophe and tells the gods not to allow Enlil to approach Utnapishtim's sacrifice, since it was this deity who had caused the deluge. When Enlil finally arrives, he is very wroth on seeing that Utnapishtim and his family have escaped the flood. Ea is accused of originating this counterplot, and the Water-God in turn denounces Enlil for having provoked the destruction of mankind without out reason. Enlil should have sent minor plagues, such as a lion, a wolf, a famine, or pestilence, to diminish mankind in the case of transgression. He, Ea, did not divulge the gods' decree to Utnapishtim; instead, the*

[174] There is no evidence for a rain flood in the Akkadian version, as there is in Gen. 7; it seems much more probable that the Mesopotamian deluge was thought to be of marine origin; perhaps it was the consequence of an earthquake or of a hurricane.

[175] Obviously Ishtar has here taken the place of Mami, Ninhursag, or Aruru as the mother-goddess.

[176] Concerning the site of this mountain, cf. E. A. Speiser, *Annual* of the American Schools of Oriental Research (1926–27), VIII, 17ff.

*King of Shuruppak perceived the divine secret through a dream. Enlil thereupon takes Utnapishtim and his wife aboard and blesses them, conferring upon them eternal life. He assigns the couple a new abode, at the mouth of the rivers.*

The Akkadian legend of the Flood presents many similarities to the Biblical Deluge story. It has therefore often been argued that the account of Gen. 6–8 is based directly on the Mesopotamian text. It is, however, more probable that both tales arose independently out of a common tradition in the ancient Near East.[177]

In Sumerian literature, too, we have an account of a flood, without any reference to Gilgamesh. The protagonist, Ziusudra,[178] escapes universal destruction in much the same way as the Akkadian Utnapishtim. The Sumerian tablet, however, is fragmentary and does not allow a close comparison with the Semitic deluge story.

In the Sumerian text, Ziusudra is informed of the impending flood by the voice of a deity across a wall. He boards a huge boat (probably together with his family and a number of animals).[179] The flood is provoked by the combined raging of all the windstorms[180] and lasts for seven days and seven nights. After the reappearance of the sun, Ziusudra offers a sacrifice to Utu. At last immortality is conferred on the survivor of the Deluge by Anu and Enlil, and he is made to dwell in the "land of Dilmun, the place where the sun rises."[181]

The supposition that the Flood episode in the Gilgamesh epic was originally an independent legend appears to find confirmation in the fact that in Akkadian literature there are still other texts alluding to a deluge and a life-saving ship. Whether they can all be considered one

[177] The problem of a dependence of the Biblical story on Mesopotamian material has been discussed by A. Heidel in his monograph, *The Gilgamesh Epic and Old Testament Parallels.*

[178] Text published by A. Pöbel in *Publications of the Babylonian Section* (University Museum of Pennsylvania, 1914), I. Ziusudra is the direct prototype of the Xisouthros of Berossus' *History of Babylonia.*

[179] This may be guessed from a later passage, in which Ziusudra is reported to prepare an ox and a sheep as offerings to Utu.

[180] Here, too, no mention is made of heavy rains as the origin of the Flood (see n. 174 above).

[181] See n. 138 above.

epic is dubious, since the extant tablets are too badly damaged for any positive conclusion.

### THE ATRAHASIS EPIC

The poem commonly called by this name has been pieced together from various fragments, designated as A, B, X, C, and D. They date from different periods, and it is not certain that they all belong to the same composition. The Akkadian text has been published by:

A. T. Clay, *Yale Oriental Series* (1922), pls. I–II (fragment A).

A. Boissier, *Revue d' Assyriologie* (1931), 92ff. (fragment B).

H. V. Hilprecht, *Babylonian Expedition of the University of Pennsylvania* (1910), Series D, V, 1 (fragment X).

F. Delitzsch, *Assyrische Lesestücke* (1885), 101 (fragment C).

L. W. King, *Cuneiform Texts of the British Museum* (1902), 49 (fragment D).

Fragments A and B are each followed by a colophon indicating that they are respectively tablets II and III (both heavily mutilated) of the epic *"Enūma ilu awēlum"* ("When God, man . . ."), which consists of 1,245 lines. The two fragments have been copied in the Old Babylonian period.

Of fragment D[182] no colophon is extant, but it clearly belongs to the same epic since passages of fragment A are repeated here. It contains no allusion to a flood.

Fragments X and C, both without colophon, may or may not belong to the epic *"Enūma ilu awēlum."* They contain portions of an account concerning a flood, bearing thus a possible connection with fragment B.

Fragments A, B, C, and D all contain the name of Atrahasis, faithful servant of the god Ea and intercessor in behalf of mankind. There is, however, no warranty that this was the real and the only name of the hero, since "Atrahasis," meaning "exceedingly wise," is an epithet which in the course of Akkadian literature has been bestowed on more than one hero, for example, on Etana and on Adapa, neither of whom is associated at all with a flood.

What renders the problem particularly intricate, however, is the

[182] Fragments C and D date from the time of Ashurbanipal.

fact that Utnapishtim, too, is once called "Atrahasis" in the Gilgamesh epic. Consequently the question arises whether there are two distinct heroes of two independent floods, or whether Utnapishtim is identical with Atrahasis.

Fragment C and especially the Hilprecht text (fragment X) might in fact belong to the Utnapishtim episode. Since tablet XI of the Gilgamesh epic is in an almost perfect state of preservation and shows no lacunae which might be filled in by the two fragments, it is to be supposed that either the succinct account of tablet XI goes back to a more elaborate description which is now lost, comprising the details recorded in X and C, or there existed two poetic versions of the same legend.

The story of the Atrahasis epic, as it is recorded in fragments A through D, appears rather entangled, and there are repetitions of entire passages within the same fragment. The logical sequence might be the following: Enlil, disturbed by the clamor of mankind, sends a number of plagues upon the people in order to diminish their noise; he finally decides on their total destruction by means of a flood.

We might divide the story tentatively into the following passages:
I. The pestilence.
II. Enlil's project to bring on a drought.
III. The drought.
IV. The effect of the famine on the people.
V. Announcement of a flood.[183]

Fragments A–B–X–C have the sequence II–V (gaps in the text probably correspond to III and IV). Fragment D has the following sequence: IV–III–IV–I–II–III.

## Passage I

*Enlil, head of the pantheon, is enraged at the great noise[184] which mankind produces, and he complains that he cannot sleep. He therefore*

---

[183] It is quite possible that Enlil sent still other plagues before he decreed the flood; in none of the fragments is there a direct transition from IV to V, and the large gaps would allow for other "paragraphs" describing more plagues after the six years' famine.

[184] Cf. Gen. 18:20: "The cry of Sodom and Gomorrah is great"; and Gen. 19:13: "We will destroy this place because the cry of them is waxen great before the face of the Lord."

*sets up the assembly of the gods and decides upon a pestilence to diminish the clamor of the people. The plague has the desired effect. But Atrahasis, the wise servant of Ea, goes to his lord and beseeches him to cause a cessation of the plague. Ea proposes prayers to the goddess and apparently agrees to intercede in mankind's behalf.* [The text is mutilated here; it may be assumed that the pestilence finally ceases.]

### PASSAGE II

*But soon a fresh uproar begins to annoy Enlil, and he decides to visit a new plague upon the land. There shall be a great drought, followed by the death of all vegetation; no grain shall sprout on the plain covered with salt crystals, fever shall come upon the people, and no children shall be born.*

### PASSAGE III

*Everything happens according to Enlil's decree: no rain falls, vegetation dies, no grain grows, and the plain turns white with salt crystals. Fever plagues the people, and no children are born.*

### PASSAGE IV

*The famine produced by the drought lasts for six years; hostility increases annually, and even within families love and disinterestedness have disappeared. At last the people resort to cannibalism, and parents eat their own children.*[185] *Then once more Atrahasis converses with his lord Ea; he places his bed in front of the river.* [These last mutilated lines seem to allude to a rite which was to attract rain.]

### PASSAGE V

*Enlil has decided to bring a flood upon mankind and is rebuked for this by Ea.* [Here occurs a gap.]

*To save his faithful servant from destruction, the water-god, speaking through the wall of a reed hut, advises Atrahasis to destroy his house and build a ship. It shall have the form of an ark and bear the*

---

[185] In a document of Ashurbanipal's campaign against the Arabs is recorded the following passage concerning cannibalism: "Famine broke out among them and they ate the flesh of their children against their hunger." See Oppenheim, "Babylonian and Assyrian Historical Texts," *ANET*, 300.

name "Preserver of Life." The structure is to be strong, and its ceiling shall be like the vault of heaven. Ea will indicate when Atrahasis is to enter the ship after it has been loaded with grain and with all his possessions. With him shall come his wife and all his kin, as well as the craftsmen. The god will conduct towards the door of the ark all the beasts of the field, "as many as eat herbs."[186] Atrahasis feels himself unable to execute the work since he has never built a ship in his life. He therefore asks Ea to draw a design of the ark on the ground. [Here the tale of the poem breaks off.]

The confusion of the narration in fragment D may be explained by the fact that this did not form a part of the poem itself but was an adaptation of the epic "Enūma ilu awēlum," to enhance a birth incantation. In fact, to the Atrahasis account of fragment D has been added, as a fourth column, a passage which has no connection whatever with the preceding text but constitutes a ritual for the facilitation of childbirth. The magical purpose of this fragment may justify the entangled sequence of events, as indicated above.

### ISHTAR'S DESCENT TO THE NETHER WORLD

This poem is the third in importance of Akkadian literature, after the Creation epic and the Gilgamesh tale. It belongs to the ancient nature religion, which is based on the alternation of the seasons.

The legend of Ishtar's descent to the *Arallu* is probably one of the oldest myths in Mesopotamia. The present Akkadian version goes back to a Sumerian prototype, but without being a mere translation of it. The myth possibly took shape in the dawn of religious life, when the cult of the mother-goddess and the fertility god still predominated over the adoration of the elements.[187]

The story consists of one tablet and has come to us in two versions, one from Ashur[188] and another one from Nineveh.[189] The Akkadian text has been published by:

[186] This is the only passage in all Mesopotamian literature which specifies that only herbivorous animals are admitted into the ark (cf. Gen. 1:30).

[187] See Chapter II above, p. 47–48.

[188] A small fragment found in Ashur, apparently pertaining to an independent version, has been published by E. Ebeling, *Orientalia*, Vol. XVIII (1949), 32.

[189] This last recension dates from the seventh century B.C., while the Ashur text

E. Ebeling, *Keilschrifttexte aus Assur religiösen Inhalts,* I, pls. 1–4 (Ashur version).

L. W. King, *Cuneiform Texts from Babylonian Tablets in the British Museum,* XV, pls. 45–48 (Nineveh version).

*Ishtar, the goddess of love, makes up her mind to descend to the realm of the dead, the House of Dust, the Land of No Return. She asks the gatekeeper to let her enter and threatens, if her request is not granted, to smash the door of the Arallu and to raise up the dead. The gatekeeper goes to Ereshkigal, queen of the Nether World, and announces the arrival of her sister, the goddess "who stirs up the Apsu before Ea."*[190] *Ereshkigal reacts wrathfully to this news; then she commands the gatekeeper to make Ishtar, her deadly enemy, enter the palace, after due compliance with the ancient rules.*

*The servant welcomes the visitor to the Nether World and opens the first gate for her. But as the goddess passes, he takes away her tiara, in spite of her protests, because "thus are the rules of the Mistress of the Nether World." At the second gate, Ishtar is stripped of her ear pendants; her ensuing indignation is met with the same evasive words.*

*At each of the next gates, the keeper takes off successively the goddess' neck chains, breast ornaments, girdle of birthstones, bracelets and anklets, and eventually her breechcloth. At last she appears before Ereshkigal, completely despoiled of her apparel.*

The reason for Ishtar's journey to the Land of No Return is not indicated here, nor do we find any mention of a motive in the Sumerian version. Until recently, it has been generally assumed that the goddess descended to the Nether World to rescue her husband, the shepherd Tammuz, who was detained in the *Arallu.* But there is no proof in the text for such an assumption; on the contrary, the last obscure lines of our text, as well as an additional fragment of the Sumerian tale, lead to quite another interpretation, as we shall see below.

is considerably older. The fragment mentioned in n. 188 above is the most ancient (end of the second millennium B.C.).

190 W. F. Albright, "The Mouth of the Two Rivers," *American Journal of Semitic Languages and Literatures,* Vol. XXV (July, 1919), 184, refers in this connection to a popular creed according to which the silt in the rivers was caused by Ishtar washing her hair in the mountain sources and muddying the waters.

In the Semitic version, Ishtar never states, even falsely,[191] the reason for her visit; and the ill fate that befalls her seems to be the consequence of her ignorance concerning the Land of No Return. She does not appear to have come down to the *Arallu* with any definite project in mind which Ereshkigal might have thwarted. Ishtar's descent is probably nothing more than a mythopoeic interpretation of the disappearance of a season, without any attempt to invent a plausible reason for it.

The seven adornments that the gatekeeper takes away from Ishtar at each of the seven doors are obviously of talismanic virtue, and, while losing them one by one, the goddess is gradually deprived of her power. The magical value of certain jewels, especially those worn by women around neck and hips, can be deduced from the prehistoric female figurines connected with the mother-goddess cult which had chains around neck and hips.[192] The other ornaments of the goddess apparently had a magical significance, too, especially the tiara, symbol of divinity. Being deprived of it probably made her subject to mortality.

*When the two sisters meet, their hatred of each other becomes evident immediately. Ereshkigal commands Namtar, her vizier, to lock Ishtar up, to direct the sixty diseases towards her, and thus render each member of her body sick.*

The deadly aversion of the two goddesses for each other is based on their mythical functions: the queen of the dead is naturally the foe of the deity who promotes life. Ereshkigal fears that Ishtar has come to endanger her position as mistress of the *Arallu*. She therefore decides to put her sister to death.

The sixty diseases which are to be directed against Ishtar seem to indicate that the Mesopotamian creed thought the human body consisted of sixty members; there was a disease intended for each part of the goddess' body.[193]

*By this time, the disappearance of the goddess of love has caused on earth the cessation of mating, in the animal as well as in the human*

[191] In the Sumerian myth, Ishtar pretends that she wants to attend the funeral rites of Gugalanna, Ereshkigal's husband.

[192] Cf. Chapter II above, p. 118–20.

[193] This creed is apparent also in the Sumerian version of the myth, in which the water of life has to be sprinkled on the corpse of the goddess sixty times in order to restore her to life.

*realm. Thereupon Papsukkal, vizier of the gods, appears in tears before Sin and then Ea to tell them of Ishtar's voyage to the Nether World and of the result of her disappearance: bull and cow, ass and jenny, and man and maiden remain apart from each other. At this news, Ea decides to create Asushunamir, a eunuch, who shall save Ishtar from the powers of the* Arallu.

The consequences on earth of Ishtar's descent to the Land of No Return are very significant. As was mentioned earlier the function of the goddess of love is limited to the promotion of mating, without extension to the bringing forth of offspring.[194] In Mesopotamian mythology this assigns a definite part of the year to her domination, a part which is not identical with the period of vegetation growth.[195] This alternation of Ishtar's function with that of the vegetation deity explained for the Mesopotamian the cycle of the seasons and is at the origin of this particular Ishtar-Tammuz myth.

Other legends (e.g., "Inanna and Bilulu"[196]) interpret the fact that Ishtar and Tammuz exercise their activities at different periods of the year, with the myth of an ephemeral wedlock[197] followed almost immediately by the young god's death.

The sexless creature that Ea creates for the rescue of Ishtar is likely to find favor in the eyes of Ereshkigal, the enemy of all who produce life.

*Asushunamir's task is to calm Ereshkigal's wrath and to make her utter the oath of the gods. The eunuch succeeds in carrying out the scheme; after Ereshkigal has pledged her word, he asks her for the bag of the Water of Life. The queen of the Nether World sees now that she has been duped, but the oath obliges her to grant Asushunamir's request. As a revenge, she curses the eunuch, allotting to him food and drink from the gutters and the open air for his habitation.*[198]

The astonishing belief that the Water of Life was detained in the realm of the dead finds its counterpart in the myth of the Water of

---

[194] Ishtar is associated with childbirth only in those cases where she usurps the role of the mother-goddess in mythology (see n. 175 above).

[195] The animals mentioned all have a gestation period of several months.

[196] Text by Kramer and Jacobsen, Vol. XII (July, 1953), 160–87.

[197] The above mentioned Sumerian myth allows even the interpretation that Tammuz was killed before the marriage had been consummated.

[198] Cf. Enkidu's curse against the harlot (tablet VII).

Death which Gilgamesh has to cross before he attains the immortal Utnapishtim.[199]

*Ereshkigal commands her vizier, Namtar, to call together the* Anunnaki[200] *and to seat them on golden thrones. Ishtar shall be sprinkled with the Water of Life and conducted out of Ereshkigal's palace. Namtar, however, has to require a ransom for Ishtar, in default of which the goddess must be brought back to the* Arallu.[201] *The vizier thereupon guides Ishtar through the seven gates and returns to her each time the ornament of which she had previously been stripped. Ereshkigal then gives instructions in behalf of Tammuz, who shall be washed and anointed; a red garment shall be given to him and a flute of lapis lazuli; courtesans are to turn his mood.*

It may be inferred from these passages that Ishtar is released only on the condition that somebody else will take her place in the Nether World.

Ereshkigal's orders concerning Tammuz are probably meant for the time when the young god is brought to the *Arallu* as Ishtar's ransom (see below). He is, however, not to be treated as Ishtar had been: no diseases are released against Tammuz, and he is not put to death. Ereshkigal receives him, on the contrary, as an honored guest[202] and does everything to make Tammuz feel comfortable in her palace. Her welcome, together with the fact that Nergal is not mentioned at all in the myth, might suggest that Tammuz is to be Ereshkigal's husband during his sojourn in the Nether World.[203]

*The goddess Belili*[204] *is stringing her jewelry when she hears a sound announcing the arrival of her brother.*[205] *At this, she shows great concern and beseeches her brother not to bring woe upon her. She wishes that the dead may rise and smell the incense on the day when Tammuz*

199 See tablet XI.

200 Cf. Chapter II above, p. 59; here the *Anunnaki* are the seven judges of the Nether World.

201 This condition is mentioned only in the Ashur text.

202 Cf. Utnapishtim's offer of a bath, ointment, and a garment to Gilgamesh, p. 182 above.

203 Cf. in Greek mythology the alternate sojourn of Adonis, the Grecised form of the Phoenician Tammuz, with Aphrodite or with Persephone.

204 Probably, but not certainly, Ishtar.

205 Perhaps the sun-god Utu, or else Tammuz himself.

*is coming up to her with his flute, accompanied by wailing women and men.*[206]

This concluding passage of the poem is extremely obscure and has been the object of many tentative interpretations, which are all unsatisfactory since they start with the assumption that the mythical relationship between Ishtar and Tammuz is an affectionate one. Such may be the case in a great part of the Ishtar-Tammuz legends, but not in all. The substantial fact which underlies all the mythic tales is the close connection of their functions. But while god and goddess appear in some legends as husband and wife, their relationship in the myth "Ishtar's Descent to the Nether World" is definitely hostile. The goddess' concern at the end of the poem alludes perhaps to her fear that Tammuz might take revenge on her as soon as he comes up from the Nether World, since she has been the reason for his sojourn in the realm of death. This appears from an addition to the Sumerian version of the myth[207] stating that Ishtar ascended from the Nether World accompanied by a host of demons who had been charged by Ereshkigal with bringing back another deity, in exchange for Ishtar, as her ransom. The goddess, going from city to city with her ghastly host, meets several minor gods, who all behave in a way that pleases Ishtar, so that she does not allow the demons to take any of the deities with them. When she arrives in front of Tammuz, however, the god's attitude of indifference arouses her anger and she hands him over to the demons in spite of his supplication to Utu. An echo of this hostile attitude of Ishtar's towards Tammuz is to be found also in the Gilgamesh epic, tablet VI, in which the hero accuses the goddess of faithlessness to her lovers, among whom he cites Tammuz first.

The Sumerian version of the myth[208] is undoubtedly the older one and appears more complete than the Semitic text. Ishtar, called here Inanna, leaves her seven temples[209] and arrays herself in her seven ordi-

[206] The passage might perhaps find its explanation in a ritual purpose; it might be supposed that the recitation of the underworld myth was part of a funeral rite, promising resurrection to the dead, at the example of Ishtar and, afterwards, Tammuz.

[207] See Kramer, *ANET*, 52, n. 6.

[208] Text published by S. N. Kramer, *Proceedings* of the American Philosophical Society (Philadelphia, 1942), pls. I–X.

[209] In Uruk, Badtibira, Zabalam, Adab, Nippur, Kish, and Agade.

nances:[210] a crown, a measuring rod of lapis lazuli, a necklace of small lapis lazuli stones, two breast stones, a golden ring, a breastplate, and a garment.[211]

A significant passage of the Sumerian text, without counterpart in the Akkadian version, consists of Ishtar's instructions to Ninshubur, her vizier and faithful messenger. Before she descends to the *Arallu,* she tells him to dress in mourning as soon as she will have reached the realm of the dead and to ask the great gods, one after the other, to save her from the Nether World. This seems rather puzzling since she does not even consider the possibility of her return to the upper world without help but appears to be convinced a priori of the failure of her enterprise. The three days which Ninshubur lets pass before he goes into action are not a term set by the goddess since she does not mention them in her instructions.

Another point at which the Sumerian version differs from the Akkadian text[212] is the manner in which Ea comes to Ishtar's rescue: he fashions two, instead of one, sexless creatures and entrusts to them the Food and Water of Life, apparently his own property, which the two beings are to carry to the *Arallu.* They sprinkle the two miraculous substances sixty times on the corpse of the goddess and restore her to life.

## NERGAL AND ERESHKIGAL

The legend of the marriage of the two underworld deities is probably more recent than the preceding myth, since Nergal is not even mentioned in the tale of Ishtar's descent to the *Arallu.*

The text is known to us from two pieces of a damaged tablet. Both fragments, one of which has been inscribed on one face only, belong

210 Mention is made later of seven ordinances which belong to Ereshkigal (probably symbols of her sovereignty), and which Ishtar perhaps wants to snatch away from her sister. In this case, we would have here the trace of a motive for Ishtar's journey: she desires to become queen in Ereshkigal's stead. In this sense we might perhaps understand also Enlil's words, on refusing to save his daughter from the Arallu: "Inanna has asked for the great above, has asked for the great below."

211 The girdle of birthstones is not mentioned in the Sumerian text. In the older period the functions of the goddess of love and of the mother-goddess were more distinct than in the later period, when Ishtar gradually absorbs all the other female deities.

212 For further instances see n. 191 and 211 above; the Sumerian version does not mention the consequences on earth of Ishtar's disappearance.

to a school text and have been found at El-Amarna; they date from the fourteenth century B.C.

The fragments have been published by:

C. Bezold and E. A. Wallis Budge, *The Tell El-Amarna Tablets in the British Museum* (London, 1892), 82 (fragment A).

O. Schröder, *Vorderasiatische Bibliothek* (1915), 195 (fragment B).

### FRAGMENT A (OBVERSE)

*The gods prepare a great feast to which all the deities are invited. Only Ereshkigal, who must not leave her abode in the Nether World, cannot personally partake of the banquet. Therefore the gods ask her to send a messenger to heaven so that he may get her portion of the meal and take it to her. Namtar, the vizier of the underworld queen, thereupon enters the house of the gods, who all rise to their feet to greet him, in token of their homage to Ereshkigal.*

(The gap between fragments A and B probably correspond to the statement that one of the gods, Nergal, does not welcome Namtar. This lack of respect, duly reported by the vizier to his queen, is interpreted by Ereshkigal as an insult to herself, and she decides to kill Nergal.)

### FRAGMENT B

*Namtar appears once more before the gods and asks them to deliver up the deity who had not risen before Ereshkigal's representative. They agree to allow the emissary to take the guilty one with him. Nergal, however, has vanished, and Namtar must return unsuccessful to his mistress. Ereshkigal sends her messenger once more, and this time there is no means of escape. Nergal, very much afraid of Ereshkigal, applies to Ea for assistance. The water-god assigns to him fourteen demons to help him against his enemy. When Nergal arrives with his host at the gate of the Nether World, he asks the gatekeeper for admittance. The servant reports the god's arrival to Namtar, who, overjoyed to recognize Nergal, announces the good news to Ereshkigal. The goddess orders her vizier to have the visitor enter so that she may kill him.*

### FRAGMENT A (REVERSE)

*Nergal stations the demons at each of the fourteen gates of the under-*

*world and bids them open the doors. Then he races toward Ereshkigal and throws her down from the throne, threatening to kill her. In the face of this danger, the goddess humbles herself and offers Nergal the lordship over the Nether World. They are to become husband and wife, and Nergal shall hold the tablet of wisdom in his hand. The god agrees, and their conciliation is concluded.*

According to this legend, Nergal had once been a celestial god. His primitive functions are not alluded to, but it is very probable that as yet he was not a deity of death. He becomes a god of the Nether World through his marriage with Ereshkigal.

There exists, however, another tale concerning Nergal's presence in the *Arallu,* which is narrated in the myth of "Enlil and Ninlil."[213] Here Nergal is the son of the divine couple, destined for the realm of the dead since his father Enlil had been banished from the upper world before Nergal was born.

It may be possible that once there existed two different traditions concerning the *Arallu* in Mesopotamia, one centering around a queen, and the other around a king, of the Nether World. In the legend of Ishtar's descent to the Land of No Return, the underworld is ruled by a female deity. The description of the *Arallu* in the Sumerian appendix of the Gilgamesh epic, on the other hand, does not mention Ereshkigal, while Nergal appears as the only sovereign over the realm of the dead.

Both underworld deities seem therefore to be of distinct mythological origin, and to have been united only in a later stage of religious conception. The present legend about the marriage of Nergal and Ereshkigal appears to be nothing more than a device—probably of the priestly class—to reconcile the two different traditions.

### Kumma's Vision of the Nether World

This text is recorded on a large tablet from Ashur. While the obverse is almost completely mutilated, the reverse is fairly well preserved. The tablet dates from the seventh century B.C. and is a rather singular specimen of Mesopotamian literature. It is written in prose, which is unusual for a literary text of this order. The scribe does not mention his name but states in the concluding lines that his recording of Kumma's vision

[213] See Kramer, *Sumerian Mythology,* 47–48.

is an expiatory act meant to obtain the favor of the underworld deities.

The text has been published by W. von Soden in *Zeitschrift für Assyriologie* (1936), 1 ff.

Since the first half of the text is almost completely destroyed, the possible political and mythological implications of the story remain obscure. The personage who has been favored with the nocturnal vision is an Assyrian prince disguised under the pseudonym of Kumma. His father probably reigns at that time over Assyria, and Kumma seems to be his first-born. Apparently a great emergency of some kind has arisen in the country, which prompts the crown prince to solicit a vision of the Nether World.

(The narration is primarily a description of various infernal personages whom the prince encounters on his progress through the realm of the dead.)

*Kumma beholds first Namtar, vizier of the underworld, who clutches the hair of a victim in one hand and holds a sword in the other. The visitor then passes fifteen monstrous deities,*[214] *to all of whom he addresses his prayers. Afterwards, he meets a personage black as pitch, with a bird's head and clad in a red cloak.*[215] *Eventually Kumma beholds Nergal, the awesome ruler of the Nether World. The god sits on a throne, a crown on his head*[216] *and a mace in each hand; lightning flashes from his arms. The* Anunnaki *stand reverently to the right and left of their sovereign.*

[214] Namtartu (the vizier's consort, with the head of a sphinx and human hands and feet); the death god (with the head of a serpent-dragon and human hands and feet); the Demon Shedu (human head and hands, the feet as the claws of a bird, his left foot treads on a crocodile); Alluhappu (the head of a lion and four human hands and feet); *Mukil-resh-lemutti* (the head and the wings of a bird, and human hands and feet) Humuttabal, the boatman (the head of a bird, hands and feet . . . [unintelligible]); another Demon [name unintelligible], the head of an ox, and four human hands and feet); Utukku (the head of a lion, hands and feet of a bird); Shulak (a lion standing upright); Mamitu (the head of a goat, human hands and feet); Nedu, the gatekeeper (the head of a lion, human hands, feet of a bird); Mimalemnu (two heads, one of a lion, the other . . . [unintelligible]); another demon ([name unintelligible] . . . three feet, two of a bird, one of an ox); two gods whose names Kumma does not know (one with the head, hands, and feet of a bird; the other with a "crowned" human head, his right hand carrying a mace).

[215] See the concluding passage of "Ishtar's Descent to the Nether World," in which Tammuz is to be clothed with a red garment on his arrival in the *Arallu.*

[216] The mutilated text seems to imply that Nergal had two heads.

*The god grasps Kumma by his hair and draws him before the throne. Overcome with terror, the prince kisses Nergal's feet, but the king of the* Arallu *threatens to kill the earthly visitor. Ishum, the infernal ruler's merciful counselor, advises against such a cruel decision and proposes that Kumma be permitted to ascend once more to the upper world and to exalt there the glory of Nergal. The god consents, and decides to spare Kumma. He nevertheless berates the prince severely for having slighted Ereshkigal, his beloved wife.*[217]

*According to the queen's own wish, Kumma shall be taken to the northwest gate, from which he may ascend once more to the earth. As a condition for the suspension of the death sentence, Kumma has to promise not to forget the god and his awesome realm. There are, however, still many troubles in store for the prince during his lifetime.*

*The king of the* Arallu *shows Kumma one of the underworld personages:*[218] *he is a shepherd, to whom Nergal's father had granted the high favors of becoming king and high priest of Ashur; he had been assigned three deities*[219] *who were to protect him in battle. Nergal then criticizes Kumma's father, who, though wise and full of experience, has disobeyed a god*[220] *and acted against divine rules. The infernal ruler has decreed that both Kumma and his father be overwhelmed soon by a fearsome divine majesty.*[221] *Then he sends the visitor back to the earth.*

*Kumma, after awakening from his dream,*[222] *darts forth into the street of his city, emitting a loud lamentation; he then praises before the subjects of Ashur the valor of Nergal and Ereshkigal.*

*The scribe, upon hearing Kumma's report, ceases to take bribes as he did before, and, in order to be protected from all evil, he decides to carry out Nergal's commands.*

[217] The nature of the offence is obscure; probably the explication would be found on the mutilated obverse of the tablet.

[218] The reference is perhaps to the "pitch-black figure" mentioned after the fifteen demons and is possibly identical with Tammuz.

[219] Yabru, Humba, and Naprushu (pertaining to the Elamite pantheon).

[220] Probably Ashur.

[221] Possibly referring once more to Ashur.

[222] For the character of reality attributed to dreams in Mesopotamia, see Chapter II above, p. 97–98.

### THE EPIC OF ERA

This legend is quite similar in tendency to the preceding poem. The extant fragments of the text, dating probably from the Old Babylonian period, are unfortunately insufficient to allow a clear interpretation of the story. Of the five tablets which, according to the colophon, have constituted the poem, the second and the third ones are almost completely destroyed, and the remaining ones are written in a language that presents unusual difficulties.

The extant text has been published by P. F. Gössmann, *Das Era-Epos* (Würzburg, 1956).[223]

*The principal personage of the poem is Era, or Irra, god of death and pestilence, also known under the name of Nergal. At his side stands Ishum, the merciful counselor who tries to bridle Era's desire for destruction.*[224] *The god is surrounded by his seven terrifying helpers, sons of Anu and the Earth, who urge Era to do battle and to exterminate all men and beasts. But in his way stands Marduk, the god of Babylon, who protects his city and is not likely to permit Era's enterprise. While Marduk sits on his throne, the god of pestilence cannot execute his plan; he therefore attempts to persuade Marduk to abandon his temple temporarily and to descend towards the* Apsu. *The pretext advanced by Era is that the crown and other jewels of Marduk have become dirty and need to be cleaned or replaced. This can be done only in the* Apsu, *and the god of Babylon must descend there personally. Marduk, however, has his doubts about the consequences of his temporary absence from his city; once before, the patron deity of Babylon had abandoned his throne, and the result was a disastrous flood. Era promises Marduk to keep watch over the earth during the other god's absence and thus disperses all misgivings. As soon as Marduk has left his throne, however, Era takes advantage of his new position and, with his seven helpers, wreaks destruction all over the land. He is hindered by Ishum, who repeatedly tries to stop the devastation. Thanks to the merciful counselor, a part of Babylon's people survive the disaster. At last Era's rage abates;*

---

[223] See also E. Reiner, "More Fragments of the Epic of Era," *JNES*, Vol. XVII (January, 1958), 41 ff.

[224] Cf. Ishum's role in the preceding poem.

*he retires to his temple Emeslam and orders Ishum to increase Babylon's prosperity.*

The poem has, according to the scribe Kabti-ilani-Marduk, the power of an amulet: whosoever places the tablets in his house or chants the words will obtain immunity to pestilence and increase of riches and fame. As a charm, the text fulfills the role of Ishum, who, though not the principal personage of the story, is yet the hero of the narration: he is extolled at the beginning of the poem as well as at the end. Through Ishum's intercession mankind has been preserved from extermination, and through reverence of the present epic the worshiper of Ishum may escape pestilence whenever Era and his seven helpers ravage the land.

An exceptional feature of the Era epic is the reference made by the scribe to an inspiration granted to him at night by Ishum. This apparently implies that the scribe was also the poet of the epic, and we therefore have in this text one of the few instances in which a Mesopotamian author's name has come down to us with sufficient reliability.[225]

### THE MYTH OF ZU

Fragments of this tale have come down to us in an Assyrian (Nineveh) and an Old Babylonian version (Susa and Ashur); together, those fragments constitute a text without beginning or end, but the import of which appears fairly well from the extant material.

The Akkadian text has been published by:

J. Nougayrol, *Revue d'Assyriologie* (1952), 87ff. (Susa).

E. Ebeling, *Revue d'Assyriologie* (1952), 25ff. (Ashur).

L. W. King, *Cuneiform Texts from Babylonian Tablets in the British Museum* (London, 1902), pls. 39ff. (Nineveh).

*Enlil exercises supreme sovereignty ("Enlilship") over all the pantheon. To convey his decrees to the gods, he makes use of a messenger, the bird-god Zu,[226] to whom he entrusts the keys[227] of his shrine and the office of providing him with clean water. While Zu is thus in constant*

---

[225] Another poem, where the scribe is probably also the poet, is the "Acrostic Dialogue on Human Misery" treated below.

[226] Zu is known also as an underworld deity; it might be that after his misdeed he was banished to the *Arallu*.

[227] The Akkadian word is not legible here; instead of "keys," is might also mean "care," or the like.

*attendance upon the god, he watches with envy the exercise of sover-*
*eignty by Enlil. Zu is aware that his master's power resides in his crown*
*and robe but most of all in the tablets of destiny, which confer upon*
*Enlil command over each of the gods. Wishing to become himself the*
*supreme ruler over the* Igigi, *Zu decides to snatch away the tablets of des-*
*tiny. He stations himself at the entrance of his master's sanctuary and*
*awaits the moment when Enlil puts off his crown and robe to wash*
*himself with water. Then he quickly seizes the tablets of destiny and*
*disappears. Zu having thus won the "Enlilship," all the norms are sus-*
*pended; Enlil has been deprived of his power, and there is great con-*
*sternation among the* Igigi. *Anu, who acts as the father of all the gods,*
*presides over the divine assembly and bids one of them go and slay Zu.*
*The god who will challenge the thief is promised supremacy over all*
*the others, once he accomplishes the act.*

*But no one has the courage to oppose Zu, who has become omnip-*
*otent through possession of the tablets. After Adad, another god (the*
*mutilated text does not indicate the name*[228]*), and Shara*[229] *have refused*
*to undertake the enterprise, the gods, deeply preoccupied, exchange*
*counsel and turn to Ea, the wisest among them.*

*He inspires them with confidence, affirming that he has decided*
*Zu's downfall. Then he asks Mah, the mother of all the gods,*[230] *to*
*send her son Ningirsu*[231] *against Zu. Mah*[232] *consents and invites her*
*first-born to fight the thief.*

*The champion of the gods shall use his seven winds as weapons*
*and cut Zu's breath, direct poisonous arrows against him, and confound*
*him with a terrible battle cry. Ningirsu thereupon sets forth on his*
*journey towards the mountains where Zu has hidden. Mah accompanies*
*her son, together with the team of the seven evil winds.*

*Zu comes up from his mountain to face Ningirsu. Wrathfully, he*

[228] Perhaps Lugalbanda, who in another text is said to have fought against Zu (see L. W. King, *Cuneiform Texts*, pls. 41–42). In the Old Babylonian version, Shara is mentioned directly after Adad and no third deity is named.

[229] Son of Ishtar and god of fire.

[230] In the Creation epic it is Tiamat who holds the role of mother of all the gods.

[231] Patron of Lagash and originally a chthonic deity, he became later a war-god. The Ashur text substitutes Ninurta, likewise a war-god.

[232] Mah or Mami is the ancient mother-goddess, also called Aruru, Ninhursag, etc.

*proclaims that the tablets of fate make him invulnerable and protect him from any aggressor. Ningirsu, undaunted, opens the battle and shoots an arrow at Zu. But the arrow does not hit the bird-god, because he orders it to disintegrate and return to the canebrake where its shaft had grown; the wings are bidden to return to the birds from which they were taken. Zu likewise commands the stave and the gut of the bow to return to their place of origin.*

*Thus Ningirsu is impotent against the owner of the tablets which confer magic efficacy to Zu's words. He sends Adad[233] to Ea with word of his misfortune. Adad obeys Ningirsu's behest and returns to the mountains with Ea's new instructions: the wise water-god has invented a plan to invalidate Zu's formula.[234]*

The result of the battle against Zu is not known, since the text fails us here. It may be assumed that Ningirsu succeeded finally in subduing the thief and recovering the all-important tablets.

The identity of the hero who won the victory is not the same in the various versions. While the Nineveh recension breaks off at Shara's refusal to fight Zu, the Ashur text always mentions Ninurta instead of Ningirsu, who is the hero of the Susa tablets. In a hymn of Ashurbanipal, the credit for having slain Zu is given to Marduk.

This legend is important for revealing the conception of "Enlilship" in Mesopotamia. The supreme god's authority is based exclusively on magic power derived from the tablets of destiny, which have here the quality of a talisman. Once deprived of the tablets, Enlil is powerless; he is not even mentioned again after the theft has occurred. Another god, Anu, presides over the assembly; it is Ea who devises the plan to destroy Zu, and Ningirsu-Ninurta recovers the tablets.

In Mesopotamian mythology Zu is a storm-god and may be of

233 Presumably he had accompanied the champion to the mountains.

234 This obscure passage might perhaps be interpreted as follows: Ningirsu is to provide his arrows with a ferrule, probably to replace the feathers usually attached to an arrow-butt. Then the south wind shall cast down Zu's pinions, and while the bird-god will be occupied with the state of his wings, Ningirsu is to shoot an arrow at Zu. Even if the thief uses his magic words again, they will not arrest the arrow, since the feathers addressed by Zu will not be those of the butt of the dart but the pinions of the bird-god himself. Another explanation could be that Ningirsu is to procure himself somehow feathers of Zu, perhaps by means of the south wind, and to attach them to the arrows. Zu's words "Wings, return to the birds," would then carry the dart unfailingly to its aim.

beneficent character when, under the form of a thundercloud, he destroys the Bull of Heaven, originator of the scorching droughts. It may be that the myth reflects an ancient rivalry between Enlil and Zu, since both are wind deities; they may even have emanated from two different ethnic groups, and the mythical struggle perhaps veils an ancient political antagonism.

The recompense offered to the god who will slay Zu is similar to the one mentioned in the Creation epic: Marduk is promised supreme sovereignty over all the gods as a reward for his victory over Tiamat.[235] Here, too, the tablets of fate confer magical power and supreme authority upon their owner,[236] but the talismanic virtue of the tablets is less stressed in the Creation epic than in the Zu myth, which is probably much older.

There exist also Sumerian fragments dealing with Zu, but none of them relate the theft of the tablets; therefore, a parallel cannot be established.

### The Myth of Etana

This legend is known through fragments of an Old Babylonian, a Middle Assyrian, and a Neo-Assyrian version, which furnish a fairly connected narrative; the conclusion of the myth is, however, not recorded.

The Akkadian text has been published by:

S. Langdon, *Babyloniaca* (1931), pls. I–XIV (Old Babylonian and Neo-Assyrian versions).

E. Ebeling, *Archiv für Orientforschung* (1944), pls. IX–XII (Middle Assyrian version and additional Neo-Assyrian fragments).

The story takes its title from the principal personage, Etana, a legendary king of the postdiluvian dynasty of Kish, who was believed to be of divine nature[237] and who exercised the function of a shepherd.

The legend, as it emerges from the various versions, appears very

235 Cf. also the fragment of the Labbu (see King, *Cuneiform Texts*), where several gods are promised the highest rank in recompense for their slaying the monster.

236 For the relationship between magic power and authority, see Chapter II above, p. 50.

237 His name, as that of Gilgamesh, is usually preceeded by the sign ⟩⟩⟨, the determinative for "god."

much in the form of a drama in two acts preceded by a prologue. We shall therefore divide the text according to the different scenes of action, rather than describe each fragment separately.

### Prologue

*The great gods sit together in counsel, at a time when on earth no king has as yet held sway over the people. The insignia of kingship— tiara, crown, scepter, and crook—are deposited before Anu in heaven. Ishtar, wishing to provide the people with a leader, searches for a man who would be a fit shepherd of the inhabitants of the land. Eventually the gods decide to lower kingship from heaven.* [Here the introductory text breaks off in both the Old Babylonian and the Neo-Assyrian versions.]

### First Act

*An eagle and a serpent have made up their minds to form a friendship. They swear a solemn oath by the Nether World, in the presence of Shamash, the god of justice, to guarantee their covenant. They establish their abode in a tree*[238]: *the eagle builds his nest in the crown, the serpent at the roots. Each time the serpent catches an animal, part of the booty goes to the eagle and his young; likewise, the eagle divides his prey with the serpent and his young.*[239]

*But once the young of the eagle have grown strong, their father plots evil against his friend: he decides to devour the young of the serpent. By flying up into the sky, he will be able to escape vengeance. His own little fledgling tries to dissuade him from his wicked design and warns his father against the consequences of breaking the oath sworn before Shamash. The eagle, however, does not take to heart the wise counsel of his son, but descends to the serpent's nest and devours the young of his friend.*

*When the serpent returns to the tree with fresh meat, he finds his nest destroyed. In desperation, he weeps for his murdered offspring and*

---

[238] The styrax tree (cf. R. Campbell Thompson, *A Dictionary of Assyrian Chemistry and Geology* [London, 1936], XXVI).

[239] In the Old Babylonian and the Middle-Assyrian versions, the eagle is not mentioned as requiting the serpent's kindness by sharing food with the reptile and its young.

*brings his plea before Shamash. He asks the god of justice to wreak vengeance on the eagle,*[240] *who has broken the oath of friendship.*

Shamash promises his help and advises the serpent to hide in the belly of a freshly killed ox, which the god will prepare for him. The eagle will surely come, along with other birds, to devour the flesh of the ox; as soon as he gropes into the interior of the dead beast, the serpent shall seize his false friend, pluck out his wings, pinions, and talons, and cast him into a pit where he will die of starvation.

The serpent follows Shamash's counsel, finds the ox, and hides in the animal's belly. As predicted, the eagle arrives to partake of the ox's flesh. The young fledgling, who accompanies his father, warns him against the possible presence of the serpent, who may plot vengeance against the murderer of his young. The greedy eagle does not heed his son's warning, thinking himself safe.

But the serpent seizes and threatens to kill his treacherous friend. The evildoer pleads for mercy and promises the serpent a rich gift. But the defrauded animal does not relent, since the eagle's punishment would be turned against himself should he show mercy to his foe.[241] The serpent therefore tears off the eagle's wings, pinions, and talons and casts him into a pit, leaving him to die of starvation.

The bird beseeches Shamash to succor him and promises that he will in return praise Shamash's name forever. Shamash refuses to listen to him, since the eagle has acted evilly and has eaten that which the gods have forbidden.[242] The god promises, however, to send a man to rescue the bird.

### SECOND ACT

*Etana, a pious man,* [243] *daily sacrifices lambs to Shamash and be-*

240 In the Neo-Assyrian version the eagle is once called "Zu."

241 Such a concept of justice, which does not allow mercy, is also found in the Middle-Assyrian laws, e.g., paragraph 40: ". . . female slaves must not veil themselves, and he who has seen a female slave veiled must arrest her and bring her to the palace tribunal. . . . the one who arrested her shall take her clothes. If a seignior has seen a female slave veiled and has let her go without arresting her . . . they shall flog him fifty times with staves . . . his prosecutor shall take his clothes" (text of the law in *ANET*, 183).

242 Note that Shamash does not condemn the break of friendship but the fact that the eagle has eaten serpent flesh.

243 The text does not mention Etana's kingship.

213

*seeches the god to grant him the Plant of Birth, so that he may have a son. Eventually Shamash answers his prayers and indicates to Etana the pit where the eagle lies; the bird will show the shepherd the miraculous plant.*

*Etana crosses the mountains and finds the pit. The eagle promises to procure a human offspring for Etana in return for being lifted out of the pit. Etana brings food and tries to fill in the pit as much as possible, but the weakened eagle is unable to rise after three vain attempts.* [The destroyed remainder of the fragment probably relates how Etana finally succeeds in helping the bird out of the pit. The narration is resumed in another fragment.]

*The eagle tells Etana a dream: he and his rescuer arrived in heaven before the gates of Anu, Enlil, and Ea, where they made obeisance; then they proceeded towards the gates of Sin, Shamash, Adad, and finally Ishtar. When they arrived before the goddess, who detained the Plant of Birth, they saw her sitting on her throne in all her splendor, with lions at her feet. At this moment, the eagle's dream ends. Taking the vision for a good presage, the bird proposes that Etana climb on his back so that they may both arrive before Ishtar. The shepherd places his hands and arms on the eagle's wings and sides,*[244] *and the bird soars toward heaven with his burden.*

*They ascend for three leagues, and after each one the eagle calls to Etana to look at the earth which lies below. The shepherd sees in wonder how the land around the Ekur temple*[245] *dwindles more and more and the sea loses its greatness. At last they arrive at the heaven of Anu and do obeisance before the gates of the three gods, as the dream had foretold.*

*Again the eagle encourages his friend to sit on his back and hold on to his wings and sides; he calls once more to Etana to look at the earth below. Land and sea have shrunk to the size of a bread basket. But when, after the third league above the heaven of Anu, earth and sea disappear altogether, Etana is seized with fear and will no longer ascend to Ishtar's gate. The eagle plunges down, one league after another, until both of them fall close to the ground of Anu's heaven. The bird*

---

[244] The Akkadian words *"kappu"* and *"idu"* have each a double significance: "wing" —"hand" and "arm"—"side."

[245] Sanctuary of Enlil in Nippur.

*has been bruised.* [What has become of Etana, and how his adventure turned out, is not known, since the text breaks off. Only from the fact that the Sumerian king list mentions as Etana's successor his son Balih may we infer that the enterprise has been crowned with success.]

As appears from the text, there are two distinct main courses of action, linked together by the figure of the eagle. It might very well be that here, too, as in many other Akkadian myths, we have two originally independent stories that have been joined only in a later period.

Moreover, the initial lines of the legend, which we have treated as a prologue, mention neither Etana, the eagle, nor the serpent; even the gods cited in the prologue do not reappear in the main parts of the text.[246] The only deity playing a role in both "acts" is Shamash, who on the other hand is not mentioned in the prologue. It is possible that the sequel to the prologue, destroyed in the Old Babylonian as well as in the Neo-Assyrian version, would have furnished the explication of a connection between the introduction and the two main parts.

The myth described in Act I reflects in all probability an ancient rivalry between two deities whose emblems were respectively the eagle (a frequent attribute of solar gods) and the serpent (usually connected with chthonic deities). The fact that Shamash actually punishes the eagle for having eaten serpent flesh—"the detested of the gods and the forbidden"—adds to the evidence that the bird's crime was considered by the god not so much a violation of justice as an offense against ritual precepts.

In the second act we note that Etana has to pass through seven gates before he arrives in the presence of Ishtar.[247] The remedy which the shepherd claims of the goddess is not a birthstone or other mineral talisman but a plant. The reason therefor lies probably in the fact that birthstones[248] were considered by the Mesopotamians only as having the power to facilitate delivery. Etana, however, is obviously in need of a remedy for his wife's barrenness. Just as Gilgamesh searched for a miraculous

[246] They merely give their names to the seven gates of heaven and accept Etana's and the eagle's homage but do not enter into action.

[247] Cf. the seven gates of the Nether World, which lead to the throne of Ereshkigal.

[248] Cf. Ishtar's ornaments laid aside at the fifth gate of the *Arallu* (Akkadian version).

plant in order to obtain rejuvenation, so Etana desires a magical herb which will procure an offspring for him.

There are no Sumerian texts bearing on the Etana myth, but it is quite probable that a Sumerian version did exist. Many old seals show the Etana story, depicting the shepherd's ascension towards heaven on the back of an eagle. A trace of the myth is still to be found in the Ethiopic version of the Alexander legend: the Macedonian hero is said to have soared towards heaven on the back of an eagle.

## THE MYTH OF ADAPA

The text of this legend is extant in four fragments. The oldest one, fragment II, dates from the fourteenth century B.C. Fragments III and IV derive from the library of Ashurbanipal in Nineveh. Fragment I, too, has been excavated at Nineveh, but belongs to another version; it is the only part of the Adapa story which is written in verses, fragments II, III, and IV being in prose.

The cuneiform text has been published by:

A. T. Clay, *Yale Oriental Series* (1922), pls. IV–VI (fragment I).

O. Schröder, *Vorderasiatische Schriftdenkmäler* (1915), 194 (fragment II).

R. Campbell Thompson, *The Epic of Gilgamesh* (Oxford, 1930), pl. 31 (fragment III).

S. A. Strong, in *Proceedings of the Society of Biblical Archaeology* (1894), 274 ff. (fragment IV).

From the fact that at least three different versions of the legend existed, it may be guessed that the story of Adapa was highly popular in ancient Mesopotamia.

Adapa shares with Gilgamesh not only the narrowly missed opportunity of gaining immortality but also the ambiguous position of being a god's "favorite." Both he and Gilgamesh incur trouble by following the directions of their personal gods: Gilgamesh offends Enlil by felling the Holy Cedar upon invitation of Shamash; Adapa incites Anu's wrath by executing to the letter the instructions of Ea.

*Adapa, the perfect priest of Eridu, has been created by Ea as the model of a man. The god has endowed his predilected son*[249] *with*

[249] Although a creature of Ea, Adapa is frequently called the god's son.

*supreme wisdom but not with immortality. Adapa watches personally
to see that the devotions and sacrifices in Eridu are properly executed
and sails into the sea to do the fishing*[250] *prescribed for the sanctuary of
Ea in Eridu. One day, while he is in his boat on the open sea, the south
wind*[251] *blows so hard that the priest is thrown into the water and nearly
drowns. Thereupon he casts a curse against the wind, wishing that its
wing be broken. As soon as Adapa has pronounced the fatal words,
the wind's wing does break, and stillness settles over the sea.*

*After seven days, Anu notices that the south wind no longer blows
over the country and asks his vizier the reason. The servant answers
that Adapa, Ea's son, has broken the wind's wing. Thereupon Anu
demands that the priest be immediately brought before his throne. At
this news, Ea instructs his priest on the behavior to be adopted during
the journey towards heaven: Adapa is to wear mourning garb and
leave his hair uncut. His apparel will then prompt the two deities who
stand at Anu's gate to inquire into the reason for the mourning garb.
Adapa is to answer that his distress is caused by the disappearance of
two gods, Tammuz and Gishzida,*[252] *from the earth. Since these are the
very deities standing at the gate,*[253] *they will be pleased with Adapa's
attitude, and the priest may count on their intercession in his behalf
before Anu's throne.*

*Ea, proceeding with his instructions, counsels Adapa not to eat the
bread*[254] *or drink the water which will be offered to him when he stands
in the presence of Anu, since these aliments will be lethal. If he is
offered a garment, he shall put it on; likewise is he to anoint himself
with the oil which will be presented to him.*

*Strengthened by his god's advice, Adapa follows Anu's messenger,
who leads him up the road of heaven. As Ea had foreseen, Tammuz and*

[250] For the connection of Ea with fish, see p. 61 above.

[251] In Mesopotamian mythology the winds appeared as winged spirits.

[252] Gishzida or Ningishzida ("Lord of the tree of Life") is, like Tammuz, a god
of vegetation with seasonal death and resurrection. His attributes are very similar to those
of Tammuz, and he is often confused with the other god.

[253] This is the only Mesopotamian poem in which Tammuz is mentioned as being
in heaven.

[254] The Akkadian word means "bread" as well as "food" (see n. 55 above concerning the consistency of Mesopotamian bread).

217

*Gishzida stand at the gate and are much pleased with Adapa's mourning over their disappearance from the earth. When the priest arrives before Anu, the god questions him about the reasons which led him to break the wing of the south wind. Adapa relates the misfortune that befell him while he was fishing and how the unmotivated interference of the wind, who nearly drowned him, had provoked the wrathful curse. When he has finished, Tammuz and Gishzida make the expected intercession before Anu in favor of Adapa.*

*Anu wonders why Ea has endowed the priest, who is but a mortal, with supreme wisdom. What is then left for himself to offer to the visitor? At last the god orders that the bread and water of life be set before Adapa. But the protégé of Ea, mindful of his master's warning, does not touch the aliments of life. He only puts on the garment and annoints himself with the oil, which are likewise brought to him.*

*Very much astonished, Anu questions Adapa concerning his refusal of the bread and water. The priest replies that he has been following the advice of Ea, his master, who told him not to touch food and drink.*

*Thereupon Anu dismisses Adapa angrily and orders him returned to the earth. But for the city of Eridu, Anu decrees release of feudal obligations and the glorification of its priesthood.* [The last lines of the fragment, partly mutilated, seem to imply that Adapa, by refusing the aliments of life, brought illness and disease upon mankind. These misfortunes are, however, alleviated by Ninkarrak, goddess of healing, who is asked to turn aside all malady.][255]

The principal theme of the legend is the offer, unwittingly refused, of immortality to a human being. This offer is made, as in the Gilgamesh epic, not as the recompense of a deserving action, but as a hospitable gift[256] which has not been expressly solicited.

[255] It may be that the end of the text consisted of an incantation formula meant to chase away the demon of illness from a sick person and to gain the favor of the goddess of healing. This would not be the only example where an incantation is preceded by a myth with an apparently unfavorable sense. So in the Atrahasis epic, the statement that the famine caused the cessation of births is followed by an incantation to facilitate delivery. Perhaps even the myth of Ishtar's descent to the *Arallu* (Akkadian version), in which the horrors of the Nether World are depicted, is to precede a magic formula meant to appease the dead.

[256] Cf. the ξένια of ancient Greece.

Ancient oriental custom obliged a host to offer a present to his guest, and it is in accomplishing this duty that Anu offers the bread and water of life to Adapa. It is not clear from the text whether Ea advised his priest not to partake of the aliments through ignorance of their true effect; it might be possible that the water-god purposely gave false counsel because he did not wish Adapa to attain immortality[257] lest he become equal to the gods.

It should be noted that it is not because of a grave offense that Adapa fails to attain eternal life: the fact that he broke the wing of the south wind is not judged harshly by Anu and apparently does not require a punishment. The reason for the failure seems tragically trivial, a mere misunderstanding, which, however, rests on a dissent between two deities.

There is no reason for seeing in the fate of Adapa a primitive account of the Fall of Man. No grave sin preceded the interview between god and man, and immortality was offered to Adapa after he had broken the wing of the south wind, not before. Even the consequence of Adapa's refusal is obviously of lesser moment than that of Adam's disobedience to God. The last lines of the fourth fragment seem to state that Adapa, by his unwise behavior, had brought misery and disease upon mankind. But at the same time Anu grants the city of Eridu, Adapa's homeland, exemption from feudal obligations and the establishment of a glorious priesthood.

The concept of guilt in a moral sense is altogether absent from Mesopotamian literature. The sentiment of honesty, too, is completely missing: the shrewd counsel of Ea regarding Tammuz and Gishzida smacks of hypocrisy. It is in perfect accord with the Mesopotamian view of life: cleverness and assiduous service of the gods assure divine favor, rather than sincerity of sentiment and rectitude of action.

[257] Cf. Gen. 3:22.

# CHAPTER V

*Speculative Literature*

T HIS GROUP OF AKKADIAN POETRY IS CHARACTERIZED by its subjective
view of man's existence and his link with the surrounding world.
It has developed from the ancient wisdom literature which was
in great favor throughout the Eastern world.[1] But while in the older
stage wisdom counsels are chiefly utilitarian and meant as a practical
guide,[2] in the later period a genre evolves which is, in a certain sense,

[1] See the "instructions" of Ptah-hotep, Amen-em-het, and others in Egypt; "Lun Yu"
of Confucius; the Book of Proverbs and the Ecclesiastes of the Old Testament; and the
Aramaic "Words of Ahiqar," etc.

[2] See the Sumerian proverbs, sometimes interspersed with Akkadian adaptations (text
published by S. Langdon in *American Journal of Semitic Languages and Literatures* [1912],

the predecessor of philosophy, especially of that branch of philosophy which tries to decipher the nature of the relationship between the human soul and the supernatural.

Akkadian speculative literature does not concern itself with cosmogonies and the problem of origins, as do the seven sages of Greece; the old myths answered such questions to the entire satisfaction of the individual. It is the position of man in the universe that occupies the speculative poet of Mesopotamia, the problem of Socrates and the Sophists.

The speculative attitude leads necessarily to a new examination of religious habits and sets up an inquiry about the basis of good and evil.

The beginnings of speculative literature are naturally to be found in religious texts. Religion, which hovers over the totality of spiritual life in Mesopotamia, is the oldest interpretation of the relationship between man and the universe. When reasoning begins to challenge faith, we arrive at the attitude of speculative literature.

In some of the Mesopotamian prayers we find, embedded between the hymnical introduction and the final supplication, the germ of a critical consideration of life and world order, as in a "Prayer of Lamentation to Ishtar,"[3] in which the supplicant demands an explanation for the evil which has befallen him. The author of "Prayer to an Unnamed God"[4] ignores the sin he may have committed and ruthfully beseeches the unknown deity whom he may have offended to reveal to him the nature of his transgression.

The conflict between human and divine judgment of a mortal's actions is explained by man's inadequacy to discern good and evil. Here emerges the realization of a discrepancy between the reward due for a pious life and the actual disfavor of the gods: the phenomenon of worldly injustice results from a difference between divine and human standards of good and evil.

The pessimism of such an attitude reaches its peak in those com-

234ff.), and the Akkadian counsels of wisdom (published by the same author in *Proceedings of the Society of Biblical Archaeology* [1916], 105ff.).

[3] Text published by L. W. King, *The Seven Tablets of Creation* (London, 1902), II, pls. 75–84.

[4] Text published by H. C. Rawlinson, *The Cuneiform Inscriptions of Western Asia*, Vol. IV, No. 10.

positions which have been characterized as the poems of the righteous sufferer. The best-known and most beautiful of these texts is the monologue "I Will Praise the Lord of Wisdom."

### "I Will Praise the Lord of Wisdom"

This poem, also called *"Ludlul bēl nēmeqi"* after the Akkadian initial words, consists of four fragmentary tablets, three of which have been excavated in Sippar, while the fourth comes from Ashur. It is probable that the poem was originally limited to the first part of the extant version, the pessimistic monologue on the misery and injustice of human life,[5] and that the second part, a eulogy on Marduk, was added at a later period.

The text has been published by H. C. Rawlinson, *The Cuneiform Inscriptions of Western Asia,* Vol. IV, No. 60 (London, 1891).

Both depth of reasoning and beauty of language mark the first two tablets as highly superior to the rest of the poem. The situation of the person involved resembles somewhat that of Job; the Babylonian speaker experiences woes of all kinds and is consequently threatened by a religious crisis.

The second part brings a rather artificial and spiritually unsatisfactory solution by introducing into the story Marduk, who restores the sufferer to his former health and glory.

(The first tablet is almost completely destroyed; it alludes to a brusque reversal of the protagonist's situation: once a lord, he has now become a slave, and his life consists of sorrow and distress.)

### Second Tablet

*Alone in this world, he is surrounded by evil and injustice. God and goddess do not listen to his prayers; the priests, whose incumbencies are divination, dream interpretation, necromancy, and magic, have all failed to help him, and his pitiable situation becomes worse every day. Where lies the reason for his misery? His present plight would seem to be the just punishment for impious behavior towards the gods; yet, he can remember how fervently he had always done his religious duties and how he had treated his king with reverence. In bewilderment, he no*

[5] Tablets I and II, with the exception of the last two lines.

*longer knows how to act since his righteous conduct has failed to attract
the favor of the deities. He suspects that the gods have another measure
for good and evil, far beyond human comprehension.*[6] *Man's life and
mood are constantly subject to changes: he who enjoyed health the
day before meets death on the morrow; merriment and arrogance
alternate with grief and despair.*

[After a small break, the sufferer complains about physical illness.]

*Disease demons have come up from the underworld to torment him
with chills, fever, and headache; he can no longer hear or see, and
weakness has overwhelmed the once vigorous body. All his limbs are
ill, and an evil ghost pursues him with terror. There is none to grant
him relief from his pains: conjurer, diviner, and enchanter do not lessen
his affliction; god and goddess show no mercy.*

*At last the hour of death arrives: while his grave is still open, the
greedy heirs seize his jewels; he is not yet dead when the dirge has
already ceased. At the news of his death, his enemies rejoice, and their
hearts are delighted.*

(The last two lines of the tablet express the sufferer's hope that
some day his affliction will come to an end through the mercy of the
gods.)[7]

### THIRD TABLET

(The first part, largely mutilated, alludes to dreams which, by
means of divine messengers, foretell the sufferer's salvation.)

*He is eventually shown favor by Marduk, who comes to his rescue.
His sins are carried away by the winds; one by one the evil demons are
chased back to the Nether World. His ears hear once more, his eyes
see again. Strength and vigor have returned to his weakened body, the
slave mark has been obliterated from his forehead. He is freed from
the evil incantation, protected through his benevolent savior from the
devouring lion.*

[6] Cf. the "Prayer to an Unnamed God" (Rawlinson, *Cuneiform Inscriptions,* Vol.
IV, No. 10): "Mankind, everyone that exists, what does he know? Whether he is committing sin or doing good, he does not even know."

[7] Cf. Ps. 102:13.

## Fourth Tablet

*Revivification is granted to him by Marduk, who pulls him out of the River of the Dead and saves him from his enemy. Ascended from the grave, he returns once more to life. In Babylon he enters the temple of his savior; as he traverses the twelve gates of the Esagil, he is relieved from all his misery. Purified from guilt and trouble, he appears before Marduk and kisses the foot of Sarpanit, the god's spouse. He offers incense and gifts to the deities, slaughters oxen and sheep, pours out libations, and provides the temple with oil and grain.*

*When he gives a banquet to the Babylonians, all of them wonder at his resurrection and praise Marduk, who saved him from the grave, and Sarpanit, who conferred life upon him. May every creature throughout the world unceasingly proclaim the glory of Marduk.*

Quite similar to this monologue in conception, though more elaborate in exterior form, is the "Acrostic Dialogue on Human Misery."

### "Acrostic Dialogue on Human Misery"

This poem has twenty-seven stanzas, fourteen of which are fairly well preserved. The eleven lines of each strophe begin with the same syllable, forming the following acrostic: "I, Shaggilkinam-ubbib, the conjurer, bless the god and the king." This is one of the rare instances in Mesopotamian literature in which the name of the author is mentioned on the tablet.[8]

The text, which belongs to the first half of the first millennium B.C., has been published by J. A. Craig, "Babylonian and Assyrian Religious Texts," *Assyriologische Bibliothek* (Leipzig, 1895), pls. 44–52.

The poem is a dialogue between an unhappy man and his friend.[9] (Hoping for comfort, the sufferer relates his miseries to his friend.)

*His misfortunes began in early youth, when father and mother were seized by the Nether World and he was left alone. He sees himself overcome with trouble; unlike an animal or a parvenu, he has always behaved piously towards the gods, yet they have forsaken him. Indeed,*

---

[8] See also the Epic of Era, Chapter IV above, n. 225.

[9] In order to avoid the fractionation of each partner's viewpoint into alternating stanzas, we have preferred to sum up the sufferer's complaints as well as the friend's replications. It is the sufferer who begins and ends the dialogue.

*the ungodly are better off in this world than the worshipers of the
deities. Since his childhood he has been devoted to the service of the
gods, but his reward has been poverty and ill treatment. It would be
better for him to mock the rites and offerings, abandon his house, and
roam in the desert like a beggar.*

*What is the effect of a god's reign over the people? The demons
are not bridled in their activity, and injustice is the rule of society: a
father works hard, while his son lies lazy in bed; of two brothers, one
behaves like a lion, while the other meekly drives a mule; one acts as
a thief, while the other practices charity.*

*People honor the evildoer who murders the righteous and robs the
helpless, but they abuse the humble and chase away the poor.*

*Oh, that Ninurta and Ishtar may have pity on him and consider
his righteous conduct! May they free him from his misery, and may
the king show him mercy.*[10]

[The friend reproves the sufferer for his pessimism and praises the
advantages of a god-fearing conduct.]

*The righteous is protected by a* lamassu,[11] *and abundance is bestowed on the worshiper of a goddess. The animals, who do not adore
a deity, will die a violent death through the arrows and the pits of the
hunter. The parvenu is thrown into the fire by the king. Only the favor
of a god brings real happiness. It is neglect of religious duties and
absence of piety that cause misery. The ungodly man who had heaped up
property will be killed by the greedy robber.*

*There are indeed many strange paradoxes in life: a fool may have
a son of outstanding qualities, while a hero's child may be quite the
contrary. But who can comprehend the designs of the gods? Who can
understand their decrees?*

*It is unfortunately true that falseness and untruth rule among the
people: they praise the wicked and rebuke the righteous; they mistake
worldly prosperity and prominence for piety and honesty.*

Thus the poem terminates on a note of profound pessimism, the
friend agreeing in the end with the sufferer's gloomy outlook on life.

---

[10] This last invocation appears to be an artificial appendix, a formula with which
the poem was to be presented to the local sovereign and his divine lords.

[11] A tutelary genius (see Chapter II above, n. 221).

## "DIALOGUE BETWEEN MASTER AND SERVANT"

An almost cynical attitude concerning the absurdity of human life is to be found in this dialogue. This poem, relatively well preserved, consists of twelve stanzas; in each of them the master first expresses a wish, then repents of it. The servant, in one case or the other, approves his lord's decision.

The cuneiform text of the composition has been published by Erich Ebeling in *Keilschrifttexte aus Assur religiösen Inhalts,* I, No. 96 (Berlin-Leipzig, 1919).

I. *The master wants to ride to the king's palace.*

SERVANT: Yes, he surely will be treated graciously by his sovereign.

MASTER: *No, it would be better for him to stay at home.*

SERVANT: Certainly, since the king will probably send him away to a foreign country.

II. *The master wants to sit down and dine.*

Yes, to eat regularly brings joy to the heart and attracts the favor of Shamash.

*No, it would be better for him to change his mind.*

Certainly, since it is vulgar to appease hunger and thirst.

III. *The master wants to ride out into the wilderness.*

Yes, life in the wilderness is full of abundance.

*No, it would be better for him to renounce the project.*

Certainly, since the wilderness is desolate and bare.

IV. and V. (mutilated; these lines seem to concern the capture of an enemy and the building of a house.)

VI. *The master wants to remain silent when he is accused by his enemy.*

Yes, silence is more effective than words.

*No, it would be better for him to answer his foe.*

Certainly, since his adversary would otherwise be angry at him.

VII. *The master wants to rebel against his lord.*

Yes, only through a rebellion will he have his stomach filled.

*No, it would be better for him to give up such a plan.*

Certainly, since a man of violence is either killed or taken prisoner.

VIII. *The master wants to love a woman.*

> Yes, a woman chases away all trouble.
>
> *No, it would be better for him to remain single.*
>
> Certainly, since a woman causes a man's ruin.

IX. *The master wants to offer a sacrifice to his god.*

> Yes, a pious man enjoys happiness and prosperity.
>
> *No, it would be better for him not to fulfill his religious duty.*
>
> Certainly, may the god run after him like a dog and beg for the celebration of the ritual.

X. *The master wants to lend food to the country.*

> Yes, the grain will remain his property, while he will gain large sums of interest.
>
> *No, it would be better for him to keep the grain for himself.*
>
> Certainly, since the people will consume the grain and afterwards curse the giver.

XI. *The master wants to benefit his country.*

> Yes, his good deed will be brought before Marduk.
>
> *No, it would be better for him not to exercise charity.*
>
> Certainly, since no one will remember after his death if he has been an evildoer or a benefactor.

XII. *The master wants to know: What is good?*

> To break both their necks and be thrown into the river.
>
> *No, it would be better for him to kill his servant and remain himself alive.*
>
> And would the master have the courage of living even three more days?

The pessimism that prevails in all these examples of speculative literature is an echo of the tired civilization which governed the last centuries of Assyro-Babylonian splendor.

The tragic problem that marks all these compositions is the religious crisis. Man appears to have grown accustomed to demanding protection and tangible favors of the gods in exchange for his worship. Once overwhelmed by the conception of the gods as tyrannical, arbitrary masters who created mankind exclusively for their service and who owe nothing to their creatures, the Mesopotamian now holds himself to be deprived of his rights, when, in spite of assiduous piety, he experiences hardships and misery. No longer content with unconditional submission, he applies standards of human justice to his relationship with the gods.

The resulting disorientation, soaring sometimes to black despair, puts him on the threshold of religious rebellion; yet the courage of crossing this threshold by an intellectual detachment from ritual habits is to belong to the thinkers of a new civilization: the philosophers of Greece.

# CONCLUSION

## POETICAL STRUCTURE

AKKADIAN POETRY DOES NOT APPEAR TO HAVE DEVELOPED complicated metrical systems. The epic tales all follow more or less the pattern of a rhymeless long line divided by a caesura into two segments; each half-line counts two beats, i.e. two word accents. The rhythmic scheme of the usual Akkadian epic verse may be rendered as follows:

$$\underline{\quad\quad}\;'\;'\quad\;/\;\quad\underline{\quad\quad}\;'\;'$$

The Assyro-Babylonian meter ignores the precision with which long and short syllables alternate in Greek poetry. A true appreciation of

Akkadian rhythm and its effectiveness is very difficult, since we do not know the nature of the musical accompaniment which probably underlined the recitation.

The rules of rhythm and meter do not seem to have been very strict in Babylonia; we often find variations and deviations from the scheme indicated above.[1]

While Sumerian poetry is characterized by frequent repetitions of identical phrases, which suggest a magical purpose as the motivation for such stylistic details, Akkadian meter seems to be less governed by extra-poetical considerations. Quite often in Assyro-Babylonian texts we find repetitions of whole passages, apparently not dictated by precepts of a ritual nature,[2] since the repeated passages are mostly reports and messages.[3] It is quite probable that many, if not all, Akkadian poems were intended for musical recitation, and we may assume for some of them also a mimic representation. This is almost certainly the case of the dialogues between "The Date-Palm and the Tamarisk"[4] and "The Ox and the Horse."[5] These poems are Akkadian examples of a genre which already existed in Sumerian literature and was called *"adamanduga,"*[6] or dispute: the opponents, usually two, but sometimes up to

---

[1] E.g., the short verses in tablet II of the Gilgamesh epic, the unusually long lines of "Kumma's Vision of the Nether World," and the prose version of the "Adapa myth," etc.

[2] The only exception is Fragment D of the Atrahasis epic, in which several passages are repeated as an incantation.

[3] In the Creation epic, Ea's report of Tiamat's plan is repeated first by Anshar, who instructs his vizier, Gaga, then by Gaga himself. In the epic of Gilgamesh the words of the hunter's father about the harlot are repeated by Gilgamesh, then by the hunter. Gilgamesh's report of Enkidu's death is repeated four times; to the scorpion men, the alewife, the boatman, and Utnapishtim.

On the other hand, there occurs in tablet XII of the epic, which is, as mentioned before (page 151 above), a translation from a Sumerian text, the repetition of three lines which have in all probability a magical purpose, in conformity with other Sumerian compositions. In the myth of Zu, the promise of supremacy in the divine assembly made to the god who will defeat the thief of the tablets, is repeated verbatim to each candidate; their answers are likewise—identical except for the reply of Ningirsu, who accepts the challenge. Ningirsu's instructions to Adad are repeated by the messenger to Ea, and Ea's reply is likewise repeated twice.

[4] Text published by E. Ebeling, *Keilschrifttexte aus Assur religiösen Inhalts*, I, 1245.

[5] Text published by C. Johnston, "Assyrian and Babylonian Beast Fables," *American Journal of Semitic Languages and Literatures*, Vol. XXVIII (1911–12), 93ff.

[6] Cf. J. J. A. van Dijk, *La sagesse suméro-accadienne* (Leyden, 1953), 32.

four, may be humans, animals, plants, tools, or even seasons; there exist, in fact, Sumerian disputes between shepherd and farmer, fish and bird, tree and cane, plow and hatchet, and summer and winter. Each partner praises his own qualities and belittles those of his adversary. The dispute is usually concluded with a judgment at the hands of a god or with a reconciliation.

The two Akkadian compositions imitate faithfully this genre and do not show in their contents any evolution. The step towards an allegorical significance, as in the Aesopian fable, has never been taken.[7] But by their structure these poems lead up to the much later Babylonian dialogues between "The Unhappy Man and His Friend" and between "Master and Servant," which have been treated in the chapter on speculative literature.

The supposition that the Mesopotamian *adamanduga* was acted might find support in the fact that passages of the Sumerian poems are often written alternatively in *Eme-ku* or *Eme-sal*[8] dialect,[9] suggesting a

---

[7] In the dispute between the two trees the tamarisk boasts to be superior to the date palm because of its utility for the farmer, who fashions his hoe and other tools from its wood. The date palm contests that it is still more useful to the farmer whom it provides with bridle and whip, rope and net. Important is the tamarisk's role in the temple; it is the chief exorcist; incense and omens come from it. But the date palm serves for the libations, and during the rites its branches are strewn on the ground. The tamarisk exalts its presence in the royal palace; the king's table, the queen's cup, the warriors' forks, are made of its wood. The date palm, however, provides orphans and widows with sweet fruit and nourishes the poor. At last the King plants both trees side by side and recommends to the palm to bring peace into the city, freshness into the wilderness.

In the dispute between the two beasts, the ox, well content with his placid life on a rich pasture, proposes to the horse to change his proper existence and to live on the meadows. But the horse rejoices in warfare and likes to be clad in a garment of brass. But the ox points out that his adversary's role in battle is a poor one; the horse has to carry the arrows and other weapons of the warriors, his master wounds him with the spur, and he is not free to go where he wants since he is limited by bridle and blinker. The horse remains undaunted and reproaches to the ox that he is bound to the water wheel and eats the dregs of the earth, while he, the horse, acquires glory equal to that of a lion. (The end of the dispute is not preserved.)

[8] Eme-ku is the regular language of Sumer, while Eme-sal ("language of women") is a dialect slightly different in pronunciation and vocabulary, supposedly spoken in the northern part of Sumer. For some obscure reason, the words attributed to female protagonists in Sumerian poetry are frequently rendered in Eme-sal.

[9] See the dispute between "Dumuzi and Enkimdu" pieced together by J. J. A. van Dijk, *La sagesse suméro-accadienne*, 65ff.

recitation by two persons or two groups of persons, one of which might be female.

Such an alternation of passages, written in two different Sumerian dialects, is also found in a composition called "Lamentation Over the Destruction of Ur,"[10] which does not belong to the *"adamanduga"* but which, too, may have been the object of a mimic representation. The lamentation was perhaps recited by a chorus of priestesses and another chorus of priests, or, more likely, by an actor and an actress accompanied by a chorus.[11]

Germs of dramatic style we perceive also within the narrative structure of Akkadian epics. Scenes which might feature a chorus and one protagonist can be found, for example, in the Creation epic. In tablet I, Tiamat listens to the evil deities who incite her to wage battle against her sons;[12] she answers with an approval of the chorus' advice. In tablet IV, the great gods as a group speak to Marduk, exalting his new power and inviting him to make a garment first vanish, then reappear; the god complies with their suggestion. In tablet VI, Marduk replies joyfully to the joint proposal of the *Anunnaki* to build a temple as a token of their gratitude to their savior.

The Gilgamesh epic, too, contains passages which employ dramatic technique. Sometimes the chorus is alone (as in tablet II, in which the people of Uruk comment upon the entrance of Enkidu into the city), sometimes confronted by one personage (as in tablet III, in which Gilgamesh discusses with the elders his project of slaying Huwawa); in the scene preceding the departure of the two heroes (third tablet of the Old Babylonian version) we have even two "actors" in addition to the chorus: Gilgamesh, Enkidu, and the elders of Uruk, the three participants in the action.

The type of lamentation appears in tablet VIII, in which Gilgamesh mourns before the elders of the city over the loss of his friend, as well as in tablet VII, in which Ishtar assembles the votaries and other

10 Edition of the text by S. N. Kramer in *Assyriological Studies*, Vol. XII (1940).

11 The words of the chorus might have been those lines called tentatively "antiphon," which intersperse the eleven songs of the poem.

12 Cf. also the Epic of Era, in which the seven helpers of the death-god incite their master to destruction. Here Ishum holds the role of the second personage.

priestesses of her temple to set up a lamentation over the thigh of the celestial Bull.

A chorus-"actor" scene of the Akkadian type is also found in the Ugaritic myth of Baal and Anath. At the god's death, messengers bring the fateful news to his father El, who wails and mourns, beating his chest and gashing his cheeks.[13] The goddess Anath then takes up the lament, roaming over the earth and emitting loud cries.[14]

In the still younger Hebrew literature there seems likewise to have existed acted poetry[15] involving a chorus, an actor, and an actress. Such a genre finds its reflection in the Song of Solomon, in which the Shulamite and her lover are accompanied by the chorus of the daughters of Jerusalem.[16]

These different types of acted poetry seem to foreshadow the alternate chants of a chorus and one or two actors of the ancient Greek drama.

The Aeschylean chorus often has a role similar to that of the elders of Uruk in the Gilgamesh epic or of the *Anunnaki* in the Creation epic; the chorus expresses fears and gives advice but remains otherwise inactive.

The lamentation dialogue between Xerxes and the elders of Susa in "the Persians" resembles the oriental genre. The actions to which the unhappy king incites the elders (to rend their garments, tear their cheeks, dress in sackcloth, beat their chests, and pluck out their hair and beards) are typical of the Semitic orient and return in the Gilgamesh epic,[17] the Ugaritic Baal myth,[18] and many Old Testament verses.

There exists also a similarity between the erotic ecstasy of the Shulamite's dialogue with the daughters of Jerusalem and the frenzy of the

---

[13] *ANET*, 139.

[14] Cf. Gilgamesh's lamentation over Enkidu's death.

[15] See the lamentations of Jeremiah, in which the prophet speaks to and is answered by the city of Jerusalem (second half of first chapter; 2, 20–22). In chapter 4, verse 17, a chorus seems to join the actors until the end of chapter 5.

[16] The chorus speaks in at least the following verses 1:8, 5:9, 6:1, and 6:13. The Shulamite addresses the chorus in verses 1:5–6, 2:7, 3:5, 3:11, 5:8, 5:16, and 8:4.

[17] The hero pulls out his hair, tears off his finery, dresses in a lion's skin, and wails loudly at the friend's death.

[18] See preceding page; it may be the counterpart to the Tammuz lamentations held in all the ancient Near East at the end of summer.

chorus of the "Bacchae."[19] The orgiastic elation of the Theban women is, likewise, of oriental origin, and it is very probable that the priestesses of the Assyro-Babylonian Ishtar temples were wont to sing chants—which have not been preserved—resembling the Euripidean songs of the bacchantes.

This consideration of the points of contact between Semitic acted poetry and the Attic tragedy is not intended to suggest that the splendid performances of the Greek theater had oriental precedents. We merely present the hypothesis that the technique of alternating chants between a chorus and one or two personages was current in the ancient Near East long before the appearances of the Thespian cart and found acceptance in Hellas along with other oriental customs.

## PERSEVERANCE OF AKKADIAN EPIC TALES

We have already seen how widespread certain Akkadian poems were in the ancient oriental world. The Gilgamesh epic and the legend of Etana had a profound influence on popular tradition. The fact that they were principally heroic tales facilitated their propagation among people of different religious customs.

There are similarities, for example, between the exploits of Gilgamesh and the labors of Heracles. The slaying of the Nemean lion finds its counterpart in Gilgamesh's killing of lions who appear often in connection with the hero on Akkadian bas-reliefs and seals.

Heracles fights against the monstrous Bull of Crete sent by the god Poseidon just as Gilgamesh slays the terrifying Bull of Heaven commissioned by the god Anu to revenge Ishtar.

After the fall of Babylonian civilization, the remembrance of the heroic deeds of legendary kings continued in the popular tradition. Stripped of the mythological background as well as of the deep meaning which the Akkadian poets had attached to the enterprises of their heroes, the tales survived only as stories of marvelous adventures. As such, they were likely to be blended with other legends, and, indeed, we find episodes from the Gilgamesh epic and the Etana myth reappearing in the romance of Alexander the Great.[20] The Macedonian conqueror,

---

19 Verses 11–13 of the second chapter of the Biblical song may be interpreted as referring, in the person of the lover, to a fertility god of the type of Tammuz or Dionysus.

like the King of Uruk, traverses many lands and crosses the dark mountain tunnel of Masius[21] in his quest for immortality, which is refused to him as it had been to Gilgamesh. The Waters of Death which the Babylonian hero crosses before arriving at Utnapishtim's abode correspond to the fetid sea situated in the great ocean, where many of Alexander's warriors die.[22] The sweet waters of the *"pī nārāti"*[23] are evoked in another episode of the Alexander romance: the king goes up a river until he finds its source. For twenty-nine days he wades through a cave whence the water issues.[24]

The Macedonian hero scales heaven on the back of an eagle, as did Etana, king of Kish.[25]

In all those adaptations of the Babylonian tales we miss a profound motivation for the heroic deeds. Alexander seeks immortality and flies towards heaven without any compelling motive for his actions. His only reason for undertaking these deeds is nothing but the presumption —very superficially treated and lacking all tragical grandeur—of a mortal who wants to accomplish something which no human being has achieved before. There is no metaphysical anguish at the idea of death, as in the Akkadian Gilgamesh epic, no ardent yearning for an offspring, as in the Etana legend.

Later authors have tried to replace the lost spiritual background by the interpolation of new religious and moral considerations, but in no case has a subsequent formulation of the ancient themes achieved the poetic level of the Akkadian epics.

[20] The many oriental and occidental ramifications of the Greek romance written in Egypt about the third century A.D., and falsely attributed to Alexander's contemporary Callisthenes.

[21] See Peckham and La Du, eds., *Alexandri Magni iter ad Paradisum*.

[22] See the Syriac version of the Alexander legend. Here appears for the first time the statement that Alexander had been provided by God with horns. This fabulous attribute, which continues also in the Quran, where Alexander is called ذو القرنين "He of the two horns" (cf. Sura XVIII) is probably based on the ancient Semitic interpretation of horns as symbols of power. But it may rest also on an early confusion of the two Hebrew words מקדון ("Macedonian") and מקרין ("horned").

[23] Cf. our comment on the "Mouth of the Rivers," p. 182.

[24] See the Hebrew poem on Alexander (M. Gaster, *The Chronicles of Jerahmeel*, in Oriental Translation Fund, NS IV Royal Asiatic Society (London, 1899).

[25] Ethiopic story of Alexander. In other versions of the pseudo-Callisthenes the king is carried upwards by four eagles attached to a board.

To examine the propagation of purely divine myths is a much more difficult task than to follow the trace of heroic legends; the religious traditions are usually much older and in the course of time have undergone adaptations to changing forms of worship.

Similarities between Akkadian myths and later legends may be the consequence, not of influence, but of separate developments of a common tradition. Thus we cannot know if the tale of the Flood, as it is recorded on Akkadian as well as on Sumerian tablets, was a direct source of the Biblical deluge story and of the Greek legend of Deucalion and Pyrrha.

It is probable that the Hebrew and the Assyro-Babylonian accounts are independent issues of a common Semitic tradition. As for the Greek legend, it might be preferable, because of the chronological priority of the Near Eastern civilizations, to assume an oriental influence on early Aegean mythology.

Without attempting to enter into the discussion about the primitive home of the Indo-Europeans, we direct attention to the fact that in the Norse cosmogony of the Edda there are certain features which point to an origin other than North European: the serpent twined around Midgard, threatening to destroy the earth, does not seem to fit into the frame of northern fauna. It may have been that in the remote past, when the abode of the proto-Germanic tribes was situated much more eastward than before the migrations, some oriental conception entered the mythological patrimony of these primitive populations.

The myth of a monstrous serpent menacing the earth with destruction, which was so widespread in the Semitic orient—Tiamat and Labbu[26] in Mesopotamia, Lotan in Phoenicia,[27] and Leviathan in Palestine[28]—perhaps had an influence on the formation of the creed concerning the Midgard serpent.

Other points of contact between oriental and Norse mythologies may be seen in the similarity of the act of creation, such as Marduk's fashioning heaven and earth from the body of his slain enemy Tiamat,

[26] For the text relating the combat against the Labbu, see pp. 150–51 above.

[27] See the Ugaritic myth of Baal and Anath.

[28] For references concerning the serpentine monster in the Old Testament, cf. references cited in n. 31, Chapter IV above.

and Odin and his brothers' creating heaven and earth from the body of the slain giant Ymir. The primeval cow which feeds Buri, the forefather of the gods, is reminiscent of the bovine deities of Mesopotamia and Phoenicia.[29] In the Germanic Freyia we find the attribute of Ishtar: she is not only the goddess of fecundity and love but also the patroness of battle.[30]

In conclusion, we can say that the old Mesopotamian civilization, much more than its Egyptian contemporary, has had significant ramifications reaching into the nascent Indo-European culture, of which Hellas has been the most influential protagonist.

Greek poetry at once absorbed and surpassed oriental traditions, erecting the marvelous structure of a new culture; its foundations, however, bear the mark—not entirely obliterated—of the people who, in the Plain of the Two Rivers, at the dawn of human history, exalted the master of the stylus who held the sacred torch of poetry:

*"mu- un  til   ki   nam-  dub-  sar-  (ra)  ka*
*"He who dwells  in   the   place   of   scribal   art*

*babbar dim₂   he₂   e₃*
*like   the   sun   may   he   shine!"*[31]

---

[29] Ninsun, the mother of Gilgamesh, is called the "wild cow of the steer-folds," and her son a "wild Ox;" the Ugaritic god El is called "Bull El," etc.

[30] See n. 33, Chapter II above.

[31] Sumerian proverb from Sippar.

# APPENDICES

*Appendix A*

### Prehistory

| | |
|---|---|
| Prepottery period | end of sixth millennium B.C. |
| Hassunah period | beginning of fifth millennium B.C. |
| Halaf period | middle of fifth millennium B.C. |
| Ubaid period | end of fifth millennium B.C. |
| Warka and Protoliterate periods | ⎱ fourth millennium B.C. |
| Gawra and Ninevite periods | ⎰ |

### History

| | |
|---|---|
| Pre-Babylonian period | ca. 2900–1800 B.C. |
|    First dynasty of Ur | ca. 2750 |

238

| | |
|---|---|
| Dynasty of Lagash | ca. 2700 |
| Lugalzaggesi | ca. 2500 |
| Sargon I of Agade | ca. 2450 |
| The Guti | ca. 2300 |
| Gudea of Lagash | |
| Third dynasty of Ur | ca. 2100 |
| Dynasties of Isin and Larsa | ca. 1800 |
| Old Babylonian period | ca. 1800–1170 B.C. |
| Hammurabi | 1728–1685 |
| The Hittites in Babylon | 1531–1530 |
| The Kassite dynasty | 1530–1170 |
| Assyrian period | ca. 1200–612 B.C. |
| Tukulti-Ninurta I | 1235–1198 |
| Tiglat-Pileser I | 1116–1090 |
| Ashurnazirpal II | 883–859 |
| Shalmaneser III | 858–824 |
| Tiglat-Pileser III | 745–727 |
| Sargon II | 721–705 |
| Sennacherib | 704–681 |
| Esarhaddon | 680–669 |
| Ashurbanipal | 668–626 |
| Fall of Nineveh | 612 |
| Neo-Babylonian period | ca. 612–539 B.C. |
| Nabopolassar | 625–605 |
| Nebuchadnezzar II | 605–565 |
| Nabonidus | 555–539 |
| Fall of Babylon | 539 B.C. |

## *Appendix B*

### List of Toponyms

| *Ancient Name* | *Modern Name* |
|---|---|
| Adab | Bismaya |
| Ashur | Qalat Shergat |
| Babylon | Hillah |
| Borsippa | Birs-Nimrud |

| | |
|---|---|
| Dur-Sharrukin | Khorsabad |
| Eridu | Abu Shahrain |
| Eshnunna | Tell-Asmar |
| Kalah | Nimrud |
| Kish | Al-Uhaimir |
| Kutha | Tell-Ibrahim |
| Lagash | Telloh |
| Larsa | Senkereh |
| Mari | Tell-Hariri |
| Nineveh | Kuyunjik |
| Nippur | Niffer |
| Nuzi | Yorghan Tepe |
| Shuruppak | Farah |
| Sippar | Abu Habba |
| Umma | Djoha |
| Ur | Al-Mughair |
| Uruk (Erech) | Warka |

# BIBLIOGRAPHY

PREHISTORY

Andrae, W. *Das wiedererstandene Assur*. Leipzig, 1938.

Braidwood, Robert J., and Linda Braidwood. "The Earliest Village Communities of South-Western Asia," *Journal of World History*, Vol. I (1953), 278–310.

Contenau, G. *Manuel d'Archéologie orientale depuis les Origines jusqu'à l'Époque d'Alexandre*. 4 vols. Paris, 1927–47.

Delougaz, Pinhas. *Pottery from the Diyala Region*. Oriental Institute *Publications,* Vol. LXIII, Chicago, 1952.

Frankfort, Henri. *Sculpture of the Third Millennium* B.C. *from Tell Asmar and Khafājah*. Oriental Institute *Publications,* Vol. XLIV, Chicago, 1939.

Herzfeld, E. *Die vorgeschichtlichen Töpfereien von Samarra. Forschungen zur islamischen Kunst,* Part II, Vol. V, Berlin, 1930.

Jordan J., *et al. Vorläufiger Bericht über die von der Notgemeinschaft der deutschen Wissenschaft in Uruk-Warka unternommenen Ausgrabungen (Abhandlungen der preussischen Akademie der Wissenschaften,* Phil.-hist. Klasse), Berlin, 1930–41.

Koldewey, R. *Das wiedererstehende Babylon.* Leipzig, 1925.

Langdon, S. *Excavations at Kish.* Oxford, 1924.

Lloyd, Seton, and Fuad Safar, "Tell Hassuna," *JNES,* Vol. IV (October, 1945), 255–89.

Mackay, E. *Report on Excavations of Jemdet Nasr Iraq.* Chicago, 1931.

Mallowan, M. E. L. *Survey of the Habur.* London, 1936.

Oppenheim, Max Freiherr von. *Tell Halaf.* 3 vols. Berlin, 1943–55.

Parrot, A. "Les fouilles de Mari," *Syria,* Vol. XVI (1935) and Vol. XVII (1936).

Perkins, A. L. *The Comparative Archeology of Early Mesopotamia.* Chicago, 1949.

Schmidt, E. "Excavations at Fara," *MJ,* Vol. XXII (1931), 193–245.

Speiser, E. A. *Excavations at Tepe Gawra.* Vol. I, Philadelphia, 1935; Vol. II by A. J. Tobler, Philadelphia, 1950.

———. *Mesopotamian Origins.* Philadelphia, 1930.

Starr, Richard F. S. *Nuzi; Report on the Excavations at Yorgan Tepe Near Kirkuk, Iraq.* 2 vols. Cambridge, Mass., 1937–39.

Woolley, Leonard. *Excavations at Ur.* London, 1954.

## HISTORY

Bauer, Theo. *Das Inschriftenwerk Assurbanipals.* Leipzig, 1933.

Böhl, Franz Marius Theodor de Liagre. *Het tijdvak der Sargonieden volgens brieven uit het koninklijk archief te Nineve.* Amsterdam, 1949.

*The Cambridge Ancient History.* 12 vols. Cambridge, 1923ff.

Contenau, G. *"L'Asie Occidentale Ancienne," Histoire de l'Orient Ancien.* Paris, 1936.

Goetze, Albrecht. *Hethiter, Churriter und Assyrer.* Oslo, 1936.

Jacobsen, Thorkild. *The Sumerian King List.* Chicago, 1939.

Landsberger, B. *Assyrische Handelskolonien in Kleinasien aus dem dritten Jahrtausend.* Leipzig, 1925.

Lewy, H. "Nitokris-Naqī'a," *JNES,* Vol. XI (October, 1952), 264–86.

Messerschmidt, L., and O. Schroeder. *"Keilschrifttexte aus Assur historischen Inhalts," Wissenschaftliche Veröffentlichungen der deutschen Orient-Gesellschaft,* Vols. XVI and XXXVII, (Berlin-Leipzig, 1911 and 1922).

Meyer, Eduard. *Geschichte des Altertums.* 2 vols. Berlin, 1907.

Moortgat, A. *"Die Entstehung der sumerischen Hochkultur," DAO,* Vol. XLIII (Berlin, 1945).

Oppenheim, A. Leo. "Babylonian and Assyrian Historical Texts," *ANET,* 2d ed. Princeton, 1955.

Pallis, S. A. *The Antiquity of Iraq.* Copenhagen, 1956.

Robinson, C. A. *Ancient History.* New York, 1951.

Schmökel, H. *Geschichte des alten Vorderasiens.* Leiden, 1957.

Soden, Wolfram von. *Der Aufstieg des Assyrerreiches als geschichtliches Problem.* Leipzig, 1937.

———. *Herrscher im alten Orient.* Berlin, 1954.

Thureau-Dangin, F. *Die sumerischen und akkadischen Königsinschriften.* Leipzig, 1907.

## RELIGION

Bottéro, J. *La Religion Babylonienne.* Paris, 1952.

Dhorme, Edouard. *Les Religions de Babylonie et d'Assyrie.* Paris, 1945.

Ebeling, Erich. *Keilschrifttexte aus Assur religiösen Inhalts. Wissenschaftliche Veröffentlichungen der deutschen Orient-Gesellschaft,* Vol. XXVIII, Berlin-Leipzig, 1915–19.

———. *Quellen zur Kenntnis der babylonischen Religion.* Leipzig, 1918.

———. *Stiftungen und Vorschriften für assyrische Tempel.* Berlin, 1954.

———. *Tod und Leben nach den Vorstellungen der Babylonier.* Berlin, 1931.

Frankfort, H., H. A. Frankfort, Thorkild Jacobsen, *et al. The Intellectual Adventure of Ancient Man.* Chicago, 1946.

Falkenstein, A., and Wolfram von Soden. *Sumerische und akkadische Hymnen und Gebete.* Zurich-Stuttgart, 1953.

Hooke, S. H. *Babylonian and Assyrian Religion.* London, 1953.

Jastrow, Morris. *The Religion of Babylonia and Assyria.* Boston, 1898.

Kramer, S. N. *Sumerian Mythology.* Philadelphia, 1944.

Langdon, S. *Semitic Mythology.* Boston, 1931.

Mendelsohn, Isaac. *Religions of the Ancient Near East.* New York, 1955.

Moortgat, A. *Tammuz, Der Unsterblichkeitsglaube in der altorientalischen Bildkunst.* Berlin, 1949.

Pallis, S. A. *The Babylonian Akitu Festival.* Copenhagen, 1926.

Sachs, A. "Akkadian Rituals," *ANET.* 2d ed. Princeton, 1955.

San Nicolò, Mariano. *Beiträge zu einer Prosopographie neubabylonischer Beamten der Zivil-und Tempelverwaltung.* Munich, 1941.

Soden, Wolfram von. *"Religion und Sittlichkeit nach den Anschauungen der Babylonier,"* Zeitschrift der deutschen morgenländischen Gesellschaft (Leipzig, 1935).

———. *"Akkadische Gebete an Göttinnen,"* RA, Vol. LII (Paris, 1958), 131–36.

Tallqvist, K. Leonard, *"Akkadische Götterepitheta,"* Studia Orientalia, Vol. VII (1938).

Ungnad, Arthur. *Die Religion der Babylonier und Assyrer.* Jena, 1921.

## KINGSHIP

Deimel, Anton. *Codex Hammurabi.* 3d ed. Rome, 1953.

Driver, G. R., and J. C. Miles. *The Assyrian Laws.* Oxford, 1935.

———. *The Babylonian Laws.* Oxford, 1952.

Ebeling, Erich. *Keilschrifttexte aus Assur juristischen Inhalts. Wissenschaftliche Veröffentlichungen der deutschen Orient-Gesellschaft,* Vol. L, Berlin-Leipzig, 1927.

Frankfort, Henri. *Kingship and the Gods.* Chicago, 1948.

Goetze, A. "Codex Eshnunna," *Sumer,* Vol. IV (1948), 63–102.

Hallo, W. W. *Early Mesopotamian Royal Titles.* New Haven, 1957.

Jacobsen, Thorkild. "Early Political Development in Mesopotamia," *ZA* (1957), 91–140.

Koschaker, P. *"Fratriarchat, Hausgemeinschaft und Mutterrecht in Keilschriftrechten,"* ZA, NF VII (Leipzig), 1–89.

Kramer, S. N. "Code of Urnammu," *Orientalia,* Vol. XXIV (Rome, 1954).

Labat R. *"Le caractère religieux de la royauté assyro-babylonienne,"* Études d'Assyriologie, Vol. III (Paris, 1939).

Landsberger, B. *"Die babylonischen Termini für Gesetz und Recht,"* Studia et documenta ad iura orientis antiqui pertinentia. Leiden, 1949, Vol. II.

Meek, T. "Babylonian and Assyrian Laws," *ANET.* 2d ed. Princeton, 1955.

Peiser, F. E. "The Neo-Babylonian Laws," *Sitzungsberichte der preussischen Akademie der Wissenschaften,* Berlin, 1889.

San Nicolò, M. *Babylonische Rechtsurkunden des ausgehenden VIII und des VII Jahrhunderts.* Munich, 1951.

San Nicolò, Mariano, and A. Falkenstein. *"Das Gesetzbuch Lipit-Ishtars von Isin,"* Orientalia, NF XIX (Rome, 1950), 103f.

Speiser, E. A. "Authority and Law in Mesopotamia," Supplements to *JAOS,* Vol. LXXIV (1954), 12ff.

MAGIC

Contenau, G. *La Magie chez les Assyriens et les Babyloniens.* Paris, 1947.

Buren, E. Douglas van. "The Sacred Marriage in Early Times in Mesopotamia," *Orientalia,* NS XIII (Rome, 1944).

Ebeling, Erich. *"Beiträge zur Kenntnis der Beschwörungsserie Namburbi,"* RA, Vol. XLVIII (January and April, 1954), 1–13 and 76–85.

Falkenstein, A. *"Die Haupttypen der sumerischen Beschwörung,"* Leipziger Semitistische Studien, NF I (Leipzig, 1931).

Furlani, G. *Riti babilonesi e assiri.* Udine, 1940.

Kunstmann, W. G. *"Die babylonische Gebetsbeschwörung,"* Leipziger Semitistische Studien, NF II (Leipzig, 1932).

Proosdij, A. A. van. *Babylonian Magic and Sorcery.* Leiden, 1952.

Tallqvist, K. *Die assyrische Beschwörungsserie Maqlû.* Helsingfors, 1895.

Thompson, R. Campbell. *The Devils and Evil Spirits of Babylonia.* London, 1903–1904.

Thureau-Dangin, F. *Rituels Accadiens.* Paris, 1921.

James, E. O. *Myth and Ritual in the Ancient Near East.* London, 1950.

DIVINATION AND MEDICINE

Contenau, G. *La Divination chez les Assyriens et les Babyloniens.* Paris, 1940.

———. *La Médecine en Assyrie et en Babylonie.* Paris, 1938.

Filliozat, J. *"Pronostics médicaux Akkadiens, Grecs et Indiens,"* JA, (Paris, 1952), 299ff.

Labat, R. *Hémérologies et Ménologies d'Assur.* Paris, 1939.

———. *"Traité akkadien de diagnostics et pronostics médicaux,"* Académie Internationale des Sciences (Paris, 1951).

Neugebauer, Otto. "The History of Ancient Astronomy," *JNES*, Vol. IV (January, 1945), 1–38.

Oefele, F. von. *Keilschriftmedizin in Parallelen*. Leipzig, 1904.

Oppenheim, A. Leo. *The Interpretation of Dreams in the Ancient Near East*. Chicago, 1956.

Pfeiffer, R. H. "Akkadian Oracles and Prophecies," *ANET*. 2d ed. Princeton, 1955.

Thompson, R. Campbell. *The Assyrian Herbal: The Assyrian Vegetable Drugs*. London, 1924.

### Cuneiform Writing

Bayer, F. *"Die Entwicklung der Keilschrift,"* Orientalia, Vol. XXV (Rome, 1927).

*The Chicago Assyrian Dictionary*. Chicago, 1956ff.

Deimel, A. *Šumerische Grammatik*. Rome, 1939.

————. *Die Inschriften von Fara I. Wissenschaftliche Veröffentlichungen der deutschen Orient-Gessellschaft*, Vol. XL, Berlin-Leipzig, 1922.

Driver, G. R. *Semitic Writing*. London, 1948.

Gelb, I. J. *Glossary of Old Akkadian*. Chicago, 1957.

Labat, R. *Manuel d'épigraphie akkadienne*. Paris, 1952.

Leander, P. *Die sumerischen Lehnwörter im Assyrischen*. Leipzig, 1903.

Rutten, M. *"Notes de paléographie cunéiforme,"* Revue des Études Sémitiques et Babyloniaca (Paris, 1940), 1–53.

Soden, Wolfram von. *"Grundriss der akkadischen Grammatik,"* AO, Vol. XXXIII (Rome, 1952).

————. *"Das akkadische Syllabar,"* AO, Vol. XXVII (Rome, 1948).

### Pictorial Art

Buren, E. Douglas van. *Symbols of the Gods in Mesopotamian Art*. Rome, 1945.

Busink, T. A. *De Toren van Babel*. Batavia, 1938.

Calderini, A. *Saggi e studi di antichità*. Milan, 1924, Vols. IV and V.

Champdor, A. *Babylone*. Paris, 1957.

Clercq, L. de *Catalogue de la Collection De Clercq*. Paris, 1885, Vol. I.

Delaporte, L. *Catalogue des Cylindres Orientaux du Musée du Louvre*. 2 vols. Paris, 1920–23.

Frankfort, Henri. *Cylinder Seals; A Documentary Essay on the Art and Religion of the Ancient Near East.* London, 1939.

——. *The Art and Architecture of the Ancient Orient.* Harmondsworth, 1954.

Frankfort, Henriette A. *Arrest and Movement: An Essay on Space and Time in the Representative Art of the Ancient Near East.* Chicago, 1951.

Furlani, G., and E. F. Weidner. *Die Reliefs der assyrischen Könige.* Berlin, 1939.

Hall, H. R. *Babylonian and Assyrian Sculpture in the British Museum.* Paris, 1928.

Lenzen, H. *"Die Entwicklung der Zikkurat," Vorläufiger Bericht der von der Notgemeinschaft der deutschen Wissenschaft in Uruk-Warka unternommenen Ausgrabungen,* Vol. IV, Leipzig, 1941.

Moortgat, A. *Die Kunst des Alten Orients und die Bergvölker.* Berlin, 1932.

——. *Frühe Bildkunst in Sumer. Mitteilungen der vorderasiatisch-aegyptischen Gesellschaft,* Vol. XL, No. 3, Leipzig, 1935.

——. *Vorderasiatische Rollsiegel.* Berlin, 1940.

Parrot, A. *Ziqqurats et Tour de Babel.* Paris, 1949.

Porada, E. *Corpus of Ancient Near Eastern Seals in American Collections.* Washington, 1948.

Pritchard, J.B. *The Ancient Near East in Pictures.* Princeton, 1954.

Rutten, M. *"L'Art de la Mésopotamie ancienne au Musée du Louvre," Encyclopédie photographique de l'Art.* Paris, 1935.

### POETRY

Bauer, Theo. *"Ein viertes altbabylonisches Fragment des Gilgamesch-Epos,"* JNES, Vol. XVI (October, 1957).

Böhl, Franz Marius Theodor de Liagre. *Het Gilgamesj Epos.* Amsterdam, 1952.

——. *Opera Minora.* Groningen, 1953.

Brongers, H. A. *De Literatuur der Babyloniers en Assyriers.* Den Haag, 1953.

Contenau, G. *Le Déluge babylonien—Ishtar aux Enfers—La Tour de Babel.* Paris, 1952.

Dhorme, E. *La Littérature babylonienne et assyrienne,* Paris, 1937.

Dijk, J. J. A. van. *La Sagesse Suméro-Akkadienne.* Leiden, 1953.

Fish, T. "The Zu Bird," *Bulletin of the John Rylands Library,* Vol. XXI (1948), 162–71.

Furlani, G. *Poemetti mitologici babilonesi e assiri.* Florence, 1954.

Gössmann, P. F. *Das Era-Epos.* Würzburg, 1956.

Heidel, Alexander. *The Babylonian Genesis.* 2d ed. Chicago, 1951.

———. *The Gilgamesh Epic and Old Testament Parallels.* 2d ed. Chicago, 1949.

Kramer, S. N. "Sumerian Myths and Epic Tales," *ANET.* 2d ed. Princeton, 1955.

Landsberger, Benno. "Die babylonische Theodizee," *ZA,* Vol. XLIII (Leipzig, 1936), 32.

Meissner, Bruno. *Die babylonisch-assyrische Literatur.* Potsdam, 1928.

Oppenheim, A. Leo. "Mesopotamian Mythology," *Orientalia,* Vols. XVI and XVII (Rome, 1947 and 1948), 207ff. and 17ff.

Pfeiffer, R. H. "Akkadian Observations on Life and World Order," *ANET.* 2d ed. Princeton, 1955.

Reiner, E. "More Fragments of the Epic of Era," *JNES,* Vol. XVII (January, 1958), 41 ff.

Rinaldi, G. *Storia delle letterature dell'antica Mesopotamia.* Milan, 1957.

Schott, A. *Das Gilgamesch-Epos.* Leipzig, 1934.

Speiser, E. A. "Akkadian Myths and Epics," *ANET.* 2d ed. Princeton, 1955.

———. "The Case of the Obliging Servant," *Journal of Cuneiform Studies,* Vol. VIII, No. 3 (1954).

# INDEX

The Orient harbors the oldest civilizations of the world, and it was there, in the valleys of the great rivers, that human speech first became poetry and inspiration was perpetuated into written word.

The Assyro-Babylonian literature instilled its ideas into Greek mythology, and thus succeeded in surviving, although incognito, until European culture began to flourish. To our inestimable advantage, Mesopotamian literature was inscribed on clay tablets which have outlived the destructive action of the ages, and which have been found in the last two centuries by archaeologists under the dust of Iraq's mounds.

*Voices from the Clay* considers Assyro-Babylonian poetry transcribed from these tablets in its cultural setting, illustrating the background upon which the epic and speculative poems were projected. Included is an assessment of the ethnic composition in prehistoric times, a political profile, and an examination of the religious system of the era.